Outlines of the history of Greek philosophy

OUTLINES

OF THE HISTORY

OF GREEK

PHILOSOPHY

by Eduard Zeller

Thirteenth edition, revised by Dr. Wilhelm Nestle
and translated by
L. R. Palmer, Trinity College, Cambridge

MERIDIAN BOOKS, INC. *New York*

M

Published by Meridian Books June, 1955
First printing April, 1955
Second printing November, 1955
Third printing January, 1957
Fourth printing December, 1957
Fifth printing June, 1958
Sixth printing August, 1959
Seventh printing January, 1960
Eighth printing July, 1960

Reprinted by arrangement with The Humanities Press, Inc.

Thirteenth Edition revised and published 1931

Reprinted 1948 and 1950

Library of Congress Catalog Card Number: 55–7579

Manufactured in the United States of America

Contents

Second period

THE ATTIC PHILOSOPHY AND THE SOCRATICS. PLATO. ARISTOTLE

Third period

HELLENISTIC PHILOSOPHY. THE STOA. THE LATER CYNICISM. EPICUREANISM. SCEPTICISM. ECLECTICISM

Fourth period

THE PHILOSOPHY OF THE ROMAN EMPIRE

Eduard Zeller

Eduard Zeller was born in 1814 in Württemberg, Germany. He taught theology at Tübingen, Bern, and Marburg, migrated to the faculty of philosophy as the result of disputes with the clerical party, and in 1862 became Professor of Philosophy at Heidelberg University. His philosophical thought was influenced by that of Kant and Hegel and his works include, besides his monumental *Philosophie der Griechen,* the *Platonische Studien, Geschichte der Christ-*

FROM THE PREFACE TO THE
FIRST EDITION

My object has been primarily to provide students with a help
for academic lectures which would facilitate preparation and
save the time wasted in writing down facts, without interfer-
ing with the lecturer's work or imposing any limitations
upon him. I have made it my task therefore to give my readers an idea of the contents of the different philosophic systems and the course of their historical development which
should contain all essential features, and also to put into
their hands the more important literary references and
sources. But as in the last respect I have not gone beyond
what is absolutely necessary, so in the historical account I
have as a rule indicated only very briefly the parts with
which historical considerations of a general nature or special
explanations and inquiries are connected, or in which it
seemed proper to supplement my earlier work. . . . My outlines are intended in the first place for beginners, who as a
rule form the majority of the hearers. But these are rather
confused than helped if the historical material is given in too
great abundance or if they are overwhelmed with the titles
of books of which they will only see a very small proportion.
Anyone, however, who wishes to study the history of phi-

losophy must not content himself with a compendium but should consult the sources and the more comprehensive works upon them.

E. Zeller

Berlin.
September 27th, 1883.

PREFACE TO THE THIRTEENTH EDITION

When eight years ago I was occupied on the twelfth edition of Zeller's *Outlines*, I confined myself to adding in the footnotes the most important modern literature and to pointing out briefly where recent research had led to different results. In the present edition this procedure was found no longer to suffice. Indeed a warning has come from an authoritative source which takes account of Zeller's personal significance: "We should not attempt to revise his work and to bring it up-to-date like a school-book." This warning was of course uttered by Wilamowitz with reference to Zeller's great work, "The Philosophy of the Greeks in its Historical Development." In my revision of the sixth edition of the first section of this work (I, 1, 2, 1920) I have closely conformed to this injunction and have merely added the literature of twenty-five years in the footnotes and left the text untouched except for a few additions which are enclosed in square brackets. By this I believe I have shown that I am not lacking in reverence towards a man of Zeller's significance or in feeling of responsibility towards a work so monumental as his certainly is. Here everyone can today still read Zeller's own conception, which will always demand consideration even in those points where research believes it has passed beyond him.

It is otherwise with these *Outlines,* which Zeller himself intended to be an aid to students and further a guide to other friends of Greek philosophy. If it is to fulfil this aim, it cannot remain in a state which the progress of research has in many points rendered out of date. In point of fact the last two decades have brought so much that is new that this could no longer find a place in the footnotes, but in view of its importance had to be worked into the text. It suffices to mention the fundamental researches of J. Stenzel on Plato, W. Jaeger on Aristotle, Erich Frank on the Pythagoreans and K. Reinhardt on Posidonius. The theories, too, of H. Maier on Socrates, which received a confirmation by the book of Chr. Schrempf that is all the more convincing because of its complete independence, could not remain out of consideration, while the account of the Sophists in which Zeller showed himself too completely dominated by Plato's views demanded recasting and all the more so that a comprehensive work on this intellectual movement is still wanting. Finally, more account had to be taken of the far-reaching influence which the Orphic mystery religion that invaded Greece in the seventh and eighth centuries exerted on the Greek way of thought and not least on philosophy. Apart from the drastic alterations in the text which the progress of research had made unavoidable, the reviser was faced with a number of methodological considerations. Zeller both in his big work and the *Outlines* had been primarily intent upon bringing out the facts which can be historically established and in giving prominence to philosophical ideas. From these two points of view he performed an inestimable service for his time. This attitude had its disadvantages in that, on the one hand, chronological discussions and the enumeration of mere names occupied a disproportionately large space, while on the other hand the characters of the great philosophers and the connection of their ideas with the culture of their time were not treated with the fulness which they deserved. I have made some attempt to remedy this defect without, I hope, detriment to the book. Since the publishers wished the book to remain unaltered in point of size I found myself compelled to omit much if the new was to be incorporated.

These omissions comprise the chronological discussions which can be found in the bigger work and the enumeration of insignificant names which gave the *Outlines* the stamp of a mere extract from the big work. Apart from this I have removed all polemic discussions which had been included in the text by the editor of the ninth to the eleventh editions, F. Lortzing, because in my opinion they are out of place in a book intended for beginners and are today for the most part devoid of interest. On the other hand the material completions and corrections which were contained in the footnotes have been incorporated in the text and the bibliographies, with few exceptions, transferred to the end of each chapter, so that the footnotes have been considerably reduced and are only used for the quotation of especially important passages and for reference within the book itself. The long methodological introduction, too, has been replaced by a shorter and the index of names confined to the ancient names. The space gained by these omissions has been utilised for the inclusion of the most important results of recent research which frequently, especially with Aristotle and Posidonius, demanded a considerable expansion of the text. In addition to this I have attempted, as far as space permitted, to give at least a sketch of the personalities of the most prominent thinkers and, where it seemed required, to indicate their relations to their environment and the influence of their thoughts. Furthermore I found myself compelled to make some re-arrangements. The so-called hedonistic Cynicism has been separated from the older representative of the school and has been discussed in a special paragraph within the Hellenistic period. Plato's physics, which form an outpost of his philosophy, I have placed at the end in order not to disturb the connection of his system. The Jewish-Greek philosophy, which Zeller, on account of inner relations, placed directly before neo-Platonism, from which it is separated chronologically by more than two centuries, I have transferred to the end of the Hellenistic period to which it belongs both chronologically and intrinsically and brought under the heading of eclecticism to which its character corresponds, so that neo-Platonism follows directly upon the neo-Pythagoreans and middle Platonism. A special paragraph has been devoted to the last representatives of Epicureanism in the Roman Empire. In the division of the neo-Platonic schools I have followed Praechter. The excellent bibliography with which he has provided his work is indispensable to anyone who wishes to undertake research in Greek philosophy. In the *Outlines* it was only possible to refer the beginner to a small selection of the most important works, especially in the case of collections of the sources. In this, older works which in their time were of fundamental importance, such as Boeckh's Philolaus and Corssen's Posidonius, etc., have not been left unmentioned. Of the ninety-five paragraphs of the book the following thirty-seven have been rewritten by the editor: 1-5, 9-12, 16, 19-23, 27, 33-41, 43, 44, 54, 55, 65, 66, 73, 78, 81, 93-95. Apart from these the others have undergone greater or smaller alterations or additions. On the whole the book is some 60 per cent. new. I cannot deny that through this the book has acquired a somewhat different aspect and that certain inequalities of presentation and style have made themselves evident. This however was unavoidable if the book was to answer to the just requirements of modern science. It is always a rather thankless and responsible task to revise the work of a dead scholar, demanding a far-going suppression of the personality of the editor which makes the creation of a harmonious and uniform whole almost impossible. I have undertaken it in order to further the cause of Greek philosophy and to help the young student who occupies himself with it. If and how far I have succeeded in overcoming the difficulties which lie in the nature of the thing is a question which must be left to the judgment of the competent reader.

WILHELM NESTLE

Stuttgart.
September, 1928.

INTRODUCTION

1. *The meaning of Greek philosophy*

Why do we occupy ourselves today with the study of Greek philosophy, 1,400 years after the Emperor Justinian dissolved the Platonic Academy, the last of the Greek philosophical schools (529 A.D.)? Have one and a half thousand years of Christian culture not been sufficient to supersede this "heathen philosophy" and make it superfluous for us? Has not the philosophy of modern times so far surpassed the results of Greek thought, as our natural science and technology the achievements of the Graeco-Roman world in these departments, so that we have no more to learn from them? Has not every people and every age its own particular philosophy and can therefore that of a long vanished people like the Greeks now have any more than an antiquarian interest for us? Those who turn to the study of Greek philosophy may well raise these questions and seek to find an answer.

In the first place it is an historical interest which attracts the modern man to this study. Greek philosophy is an important constituent of European intellectual life, the development of which cannot be understood apart from it. But from this purely historical point of view the history of philosophy appears merely as a part of the history of civilisation, and primarily that of the Greek people. That is doubt-

less true, in so far as the individual philosophic systems and
their personal creators have their roots in the general mental
character of their age, and are therefore historically conditioned, even when they rise above their generation and with
their ideas point out paths for the future. But the history of
philosophy too has its own system of laws, in so far as the
various attempts to solve philosophic problems of knowledge
of the world do not merely follow an external more or less
accidental order. One problem rather grows out of another
by an inner necessity and one system draws another after it
by way of progress or completion, contradiction or contrast.
Thus the history of the philosophy of a people mirrors the
development of its thought, while the history of knowledge
for its part becomes to some extent knowledge of history.

But can we in general speak at all of a history of philosophy? Not every people, not even every civilised people has
produced a philosophy. Many peoples have saints, prophets
and religious reformers, but only very few philosophers. Of
the peoples of antiquity, apart from the Greeks, only the
Chinese and the people of India come into consideration.
Scholars who are acquainted with the philosophic literature
of the Chinese inform us that the language is badly suited
to philosophy and that their profoundest system, the Tao-
ism of Laotse, is more mysticism than philosophy, while
Kongtse, who on his own confession was "a transmitter
but no creator" and held firmly to religion, was more a
moral preacher than a philosopher and had no understanding of metaphysical questions. The Indians have indeed
produced various philosophical systems, but Indian philosophy never lost contact with religion and never became
independent. Its other-worldly character seems strange to
our minds. Nevertheless there is no connection between the
philosophic systems of the Chinese and the Indians, nor
between theirs and that of the Greeks, but each of these
three peoples developed its own philosophy from its own
peculiar nature. From Greek philosophy, however, the
whole of European philosophy has descended. For the ideas
which the Romans express in their philosophic literature
were not original, but were taken over from the Greeks,

clothed in the Latin language and passed on to the mediæval and modern worlds.

Greek philosophy, in common with the other products of
the Hellenic spirit, was an original creation and has been of
fundamental importance in the whole development of western civilisation. Never did a people judge its own nature and
the institutions, morals and customs which it produced with
greater impartiality than the Greeks. Never did a people regard the world about it and peer into the depths of the universe with clearer gaze than they. It was this impartiality, in
combination with a strong sense of reality, and an equally
strong power of abstraction, that enabled them at a very
early date to recognise their religious ideas for what they
actually were—creations of an artistic imagination—and to
set in the place of a mythological world a world of ideas
built up by the strength of independent human thought, the
Logos, which could claim to explain reality in a natural way.
It would have been no mean achievement merely to have realised and raised these problems—since the impatience of
the naive, traditional ideas, a sense of wonder, is the beginning of all philosophy; but the Greeks in addition made im-
mense contributions to the solution of these problems. They
formulated all fundamental questions of philosophy, both
theoretical and practical, and answered them with the trans-
parent clearness which is peculiar to the Hellenic mind.
They fashioned for philosophic thought and since philosophy and physics are originally inseparable, to a considerable
extent for the natural sciences, the basic ideas in which the
whole of later European philosophy and science moved
and with which they still work. They founded the chief dis-
ciplines of philosophy and developed all the typical forms
which philosophy assumes. Even the ecclesiastical philosophy
of the middle ages, scholasticism, could not dispense with it
and when philosophy threatened to become frozen in the
form of misunderstood Aristotelianism, it was once again
the pure Greek spirit released from its bonds, which in the
Renaissance awoke thought and inquiry to fresh life and
broke a way for the philosophy of the modern age. If in consequence of the progress of the separate sciences philosophic

problems have become more complicated, it is the man who keeps clearly in view the main lines of philosophic thought which have been drawn once and for all by the Greeks, and who has learnt to trace back the complicated to the simple fundamentals and to reach an understanding in the light of these, who will first find a way in these difficult processes of thought.

But the systems built up by the Greek philosophers are not to be regarded merely as a preparation for modern philosophy. They have a value in themselves alone, as an achievement in the development of man's intellectual life. It was the Greeks who won for man freedom and independence of philosophic thought, who proclaimed the autonomy of reason and gave it a two-fold application. Wisdom in the Greek sense included not only a theoretical explanation of the world but also a definite practical attitude to life. Thus, apart from independence of scientific thought, it was the freedom to live life as he pleased, "autarchie," that distinguished the Greek "wise man." The leading Greek thinkers always *lived* as philosophers. That is what Nietzsche called "the bold openness of a philosophic life" and what he missed in the lives of modern philosophers. The absence of a religious dogmatism favoured the formulation and dissemination of philosophic attempts at explanation of the world. At the same time, in the absence of an ethics founded on religious authority, practical philosophy filled a gap in the spiritual and moral life of the people, where in the same place other peoples had their belief in a religion based on revelation which also regulated their practical life. This it was that lent to Greek philosophy its catholicity and gave it a place in the life of the Hellenes far more important and significant than modern philosophy has ever possessed, which in spite of the theoretical claims to independence, is in reality limited by the power of the church and of a religiously conditioned ethics, and has remained a specialist subject confined to a relatively small circle. Greek philosophy, on the other hand, like art and poetry before it, grew out of the mind of the people and formed an organic component of Hellenic culture. It has attained that supertemporal character which the other creations of the Greek world have won, and like them, in its best works is distinguished for perfect artistic form in presentation. Like the poems of Homer, the masterpieces of Attic tragedy and of Periclean art, this product of the Hellenic spirit stands before us in unfading freshness.

2. *The sources of Greek philosophy*

It is only of relatively few Greek philosophers that the works have been preserved complete and then of only one of the really great, Plato, while much of Aristotle has been lost, particularly his early writings. In point of fact, Plato by no means regarded his literary activity as the most important side of his life, but called it merely "a pleasant amusement." He placed most value on oral communication with his pupils. A large number of philosophers wrote nothing at all: for instance Thales, Pythagoras, Socrates, the Sceptic Pyrrho, the heads of the middle and later Academy, Arcesilaus and Carneades, the Stoic Epictetus, the founder of neo-Platonism Ammonius Saccas and many others. What we know of the lives of these philosophers we owe to the works of their disciples. It is not unimportant to realise this, for we moderns are too inclined to imagine Greek philosophy as predominantly a literary phenomenon, whereas with the Greeks the primary thing was the spoken word and personal contact between teacher and pupil. Nevertheless in the course of time literary publication reached considerable proportions. Most of this, of course, and in particular the whole of the pre-Socratic philosophy and Hellenistic with few exceptions has been lost so that for long stretches we have to fall back on the collection of fragments scattered in authors of every kind. Fortunately in later antiquity work had already begun on the history of philosophy. The following kinds of writings are of value in this respect: the doxographical, the biographical and those of the schools of philosophy. To these may be added chronological researches, critical and polemical writings, commentaries and collections.

Most important for us are the sayings of the philosophers. The records of these at second or third hand are called the doxographical literature. Aristotle set a precedent in his works, particularly in the *Metaphysics,* where he preceded the exposition of his own theories by a summary sketch of his predecessors. His example was followed by his pupil Theophrastus in his *History of Physics* (18 B), which was the first work in Greek to deal with the history of philosophy. It was arranged according to problems: principles, God, Kosmos, meteora, psychology and physiology. Apart from numerous isolated passages a considerable fragment on sense perceptions has been preserved. This work remained for the whole antiquity the main source for pre-Socratic philosophy. The so-called Vetusta Placita, which was put together in the first half of the 1st cent. B.C. by an author from the circle of the Stoic Posidonius, is an extract from this work of Theophrastus. These in their turn were the source of Aetius's (*c.* 100 A.D.) *Collections of Opinions* (of philosophers), from which the Placita philosophorum (*c.* 150 A.D.), falsely attributed to Plutarch, and the extracts of Johannes Strobæus in the first book of his *Extracts* (5th cent. A.D.) are derived. Aetius had carried down doxography from Plato until the middle of the 1st cent. B.C.

The second kind of writings which are of importance as sources is the biographies of the philosophers. This began too with the Peripatetic school, the genre being founded by Aristoxenus of Tarentum, a pupil of Aristotle with leanings towards Pythagoreanism. While anecdote, legend and occasionally personal animosity occupied a considerable space in these accounts, the Alexandrine scholars, particularly Callimachus of Cyrene in his gigantic catalogue in which the philosophers occupied a special place, endeavoured to collect documentary evidence of the life and works of the Greek philosophers. The indexes of writings which are preserved in Diogenes Laertius (p. 23) in particular go back to the original sources. A combination of these two elements, the authentic and the anecdotic, was attempted by Hermippus of Smyrna, a pupil of Callimachus (*c.* 200 B.C.), the author of the most important of the Alexandrian collections of biographies. Antigonus of Carystos stands outside of this and the Peripatetic circles. In his biographies he endeavoured to

bring out the personal character of the philosopher together
with the external account of his life (second half of the 3rd
cent. B.C.). Of course it is only very late works of this kind
which have been preserved. Among them may be mentioned
Lucian's Demonax, the life of the neo-Pythagorean Apollonius of Tyana, by the second Philostratus and the legend-
ary biography of Pythagoras by the neo-Platonists Porphyrius
and Iamblichus.

A third group of writings deals with the philosophic
schools, partly according to their attitude towards the fundamental problems of philosophy, such as the authors of the
On the Schools of Philosophy, among whom the Academician Cleitomachus (2nd century B.C.) and the Stoic Areius
Didymus (time of Augustus) may be mentioned; partly according to the external development of the schools and their
historical connection. Among the latter are the authors of
the *Philosophical Successions.* The founder of this type was
Sotion of Alexandria, who wrote between 200 and 170 B.C.
According to him there were two parallel lines of development—an Ionic, which led from Thales to the middle Academy and Chrysippus, and an Italic, from Pythagoras to the
Eleatics and the Atomists and thence to the Sophists, the
Sceptics and finally Epicurus. His mistake was to attribute
quite uncritically to the older pre-Socratic philosophy the relations which existed between the various schools in the 4th
and 3rd cent. B.C. In order to establish a connection between
these schools, he not seldom invented quite arbitrarily a
master-pupil relation between a later member of a philosophic sect and its first founder. Other authors of such
works were Philodemus of Gadara (1st cent. B.C.) from
whose *Outline of Philosophy* the sections on the Academics
and Stoics have been preserved, and Diocles of Magnesia,
whose work *Compendium of Philosophy* or at least an extract from it was used by Diogenes Laertius (3rd cent.
A.D.). The latter's work *The Lives, Opinions, and Apo-
thegms of Famous Philosophers* (10 bks.), which has been
preserved in a complete state, is the last representative of this
genre. It is a compilation made in its turn from previous
compilations, with the rejection of some material and the

addition of new which the author derived from Diocles (*q.v.*) and Favorinus *Memoirs* and *Miscellaneous History*. While much of the material is worthless, it nevertheless gives us on many points valuable information.

For the chronology of Greek philosophy the fundamental source is the *Chronology* of Apollodorus, consisting of iambic trimeters intended to be learnt off by heart. The period covered extended to about 110 B.C., and in its older parts the book was based on the *Chronographia* of Eratosthenes. The prime of life was assumed to be the fortieth year and this year was identified with some event of historical importance which fell within the life time of the particular philosopher. In this way the date of his birth was approximately calculated.

A further group of sources for Greek philosophy are the miscellanies or collections, such as the Noctes Atticæ of Gellius (*c.* 150 A.D.), the *The Banquet-Philosophers* of Athenæus (*c.* 200) and the roughly contemporary *Varia Historia* of Aelian, and in addition to these critical writings such as those of Cicero and Plutarch, the physician Galen and the Sceptic Sextus Empiricus, the works of the Christian fathers and the great collection of excerpts by Johannes Strobæus.

Finally, the commentaries must be mentioned, which were written from the beginning of the 1st cent. B.C. onwards, especially in the Peripatetic school, on the works of the philosophers who had now become classics. Foremost of these was Andronicus of Rhodes who wrote explanatory notes to Aristotle and Theophrastus. Most important is the commentary on Aristotle by Alexander of Aphrodisias (*c.* 200 B.C.) and that by the neo-Platonist Simplicius on Aristotle's *Physics* and *On the Heavens*. We owe to the latter work the preservation of many fragments and much valuable information.

3. *Prehistory and rise of Greek philosophy*

Ionia in Asia Minor was the cradle of Greek philosophy. It was here, in the colonies on the other side of the Ægean Sea, where Homer's song first resounded, that Greek philosophy came into being. Both were the product of the Ionic mind. This is undeniable however great the chronological difference may be, and however far the cry from the Homeric hero to the Ionic thinker and researcher. Homer and philosophy —these are two poles between which the world of Greek thought rotates. Even Homer's language betrays the intellectual structure of the Greek mind. For even in the violent world of warrior heroes it is mind that is superior and not the will, for which there is actually no word. That a man's actions depend on the state of his knowledge was as axiomatic to the Homeric poets as it was to Socrates. They regarded what we call "character" as knowledge: a king "knows justice", a woman "knows chastity", the savage Cyclop "knows wantonness", the hate-filled Achilles "knows wrath like a lion". And although the word occurs only once, and then with reference to practical skill of a shipwright, nevertheless Odysseus, the master of his fate, with his never-failing cleverness, appears as the prototype of the Greek "wise man." The Apolline clarity of the Ionic mind, sifting and arranging, created out of the welter of local cults the Olympian hierarchy, a model of the Ionic aristocracy with their king at the head, a point which was made by Herodotus. These human, all too human, gods are, with all the might that is theirs, more products of an artistic imagination than objects of serious worship. Not seldom we find their character and actions put to ridicule, so that Homer appears as the creator of the burlesques of the gods which are found in the later comedies. But behind and above these "carefree Gods" there stands a power to which the Homeric man looks up with almost greater seriousness than to the Olympians—Moira, immutable fate. In comparison with their pulsating vitality it is a bloodless abstraction, the creation of men who were beginning to grasp the fact that all events are governed by natural laws. In this Homeric world the fantastic beliefs and superstitions which existed among the lower strata of the population not only in the earliest times, but until far into the historical period, are completely lacking— fear of demons, witchcraft, exorcism, of which we catch only a faint occasional echo. Even death, sad as he is, is accompanied by no terror other than that of an unescapable, but, through its very commonness, supportable fate, and is represented as the twin-brother of sleep. And although naiveté has been with justice recognised as the most pronounced characteristic of the Homeric poems, we should not overlook the fact that they contain much reflection on the world and life. Perhaps no great stress should be laid on the fact that occasional doubts are expressed about prophecy, or that there are traces of an acquaintance with cosmological speculation; more important however is the deep feeling for the transience of all earthly things which animates the Homeric man and is all the stronger because for him life in the light of the sun is alone the true life, against which the shadow existence in Hades is of no significance. The shortness of life and the suffering of earthly existence gives rise to a variety of observations on the lot of the "poor mortal". Sometimes we find moods of actual pessimism, such as in the wonderful conversation of Priam with Achilles, where "Life in suffering" appears as man's natural existence or in the compassionate utterance of the greatest of the gods, that man is the most lamentable of all creatures. Once indeed the question of the origin of evil is raised and the problem is touched, which later evoked in philosophy the theodicy. Of course all these ideas are scattered and always occasioned by quite definite experiences and situations. There is nowhere any trace of a systematic working out of such ideas, and the personality of their authors is always hidden beneath the anonymity of the Homerides. But the notes, thus struck, continue to sound. Beneath the surface of the heroic poetry and its myths the Logos begins to stir, soon to grow bold and raise its head.

An essentially different picture is revealed when we follow the second great epic writer of Greece, Hesiod, from the home of his father, the Æolic Cumæ, to the poor peasant village of Ascra in Bœotia, which was sighing under the harsh tyranny of a rapacious nobility. Hesiod is the first definite individual personality in Greek literature, and it is in his writings that we meet the first efforts at systematisation which is completely lacking in Homer. He is consciously opposed to the Homeric poetry and will tell no "lies" but "reveal the truth". In his Theogony he endeavours to introduce some coherence into the multitude of the gods by means of a genealogical arrangement. In addition to this he made notable contributions to cosmological speculation. Among these are ideas such as that of Chaos and the Aether, and, as Aristotle points out, that of Eros as the moving force, without, however, abandoning the mythical form of personal creation. Hesiod's philosophy of life is distinctly pessimistic. This is revealed most clearly in the myth of the five ages of the world, a sort of primitive philosophy of history, which rests on the idea of a continued deterioration of mankind. Now it has gone so far that Shame and Justice have fled to Olympus, since they could find no abode on earth. But although he has doubts of the justice of the divine rulers of the world, Hesiod is far from being a free-thinker. He lived in the belief that the blessing of God depends on diligence and industry. He turns his attention to ethics and shows in the fable of the hawk and the nightingale that, according to the will of Zeus, the human and animal worlds are governed by different laws, the latter by might and the former by justice. Thus Hesiod, with his serious and meditative mind and his intention to tell men the truth and improve them morally, stands on the border line between two epochs as the forerunner of speculative thought. But he remains within the pale of traditional ideas. Nowhere do we find an attempt, in theory or practice, to set up in opposition to the community or to break loose from it.

In the two centuries which followed Hesiod, however, a process was completed which was of great importance for the rise of philosophy—the emancipation of the individual. In this period, the Greek people extended their territorial possessions to a remarkable extent. The so-called Dorian migration had led to the founding of the earliest colonies on the coast of Asia Minor and the islands of the Archipelago. Now a second period of colonisation embraced the Black Sea, the Propontis, the coast of Thrace and new cities sprang up on the north coast of Africa. But it was especially to the west that the movement tended. In southern Italy and Sicily, Magna Graecia was created as a new area of Hellenic culture, which sent out its furthest outposts to Corsica, southern Gaul and Spain. This great emigratory movement, which brought the Greeks into contact with numerous foreign peoples and revealed to their gaze hitherto unknown lands, different morals and customs, was occasioned by profound social and political changes in the motherland. Just as the heroic kingdoms had broken up, now the power of the nobility began to totter. The gradual change from the barter-system to a monetary system replaced the landed aristocracy of birth by a prosperous and ambitious bourgeoisie. The conflicts were fierce and bitter. It often happened that in the struggle of the Demos with the nobles, a strong individual succeeded in establishing himself as a despot, or that the opposing parties entrusted the settlement of the quarrel to a man distinguished for ability and sense of justice. Finally all these stormy movements ended with the transition to an established constitution of an oligarchic or democratic nature. Thus the Greek Polis in a constitutional sense was created, in which the citizens watched jealously over their freedom and by zealous participation in public life made a continual effort to extend it.

Just as in politics, so in the realm of poetry, the individual rose in these times above the masses, demanding attention and recognition. The individuality of the Homeric poets had been hidden behind their work. In Hesiod we found the first, still diffident attempts at expression of personal feeling and thought. Now the Lyric was created, the most personal of the poetical genres; while the epic narrated in quiet materialism the heroic deeds of bygone generations, the lyric poet, under the impulse of passion, poured out his purely personal experience in song. The world of feeling received a new prominence. The attitude to nature was no longer observational and descriptive, but emotional. In the elegy poetry became a battle-cry, a weapon in political strife or a channel through which the poet expressed his personal views on God, the world and life to his fellows. Iambic poetry not only lashed individual opponents with its biting ridicule, but was turned against particular groups. Melic poetry, the lyric song, sang of passion, friendship, natural beauty and joy of life. The writer of choral lyrics, who praised God and heroes or celebrated princes and other contemporaries victorious in war and peace, did not fail to put his own personal stamp on his poems. All these strong and passionate feelings were expressed in metrical forms of the utmost intricacy, the strictness of the artistic form acting as a wholesome restraint. All these poets endeavoured to make an impression on their contemporaries and to gain influence over them. In the gnomological poetry especially a moral and educational intention is unmistakable. We can recognise this tendency more clearly and in a still more intellectual way in the fable, which in this period became a literary genre.

Just as in politics and art (at first in descriptive and later in representational art) the individual became conscious of himself and his own strength and significance, burst the bonds of custom and put new in the place of the traditional. We observe in the course of the 7th and 8th cent. a similar process in Greek religion. Hitherto it had been the creation of the super-individual spirit of the community; now individual priests and prophets make their appearance and gain influence. Religion seemed to have entered upon a critical stage. The old popular cults no longer satisfied the new strong emotions and the necessity for a personal relation between the individual man and his God made itself felt. The reasons for this are closely connected with the changes in the life of the Greek people which have previously been described. The insecurity of property and life which the political revolutions brought with them could only intensify the deep innate feeling for the transience of all earthly things and cause him to look for some superterrestrial support which would assure him security and permanence amid all the change of mortal things. But together with this external insecurity we can observe at this time a wide-spread internal uncertainty which makes a striking contrast with the self-assured bearing of the Homeric heroes. Their minds are possessed by a remarkable religious fear. The fear of having committed any sin of deed or omission against the gods, or of defilement by any contact with impurity made whole states as well as individual persons feel the necessity for atonement and purification. Priests and prophets were often called from distant places to perform the ceremony, e.g., Epimenides of Crete, who purified Athens by an oriental rite after the defilement of the city by Cylon at the end of the 7th cent. He, like other similar figures of these times, was credited with ecstatic trances during which he was supposed to receive divine revelations. His peculiarly close relations with God were signalised by a mode of life made holy by asceticism—a completely new phenomenon on Greek soil. For divination of the future the old augury of signs known from Homer was no longer felt to be sufficient. Inspired prophets and prophetesses Bacides and Sibyls now appeared on the scene, who, full of the God, made their prophecies in ecstatic trances. Spirit-conjuring, too, a practice which was quite foreign to the Homeric world and is first mentioned in one of the later poems, the Nekuia of the *Odyssey,* achieved in this time wide-spread popularity.

Thus the ground was prepared for a new religion independent of the traditional cults, which came from abroad, from Thrace or Lydia and won an entrance to the Greek world. This new God, Dionysus, who had not yet taken up his abode on the Homeric Olympus, and whose invasion of Greek territory met with a vigorous opposition, won for himself in the course of time a place among the native gods. His worship was combined with indigenous cults like that of the Attic wine-god. At Delphi he made a truce with Apollo, where the old oracle of signs under his influence assumed the form of divination by ecstatic inspiration. He was received into the divine circle of the Eleusinian mysteries under the name of Iacchus. Dionysus is the god of creative nature. He was celebrated in nocturnal rites by torchlight on mountain tops to the accompaniment of wild music. His worshippers were usually women who followed him as Mænads and swung the thyrsus in wild dance, until in their ecstasies they believed they saw the god himself or his sacred animals, the lion and the panther, overpowered them and tore them to pieces. This cult was established as a dogmatic creed which was connected with the name of the Thracian

bard Orpheus. Dionysus is here the lord of life and death.
He himself in the form of an ox—so the legend goes—was
torn to pieces by the Titans, who swallowed his limbs. Only
the heart was retrieved by Athena and brought to Zeus, who
made from it the new Dionysus-Zogreus. Zeus blasted the
Titans with the lightning and from their ashes men were
created. Thus they have a double nature; they are a combination of the Titanic element which has its seat in the
body, and the divine Dionysiac element, from which the
soul takes its origin. The body is mortal and the soul eternal,
that is without beginning and without end. The soul is imprisoned in the earthly body as a punishment for some transgression committed during its divine existence. The body is
not the instrument of the soul but rather its bonds, its
prison, its tomb. For many thousands of years the soul must
undergo new births alternating with periods of purgation
in Hades and enter into a variety of plant, animals and human bodies. Only if it follows the path of salvation in conformance with the precepts of Orpheus, the master, leads a
pure life and abstains from flesh and other forbidden foods
(e.g., beans) and keeps away from all blood offerings, can it
finally be freed from the circle of births and return to the
lost state of divine bliss. Round this dogma of the transmigration of the soul the Orphic communities were built up,
which spread on the mainland especially in Attica, and to a
great extent in the western colonies of southern Italy and
Sicily. We possess, although from a later date (1st-2nd
cent. B.C.) gold plaques from Petelia, Thurii, Eleuthernae
in Crete and Rome, which were put into the graves of the
members of Orphic communities. The inscriptions on them
testify that the soul of the dead man or woman "comes as
pure from pure", that it "has escaped from the grievous circle of births". It is addressed "O happy and blessed one!
Now you are to become a God instead of a man". This doctrine of transmigration was combined in Orphicism with cosmological speculation the details of which are not quite
clear. This much we know definitely however: that in the
beginning of all things were Chaos and Night and these produced an egg from which sprang the winged Eros. It is also

certain that the Orphic theology did not completely supersede polytheism. It regarded the names of gods as nothing
more than different terms for the manifold effects and manifestations of the One divine Being which formed the kernel
of the whole world. Thus in doctrines like the following:

*Zeus is the beginning and the middle, from Zeus is every-
    thing made.*
*Zeus is the foundation of the earth and the star-gleaming
    heavens;*

or:

> *One is Hades and Zeus and Helius and Dionysus,*
> *One God dwells in all.*

The Orphic theology borders on pantheism without however taking the final step. It sought to comprehend the
world as a unity in which an immutable law reigns. It never
however succeeded in surmounting the difficulty which the
contrast of mind and matter, God and the world, soul and
body offers. By the doctrine of transmigration man is enclosed in the cosmic circle of becoming and passing away,
and his fate is fulfilled according to the stern law: "what
you have done, you must endure".

This Orphic mystery religion is a complete reversal of the
true Greek view of life, according to which the corporeal
man is the real man and the soul merely a sort of strenghless
shadowy image. In the Orphic philosophy on the other
hand the eternal and indestructible is the soul, while the
body is transient, unclean and contemptible. To the Greek,
life on earth in the sun is the true life, and the other world
is merely a gloomy imitation of it; to the Orphic life here on
earth is a sort of hell, an imprisonment, a punishment. It is
only in the other world, after the liberation of the soul from
the prison of the body, that the true divine existence awaits
us. Euripides felt this contrast so strongly, that he puts the
following words into the mouth of a character in a lost tragedy:

Who knows then whether life is not death
And what we call death, in the underworld is called life?

This complete reversal of the original, pure Greek view of life and the consequent change of values, especially the contempt and repudiation of the flesh, together with the practical asceticism arising from this belief, is wholly foreign to the Greek nature. It indicates, rather, a non-Greek, oriental origin. It may be that this mystical tendency struck responsive chords in the Greek character and satisfied certain needs which made themselves strangely felt about the time of the rise of this cult; it may be that the passionate Greek suddenly threw himself into religion and found there his satisfaction; nevertheless the dualism of this mysticism which divides the nature of man into two hostile elements remains a foreign strain in Greek blood. This idea of salvation, of the liberation of the god-like soul from the shackles of the earthly body doubtless originated in India, where it makes its appearance in the so-called Upanishads, the explanatory commentaries on the Vedas written between 800 and 600 B.C. when the Vedic beliefs were dying out. Here the cult was of a more speculative character, but in Iran the religion of Zarathustra combined it with the old national gods of the Persians. The oldest *Gâthas* of the *Avesta* are familiar with the belief and in a newly discovered fragment of Zarathustra he appears as a saviour sent from heaven to free the soul from the "embrace" of the body. It was Thrace which formed the bridge over which this oriental doctrine of deliverance crossed into Greece. Here, at a very early date, traces are found in different nations not only of a belief in immortality, but also of a reversal in the respective values of this world and the next which found expression in the custom of bewailing newly born children and felicitating the dead at burial on their blessed lot. Thrace was of course also the native country of Orpheus, under whose name this cult spread in Greece. Orphicism, however, never succeeded in displacing the native religion of the Hellenes; but it soon became strong and tenacious enough to occasion lively philosophic speculation among the Greeks. It is hardly justifiable to derive the "Origin of natural philosophy from the spirit of mysticism", for the Greek mind in its maturity acquired an independence of thought that was strong enough to break

unaided through the shell of myth and to fashion a new picture of the world in the light of reason. Nevertheless this
new religion helped to shake the authority of the old and
here and there to change its forms. It may have worked
like a ferment in the minds of the men of that time and
thus far have given a new impulse to thought. The Greek of
the 6th cent. B.C. who was no longer satisfied with the traditional religion had two courses open to him: that of
rational thought and investigation, which the Ionic physicists
followed, and that of religious mysticism, to which Orphicism pointed the way. These different lines of development
were however not completely separated, but crossed and re-
crossed; for religion and philosophy have a common end
when they deal with the ultimate questions. The whole development of Greek philosophy appears as a continual controversy and, in important phases, a compromise between
national Greek monistic and oriental dualistic thought, in a
word between intellectualism and mysticism. At one time
these two streams divide and run separate courses; at another they combine to form new and fruitful ideas, in which,
however, the non-Hellenic element is always unmistakable.
It was always in the times of great internal and external
disturbances, such as in the 6th cent. itself, after the catastrophe of the Peloponnesian war, in the 1st cent. B.C. at the
end of a hundred years of Roman revolution and finally
from the 3rd cent. A.D. onwards until the time of the decline
of the ancient world, that the dualistic-mystical tendency
came to the fore. Finally, in the form of neo-Platonism,
after the exhaustion of rational thought, philosophy was
transformed into mysticism.

Thus the first precursors of Greek philosophy, whom Aristotle called "theologians" are revealed to us in a curious twi-
light of religion and philosophy. Apart from Orpheus we
know of a Musæus and Epimenides and the most remarkable of them Pherecydes of Syros. This man, half theologian and half natural scientist, was the author of a work
with the peculiar title *Five Chasms* in which he propounded a phantastic theory of creation. According to this
there are three eternal beings: Zas, Chronos and Chthonie.

Zas marries Chthonie and bestows upon her a great, multi-coloured robe, which he spreads upon a winged, that is to say a wide-spreading, tree. On the robe the earth and the ocean ("Ogenos") are depicted. The book contained also the story of the world-creating Eros and the struggle of Chronos with Ophioneus. In the five chasms with their pits, cavities, doors, and portals the neo-Platonists sought to find an allegory of the transmigration of the souls, while the Aithalides mentioned in the same work, whose soul in virtue of a gift bestowed on him by Hermes could spend part of his time in Hades and part on earth, was considered in later times to have been a previous incarnation of Pythag-oras. In still later times the sun-dial constructed by him was pointed out on the island of Syros. Around his death many contradictory legends gathered, in some of which he appears as the teacher of Pythagoras. Thus in this miraculous figure a remarkable combination of mystical and rational elements is contained.

The second preliminary phase of Greek philosophy is the proverbial wisdom, which appears in connected form in the gnomological works of Solon, Phocylides, Theognis, etc., and in isolated prose maxims. Here belongs the group of the so-called seven sages, who however were rather men of practical life. Short sayings were attributed to them, which contained precepts for the conduct of life, such as: "Know thyself!" "Nothing in excess", "The beginning shows the man", "Occupy thyself with serious things", "Go bail for someone and you will regret it", "It is difficult to be hon-est", etc. The composition of this group of seven varies in different accounts; but of the twenty-two names mentioned the following occur in every list: Solon of Athens, Bias of Priene, Pittacus of Mitylene, and the man who was really the first Greek philosopher. This was Thales of Miletus, to whom legends assigned a special place among his contempo-raries.

Thus we find an explanation for the rise of Greek philoso-phy primarily in the peculiar gifts of the Greek people, in which understanding and imagination, rational and instinc-tive forces were united in a fruitful combination. The enthusiastic element, which was undeniably present in the Greek character was tempered by a feeling for truth and clarity. Their passionate disposition was held in check by a sense for order and a love of moderation and restrained by law, both in the realm of politics and formal art. The Greeks themselves connected their mental character with the climate of their sunny land, which however was not so rich that work was unnecessary: for poverty is the mother of virtue. At the same time their land pointed to the sea and traffic with foreign peoples. From there they received various stimulations; but what they borrowed they made their own and developed in their own way. Their philosophy is their own peculiar creation which was bound to well up from the depths of their nature, as soon as the progress of mental development had brought them beyond the childhood stage of myth and the Logos boldly spread its pinions in quest of knowledge and truth.

4. *The main periods of Greek philosophy*

A cursory survey of the development of Greek philosophy reveals the fact that it falls into four distinct periods.

1. *The pre-Socratic philosophy* from the beginning of the sixth until the middle of the fifth century. It consists mainly of natural philosophy, although it makes certain significant departures from this field. Its main interest is concentrated on the world that surrounds man, the Cosmos. It came to an end with the scepticism of the Sophists, who turned the attention of philosophy to man, to his mental and moral nature and to the practical problems of life.

2. *The Socratic philosophy*. With Socrates, men become even more exclusively than with the sophists the central problem of philosophic thought, with the main interest in the correct conduct of life. The solution of this problem was the aim which inspired Socrates to search for objective knowledge. It was this striving after knowledge that led on the one hand to the epistemological foundation of philosophy and on the other to a new expansion of the field of its activities, which consisted in the working out of problems

which had been raised in the pre-Socratic philosophy and Sophism. A temporary solution was reached in the two great systems of Plato and Aristotle, which however are completely different. Side by side with these are found the minor Socratic schools, which were occupied partly with epistemological and partly with ethical questions. The period of their activity falls in the 4th cent. b.c.

3. *Hellenistic Philosophy*. Side by side with the Platonic Academy and the Peripatetic school founded by Aristotle in the Lyceum, there arose about 300 b.c. the Stoa and Epicureanism, which in their physics linked themselves up with the pre-Socratic systems and in their individualistic cosmopolitan ethics developed the doctrines of the Socratic, the Cyrenaic, and the Cynical schools. In this they gave expression to the change in world conditions which had been brought about by the destruction of the Greek Polis and the mixture of peoples in the empire of Alexander the Great and those of the Diadochoi. Scepticism, though resembling them in its individualism, was rejected by these four schools, but was taken up in the doctrines of the Megarean school (which was likewise descended from Socrates) and exercised a strong influence on the middle and later Academy.

4. *The philosophy of the Roman Empire*. This is not fundamentally different from Hellenistic philosophy, for the four main schools lived on in this period and both the Stoa and Scepticism received a new impetus. But this was not strong enough to offer and sustain a successful resistance to the influx into Greek thought of oriental and mystical elements, which from the middle of the first cent. b.c. onwards set in with increasing force, gained the upper hand in the Hellenistic-Jewish philosophy, and in neo-Pythagoreanism and led finally in neo-Platonism to the extinction of Greek philosophy.

THE PRE-SOCRATIC PHILOSOPHY

5. *Its character and development*

Pre-Socratic philosophy can also be termed Ionic philosophy, after its country of origin, for it was in the great commercial sea-ports of Ionia, at first under Lydian, and later (from 546 B.C. on) under Persian sway, in Miletus, Ephesus, Klazomenæ, Samos that first philosophy was born, where in favourable contrast to the sensitiveness and narrow-mindedness of the Athenian democracy, the habitual tolerance exercised by the Persian government in questions of belief permitted it to develop without hindrance or molestation. From here they sent out apostles carrying their wisdom to the Attic Athens and to the Thracian Abdera and not least to the colonies of the Greek west, where they founded new centres for their activities.

The creators of this philosophy were a succession of individuals most of whom were members of distinguished families and for the greater part engaged in political activities. They bear the names physicists, wise men, and professors of wisdom. The term lovers of wisdom, although it existed at that time, was not applied to them. It seems first to have acquired its technical sense in the circle of Socrates and Plato and only after that to have attained general currency. It was a characteristic of the Ionic wise man that he combined theoretical knowledge of the world with mastery of practical life. It would seem therefore not improbable that practical needs and interests were an important factor in this Ionic philosophy. The mariner had always had to rely on observation of the stars for his orientation at sea. That may have given an impulse to the systematic observation of the heavens, so that it was in a good sense that later writers ascribed a "nautical astrology" to Thales. Soon after him men like him began to commit their thoughts to writing. Their works were at first circulated in prose or verse among a small number of friends and were only later given publication. The constantly recurring title of their writings seems to have been "On Nature." Their circulation should not be imagined as confined to a small clique; the works of Heraclitus were known in Elea and Athens, while those of Anaxagoras could be bought in the book shops. There is no doubt that personal relations existed between the oldest Greek philosophers. How far they combined to form schools is less clear. The later evidence on the question is open to the justifiable doubt that it merely projects the relations which existed later in Hellenistic philosophy into the past. It is however certain that among the Pythagoreans such a school existed and we find some traces of the same phenomenon elsewhere. Thus Plato (Soph. 224 D) assumes the existence of such a guild among the Eleatics and he speaks of "men of Ephesus" (*Theæt.*, 179 C) and of "Anaxagoreans" (Crat. 409 B), and when Simplicius (after Theophrastus) calls Anaxagoras "an associate of the philosophy of Anaximenes" that seems to point to the continuance of a school of this philosopher in Miletus, since it is not possible that Anaxagoras could have known him personally.

What particularly distinguishes this oldest period of Greek philosophy is the complete fusion of philosophy and science. There is still no distinction of any kind made between speculation and empirical research. Astronomy and mathematics as well as all branches of natural knowledge, and in the beginning even medicine, were all included in the scope of philosophy, the last named science being the first to detach itself as a practical *technē*. Only *historiē*, the combination of history and geography, as practised by the Ionic logographers and Herodotus, stands apart, and even here the dividing line is not always sharply drawn. Ionic philosophy in its first representatives, considered from a methodological point of view, is pure dogmatism. Without first making any sort of inquiry into the possibilities of human knowledge, they made an immediate attack on the ultimate problems of the origin of the universe. Their philosophy is rightly called "natural philosophy" after the chief object of their inquiries. They first raised the question of the basic substance underlying all things, to which the three Milesians gave different answers. From this supposition of a uniform basic substance the problem of change and, together with it, of being and not being, becoming and passing away, rest and motion followed as a logical consequence. This problem was all the more likely to occur to the Greek in that the etymological meaning of his word for nature led him to regard it not as something complete and finished, but rather as something still in the stage of formation and growth, as a process. The two diametrically opposed attempts by Heraclitus and Parmenides to solve this problem were followed by the three compromise-systems of Empedocles, Anaxagoras, and the atomists. They all denied an absolute becoming and passing away and postulated a number of eternal and unchangeable basic substances (elements). They then endeavoured to explain becoming and passing away from the combination and separation of these elements. This explanation gave rise necessarily to a third problem: the question of the reliability of sense-perception and its relation to thought. It is here that we find the beginnings of a theory of knowledge.

The philosophical tendency, represented by the pre-Socratics, has been given the name of materialism, with the possible exception of the system of Anaxagoras. It is important however to bear in mind that the separation of nature and mind was wholly foreign to original, pure Greek thought. The Greek always imagined nature as animate. On the mythical plane, everything, land and sea, mountains and rivers, trees and bushes were all for him full of divine beings; on the philosophic plane he imagined all matter as animate, not excepting even stones, for they too develop a force. It would be therefore more correct to speak of hylozoism or panpsychism. The problem of life and mind does not exist for these thinkers, since everything is living and infused, although in varying degrees, with mind. A nature deprived of the vital principle was for the Greek unimaginable, so long as he followed the trend of his own thought, independent of foreign influences. Even the "mind" of Anaxagoras had its position within the Cosmos and not outside it. With him of course a further problem crops up: the question what is the first cause of movement and order in the construction of the world and in the course of world-history? That however did not change the idea that mind, too, belongs to nature, so that not only for the pre-Socratics but also for the Stoics and Epicureans, psychology and theology still formed part of physics. The dualism, which separates matter and mind, body and soul, God and the world, won however a place in Greek philosophy even at this early period, when Pythagoreanism arrayed Orphic mysticism in a cloak of science. This school through its influence on Empedocles and Plato was of profound importance for the course of later philosophy. It was, too, the serious interest of the Pythagoreans in the practical regulation of life that first made questions of ethics and social theory subjects of philosophical inquiry. The beginnings of anthropology are found as early as Xenophanes and Heraclitus and interest in such questions was intensified at the end of this period in Democritus and the sophists, who drew the philosophical consequences of the facts which the Ionic *historiē* had established. In sophism, too, the growing feeling for scepticism indicates that natural philosophy had exhausted its strength. The Sophists had performed a valuable service in laying the foundations of educational theory, but by their denial of objective knowledge and the shock they gave to established moral beliefs they stimulated the individualism which was already inherent in the Greek nature and provoked a powerful reaction on the form of the Socratic philosophy.

Thus the pre-Socratic philosophy contained in itself all the seeds of development which later came to fruition.

I. THE MILESIANS

6. *Thales*

Thales of Miletus, a contemporary of Solon and Crœsus (*c.* 624-546) was the son of a Carian father and a Greek mother. We find him in the train of the Lydian king on his expedition against Persia, when he made possible the crossing of the Halys by diverting the course of the river and after the defeat of Crœsus he advised the Ionians to join in a close political combination against the threatening peril of Persia (Herodotus I, 75, 140). Further travels carried him to Egypt where he calculated the height of the pyramids by the length of their shadows and doubtless made his acquaintance with the Babylonian Saros-period (of 18 years 11 days), which enabled him to predict the eclipse of the sun which took place on the 28th of May, 585 B.C. (according to the Julian Calendar). He also put forward an explanation, which was however false, of the inundation of the Nile (Herod., II, 20, Athen., II, 87 A). In Miletus he constructed an instrument for determining the distance of ships sighted at sea and he referred sailors to the Little Bear as the safest guide for determining the direction of the north. A few elementary geometrical propositions were also ascribed to him. These mathematical studies and the scientific sense awakened by them had doubtless a considerable influence on his attempt to explain the ultimate basis of things on other than mythological terms. On the other hand it is in keeping with the elementary character of Greek mathematics that his physics never got beyond its first beginnings. He explained water as the substance of which everything is made and consists. Furthermore earth floats on the water like a piece of wood, an assumption which made comprehensible the fixed position of the earth in the centre of the world. Aristotle can only conjecture the reason for this hypothesis, since he was not in possession of any writings of Thales and doubtless no such works ever existed. Those which are mentioned by later writers, together with the doctrines which they contain are to be regarded as spurious. Thales seems to have given no more detailed explanation of the way in which things are created from water. He probably regarded the moving force as directly bound up with the material, and this, in the spirit of the old nature-religion as something analogous to the human soul. This is also indicated by the sayings (Aristotle, *De an.*, I, 5, 411, a, 7 405a 19) that everything is filled with God and the magnet has a soul (i.e., life) since it attracts iron. He regards the substance as having life and soul, a view which recurs in his successors and which has been aptly named hylozoism or hylopsychism. We have no grounds for assuming that he distinguished expressly between matter and the creative force as deity or mind or world-soul. However meagre these first beginnings of a physical theory may seem, the important thing is that a beginning was made at all with such a theory and that the great thought of the unity of the world was conceived.

7. *Anaximander*

This significant and influential thinker was a fellow-citizen and younger contemporary of Thales (*c.* 610-545). That he was of distinguished family is indicated by the fact that he led a Milesian colony to Apollonia on the Black Sea. Remarkable in his own time for his astronomical and geographical knowledge, he carried on by independent research the cosmological studies which Thales had stimulated. His results he embodied in a work which was however lost at an early date. He was thus the oldest Greek prose-writer and the earliest philosophical author. From this work the following sentence is preserved: "The beginning of that which is, is the boundless but whence that which is arises, thither must it return again of necessity; for the things give satisfaction and reparation to one another for their injustice, as is appointed according to the ordering of time". This sentence has undergone different interpretations. Some see in it an application of the Orphic doctrine of the sinful existence of mankind in the whole universe. Others are of the opinion

that it gives a picture of a law-suit which the things contest
before the judgment seat of Time, in which they bring forward their rival claims of a right to exist. For his primary
substance Anaximander chose neither one of the four elements nor a substance which lay between air and fire or air
and water, nor of a mixture of the individual substances in
which these were contained with definite qualitative differences. We may conclude not only from Theophrastus' definite account (in Simpl. *Phys.* 27, 17ff, 154, 14ff; Diels,
Doxogr. 479), but also from Aristotle's statements, that Anaximander either expressly distinguished his "Boundless" from
all definite substances, or, what is more probable, that he
gave no detailed explanation of its nature, but merely wished
to specify that substance which possessed none of the distinguishing characteristics of the particular substances. Thus
the boundless was conceived by him as something spacially
unbounded (infinitum) and at the same time of indefinite
quality (indefinitum). To support his view of the boundlessness of this primary substance Anaximander pointed out that
if this were not the case, this substance would exhaust itself
in the process of creation. The "boundless" as the primary
substance is unoriginated and indestructible and its motion
is likewise eternal. A consequence of this motion is the "separation" of particular substances. At first Warm and Cold
separated out and from these two arose the Moist; from this
came Earth and Air and the Circle of Fire, which surrounds
the earth like a spherical shell. This burst asunder and
formed circles like the felloes of a wheel. These felloes are
filled with fire and provided with apertures. They are moved
by air currents and revolve around the earth at an angle inclined to the horizontal. The fire which pours out of their
apertures while they revolve and is continually renewed by
evaporation from the earth gives the appearance of stars
sweeping through the space of the heavens. This idea seems
strange enough to us, but it is in reality the first attempt
known to us to give a mechanical explanation of the regular
motion of the stars on the lines of the later theory of spheres.
Anaximander regarded the earth as a cylinder whose diam-

eter is three times as great as its height. He conceived the bold thought that it swung free in the middle of the universe and through being equidistant from the boundaries of the world (which seems to be regarded as a sphere) is maintained in a state of rest. In the beginning the earth was in a fluid state and then, as it gradually dried up, it brought forth living creatures. Men were at first enclosed in fish-like coverings and lived in the water which they abandoned only when they had evolved sufficiently to support themselves on land. A trustworthy tradition which we can trace back to Theophrastus asserts that Anaximander in accordance with the postulates of his cosmology assumed a periodic alternation of creation and destruction in the universe and hence a succession of worlds without beginning or end. Apart from this he seems to have assumed the simultaneous existence of innumerable world-systems in endless space.

Anaximander constructed a sun-dial and a globe of the heavens and designed a map of the world for which in later times his fellow-countryman Hecatæus provided a text in his *Description of the Earth*.

8. *Anaximenes*

Anaximenes, also a Milesian, is described by later writers as the pupil of Anaximander, whose influence he clearly betrays. His *floruit* according to Apollodorus is to be placed between the years 585/84 and 528/24. Of his writings, which were composed in Ionic prose, only a small fragment has been preserved. In his physical theory Anaximenes differs from Anaximander in that his primary substance is not merely something infinite without any more exact definition, but in common with that of Thales a substance with definite qualities; but he agrees with Anaximander in that he chooses for this purpose a substance which seems to possess the real qualities of the latter's primary matter, that is boundlessness and perpetual movement. Both these qualities are to be found in air. It does not only spread itself out into the "boundless" but is also in a state of continual motion and change, and is thus shown (according to the ancient belief whereby the soul is identified with the life-force) to be the cause of all life and movement in living beings. "Just as our souls, which are made of air, hold us together, so does breath and air encompass the world." (Anax. in *Aet.*, I, 3, 4, Diels, *Vors.*, 3 B 2). Through its beginningless and endless motion the air undergoes a change, which is actually of two kinds—rarefaction or "loosening" and condensation or contraction. The former process is at the same time "warming" and the latter "cooling." By rarefaction air becomes fire and by condensation wind and progressively clouds, water, earth and stones. This theory Anaximenes probably derived from observation of atmospheric processes and precipitation. In the process of creation the earth was formed first; according to Anaximenes it is flat like a tabletop and on this account is sustained by the air. The vapours which rise from it are rarefied and become fire, parts of which, when pressed together by the air become stars. These are of similar shape to the earth and revolve around it, floating upon the air (unless this applies merely to the planets) in a lateral direction, like a hat turned round a head. Anaximenes was the first to recognise that the moon derives its light from the sun and he gave a natural explanation of eclipses of the sun and moon, which he regarded as caused by bodies, similar to the earth, revolving in the universe. He observed also moon-rainbows and marine phosphorescence. He explained the rainbow as the effect of the sun's beams on a thick cloud which its rays could not penetrate. According to a trustworthy tradition, Anaximenes, like Anaximander, held the theory of successive alternations of world-creation and world-destruction.

However naïve and extraordinary many views of the three oldest Greek thinkers may seem to us, it marks a powerful, fundamental change from a mythical conception to a natural, that is scientific, explanation of the world, when Iris, who is in Homer a living person, the messenger of the Gods, is here transformed into a physically explainable, atmospheric phenomenon.

II. THE PYTHAGOREANS

9. *Pythagoras and the Pythagorean order*

With Pythagoreanism begins the transformation of the Greek mode of thought by a foreign element which originated in the Orphic mysticism, a cult strange to the Hellenic nature, and by its fusion with Greek thought, gave rise to many remarkable new forms which were of great significance for the time to follow. Our trustworthy information about Pythagoras, the son of Mnesarchus of Samos, is so meagre that we only see him as a gigantic shadow striding through history. As a matter of fact we possess two biographies of him, but they are written by the neo-Platonists Porphyrius and Iamblichus and merely repeat the legends about Pythagoras the beginnings of which we find in the fragmentary remains of the Aristotelian treatise *On the Pythagoreans* (*Fr.*, 191, Diels 4, 7), and which sprang up in rich luxuriance after the time of the neo-Pythagoreans. Nevertheless we possess apart from these a few ancient testimonies which carry all the more weight because they were inspired by a spirit of criticism. Thus Xenophanes, a contemporary of Pythagoras and only a decade younger, derides him on account of his doctrine of transmigration and Heraclitus levels against him the charge of dilettantism, to say nothing of another utterance by the same philosopher, in a still more biting tone the authenticity of which however is contested. About half a century after Pythagoras' death, Herodotus (IV, 95) calls him "not the weakest sophist of the Greeks". He gives a clear testimony, although without actually mentioning any name, that Pythagoras taught the doctrine of transmigration which he erroneously supposes to have been borrowed from the Egyptians, whereas they of course know nothing of it (II. 123). Pythagoras appears already as a superhuman form in the writings of a philosopher of similar mind, Empedocles (*Fr.* 129), who ascribes the former's extraordinary knowledge to his power of retaining the experiences of twenty or thirty previous existences. Apart from this, we hear that he wrote

nothing but that in his school they held the spoken judgments of the master to be authoritative. It was conjectured
with great probability even in ancient times that Pythagoras
left his native town Samos during and because of the tyranny
of Polycrates 532 B.C. and migrated to Croton in southern
Italy, where he founded the Pythagorean order. Later, political enemies caused him to remove to Metapontum, where
he died in 496 B.C. These accounts of Pythagoras establish
three certainties: that he adopted the doctrine of transmigration which first made its appearance in Orphic societies, that
he pursued scientific studies which aroused great interest in
his own time, and that he founded a society whose members
bound themselves to a life regulated by definite religious and
ethical principles. The Legends which at an early date grew
up around his person show at least that he was a man of
supreme mental gifts and of powerful influence. a personality
well fitted to be ranked among the "theologians" of the sixth
century, men like the later Empedocles who could combine
religious speculation with scientific thought and research.

The spirit, the principles and the practices of the Pythagorean order all have their root in the doctrine of transmigration. This should not be regarded as a subordinate or more
or less indifferent appendage of the Pythagorean "philosophy"; for what distinguishes the Pythagoreans is a particular
mode of life. Just as in the "Orphic life" (Plat. Laws VI,
782c) their aim was to be freed from the circle of births and
to enter again into the last, divine state of bliss. The road to
it, the way of salvation, is here fundamentally the same: the
purification from sensuality, and the renunciation of the
earthly. In the method of this purification we may observe
a distinction between the Orphics and the Pythagoreans, in
that the purely ritual character of the former is here intel-
lectualised and moralised. The Pythagoreans indeed took
over certain ascetic observances such as abstinence from
flesh-food (in which however they seem to have been less
strict), the prohibition of beans and a large number of precepts which are usually explained as the survivals of a primitive tabu-belief or as symbolical. But they went further. They
regarded men as the property of the gods, as a sort of flock,

which may not leave its fold without the consent of the gods. Life is therefore something extremely serious and its correct conduct requires a systematic training. This is the reason for injunction of prolonged silence laid upon the novice and the demand for a strict daily self-examination. The highest form of purification is however mental work: it is the safest means of freeing oneself so far as is possible in this life from the body, this evil with which the soul is sullied, so that the sensual in us is mortified before death actually comes. To these methods of purification adopted by the Pythagoreans belongs further music, and in a particular sense gymnastics. We should imagine that this attitude to the body and its needs according to which these were regarded only as impediments to the development of the spiritual powers would not have been favourable to physical culture; and as a matter of fact, the comedy of the 4th cent. B.C. censures the Pythagoreans of that time for the neglect of the body through insufficient food and lack of cleanliness. The old, true Pythagoreans such as Milo of Croton, who created a stir by his victory at the Olympic games, always paid the greatest attention to dietetics and gymnastics. They must have been influenced by the idea of "hardening", which sought to limit the needs of the body, to give it resistance against external influences and make it an efficient instrument of the mind. We see that the idea of purification was later modified by the Pythagoreans, when it came to signify no longer purification of the soul from bodily influences but a purification of the soul by Science and Music and a purification of the body by Gymnastics and Medicine, a science which was cultivated intensively by the oldest Pythagoreans. The whole idea of brotherhood which was the basis of the Pythagorean order rested on the doctrine of transmigration. All living and organic beings (including the plant-world) were regarded as interrelated, since they represent embodiments of the soul-dæmons. This resulted in a strong social tendency which found its expression in the admission of women on an equal basis, their sex being represented by numerous names in the list of members which is preserved in Iamblichus; furthermore, in the cultivation of a spirit of friendship ready to render any help and make any sacrifice, even of life—the story of Damon and Pythias comes to mind—and finally in the humane treatment of slaves. In spite of this the Pythagoreans by no means thought that a remedy was to be found in the mechanical equalisation of all men, but in a social order which, like nature, itself had different grades. They called this in contrast to arithmetical, i.e., mechanical equality, geometrical, i.e., proportional equality, according to which the rights of the individual correspond to his merits. This principle of gradation they saw realised in transmigration, since the form in which each soul was from time to time embodied depended on the sort of life it had led previously, on the basis of which it was tried in Hades and rewarded or punished accordingly. The highest grade of earthly existence was considered to be a life as bard, physician or prince. After such a life the soul returned directly to the state of divine bliss which it had once possessed. We see in this choice of professions how the idea of purification discussed above won general acceptance.

In the light of these principles it is not to be wondered at, that the Pythagoreans felt themselves called to the spiritual guidance of their fellow-countrymen—i.e., to rule. In fact the Pythagorean order for nearly a century played a prominent part in the politics of the cities of Magna Graecia. Under the government of the Pythagoreans, Croton succeeded in establishing a hegemony over a territory about four times the size of Attica, to which belonged the cities of Metapontum, Locri, Rhegium and even Zancle in Sicily. The character of the Pythagorean politics, from the nature of its view of life can only have been that of an intellectual aristocracy which as such laid claim to the guidance of state business. This aristocratic tendency brought about the fall of the Pythagorean power about the middle of the second half of the 5th cent. B.C., when the democratic party in Magna Graecia too raised its head and gained strength. We hear of a cruel massacre of the order in Crotona, when its members were surrounded in their assembly house and the greatest part of them burnt to death. In other towns of southern Italy similar persecutions seem to have taken place. Only Archippus,

Philolaus and Lysis seem to have escaped, of whom the last became in later times the tutor of the young Epaminondas.

10. *The Pythagorean doctrines*

Our evidence shows without a possibility of doubt that Pythagoras himself, besides the doctrine of transmigration, pursued scientific studies. These were concentrated mainly on mathematics, their purpose being "purification" or liberation from sensual. On the other hand in the state of the tradition we are not in the position to distinguish the doctrines which belong to him personally from the general tenets of the school. At best we can distinguish the earlier Pythagoreanism, which lasted until the dissolution of the order in the second half of the 5th cent. B.C. from the later Pythagoreans whose head at the beginning of the 4th cent. was Archytas of Tarentum. Plato had close relations with these philosophers, who were called by Aristotle "the so-called Pythagoreans". Their doctrines will be discussed in a later chapter; here only a brief outline of the fundamental doctrines of the older Pythagoreanism will be attempted.

The fundamental doctrine of the Pythagoreans is the proposition that the nature of things is number. There can be no doubt that the Pythagoreans were led to this surprising statement by their musical studies which served ethical ends (p. 49). They recognised indeed that the pitch of tones depends on the length of the strings on musical instruments and that musical harmony is determined by definite mathematical proportions. The recognition of this fact led them to the principle which was not contained in matter itself but was supersensual. Thus the anthropological dualism of body and soul was extended to the cosmic dualism of matter and form, or, as they expressed it, of the unlimited and the limit. Hence number was for them something essentially different from water for Thales, or the Apeiron for Anaximander or air for Anaximenes; it was something opposed to matter and distinguished from it although closely connected with it, something which limits it and gives it shape. Matter as such is presupposed by the Pythagoreans and they seem to have imagined it in much the same way as Anaximander and Anaximenes, the latter of whom seems to be indicated by the theory of the unlimited breath, i.e., the endless expanse of air beyond the cosmos from which the world draws its breath. Now that number was established as a world-principle, they proceeded to make remarkable speculations on its nature. They drew distinctions between straight and not-straight, unity and duality and thus received two further pairs of opposites, whose number was later rather arbitrarily made up to ten. Individual numbers were considered particularly sacred, especially the "Tetractys of the Decad," by which they were accustomed to swear, i.e., the representation of the number ten by $(1 + 2 + 3 + 4)$ dots arranged as a pyramid. This method representing numbers led them to geometrical problems. From the points lines were derived, from the lines planes and from the plane solids. The so-called Pythagorean triangle, i.e., a right-angled triangle whose sides stand in the relation $3 : 4 : 5$, the terms of which, hypotenuse and cathetes, are reminiscent of the primitive mensuration methods of the Egyptian geometer could have provided an early opportunity for the discovery of the famous Pythagorean theorem, which there are no adequate grounds for not ascribing to Pythagoras. It cannot be determined with certainty when the epoch-making idea of the spherical shape of the earth and the other celestial bodies first appeared in the Pythagorean school. We know from Theophrastus that Parmenides was the first to speak of the spherical shape of the earth; but that may be the first literary authority for the new theory and that cannot exclude the possibility that Parmenides, who was a disciple of the Pythagorean Ameinias, may have learnt of the theory in the circle of the Pythagoreans. The theory of planetary movement and the harmony of spheres must also be ascribed to the old Pythagoreanism. That this was an attempt to apply to nature the idea of harmony discovered in music is supported also by medical theories of this time (vid. infra., p. 57). Finally an endeavour to refine religious ideas seems to have formed part of the work of the older Pythagoreans. At least that seems indicated by the legend found in a Visit to Hades; that Pythagoras saw Homer and Hesiod suffering punishment in the underworld for what they had said about the gods. Furthermore the allegorical moralising interpretation of myths seems to have found a footing in the school at an early date. The theories of the school were for a long time treated as secret doctrines (*Phædr.* 62B) and in one case we have an express testimony (Diog. L. VIII, 85) for the fact, that until Philolaus (p. 55) there were no writings on the Pythagorean philosophy.

11. *The Pythagorean Philosophers*

The Pythagorean league was, as far as we know, the cradle of scientific medicine in Greece, the Crotonian school of physicians flourishing long before Hippocrates. The first Pythagoreans were also physicians who committed their theories to writing and published them, while the other dogmas of Pythagoreanism, especially that of transmigration were still secret doctrines. The first of these physicians, who however wrote nothing, was Democedes of Croton. We find him in the service of the cities of Athens and Ægina and the tyrant Polycrates and at the court of the Persian king Darius, where his professional success overshadowed the Egyptian physicians. The first of the Pythagoreans to publish scientific books, however, was Alcmæon of Croton, who as a young man is said to have known the aged Pythagoras. He was both physician and philosopher, and this double character appears on his book, which was dedicated to the Pythagoreans Brotinus, Leon, and Bathyllus. He took his point of departure obviously from empirical investigation and may be called the first physiologist. On the basis of dissection of animals he recognised the brain as the central organ of mental life. As a surgeon he ventured upon the operation of removing an eye. According to him health depended upon an equal distribution of the qualities warm and cold, dry and wet, bitter and sweet, etc., in bodies, while the predominance of one of them caused illness. In this theory of the isonomy of substances in the body we recognise again the Pythagorean principle of harmony. When he said that men perish "because they cannot join the beginning to the end", he means that the bodily development of a man is not a circle but a straight line and finally a continuous decline. In the field of psychology, too, he made the first steps, in that he distinguished between sense-perception and thinking, which occurs in men alone, and within thinking he distinguished memory, idea and knowledge. He regarded the sun as a flat disc and therefore knew nothing of the spherical shape of the stars, which, since they are in spontaneous and eternal motion, he declared to be animate. On the same grounds he regarded the soul as immortal, and the context in which Aristotle credits him with this view, is an indication that he had given up the doctrine of transmigration. Moreover he thought very little of the possibility of human knowledge: "only the gods possess clearness about the invisible as well as earthly things; we men have to depend on conjecture alone (*Fr.* 1)".

Hippasus of Metapontum must have been considerably younger, since, following the precedent of Heraclitus, he made fire his principle and attempted to combine this with Pythagoreanism. According to one tradition he is said to have left no writings behind, according to others he is said to have been banished from the order on account of publishing mathematical discoveries of the Pythagoreans, which he gave out as his own. As a punishment for this offence he is said to have found his death at sea.

One of the last of the older Pythagoreans and the figure who of this circle has been most hotly disputed by modern scholarship is Philolaus of Croton. He was one of the few who succeeded in escaping from the catastrophe which befell the order. He, too, like Lysis, according to Plato, taught in Thebes. His disciples Simmias and Cebes are present at Socrates' death in the *Phædo* and the Pythagoreans from Phlius (*Fr.* 39, 4) are called his disciples (Diog. L., VIII, 46). Later he is supposed to have gone to Tarentum. It is certain that he was a physician and was also active as a writer. Mention is made of him in a collection of medical theories since the beginning of the 5th cent. B.C., put together by Meno, a pupil of Aristotle and we have some knowledge of him from a papyrus of the British Museum. He appears here as a medical eclectic. The warm, which he regards as a substance, constitutes human and animal bodies, and the cold air from outside flows in and is breathed out again. The causes of illness are to be found in the bodily juices, the blood, the gall and the phlegm. Apart from that, an excess or a lack of warm or cold or food can also bring about an illness. It is questionable whether Philolaus wrote anything besides the medical writings in which these views are expressed. It is quite possible however that these, like those of Alcmæon, were of anthropological content, so that other fragments, which we may with some probability ascribe to him, may belong to these works. Connected with this theory is the conception of the soul which stands in sharpest contradiction to the old Pythagorean doctrine of transmigration and which is expounded by his pupil Simmias in Plato's *Phædo* (85 E ff). According to this the soul is "a mixture and a harmony" of the substances combined in the body and accordingly perishes with it. This doctrine can be brought into line with Philolaus' medical views, and since his residence in Thebes is mentioned before (61 E) we may refer to him the playful designation of this doctrine by Socrates as "Theban harmony" (95 A), while the two disciples of Philolaus have heard nothing of the transmigration dogma from their master. Less certain is it if we may ascribe to him the world-system which is also expounded by Plato in the *Phædo* (108ff), according to which the spherical earth is poised in the middle of the universe and the stars rotate around it—a view which is put forward here as something quite new and differing fundamentally from previous theories. Yet it is immediately accepted as correct by Simmias without any expression of astonishment. In any case this cosmology, which was still new to Plato in 380 B.C., cannot be older than Philolaus. The system, however, which after the time of Posidonius was known to the ancients under his name and which abandons the theory that the earth is in a state of rest, is not consistent with the above theory and must accordingly be of later date (p. 90). Moreover it is hardly possible today to believe any longer in the authenticity of the fragments which are preserved of two books supposed to be by Philolaus, *On Nature* and *Bacchæ*. They are written in the Doric dialect and contain theories on the nature of number and harmony, on the five elements and the soul. These books, according to an anecdote current in ancient times, are said to have been acquired by Plato for a large sum, who then made them the basis of his *Timæus*. In reality these fragments belong most probably to the work of the Academician Speusippus, the nephew and successor of Plato, *On Pythagorean Numbers,* in which the author appeals to the authority of Philolaus and puts into his mouth a Pythagorean theory of the creation of the world. Apart from this we know of Philolaus only that he engaged in the allegorical interpretation of myths which was usual in Pythagorean circles.

Apart from these men a few prominent personalities of the 5th century show themselves indirectly influenced by Pythagorean ideas, although they were not actually members of the Pythagorean order. Among these was the tragic poet and philosopher Io of Chios, a contemporary of Sophocles and Pericles, who in his work entitled *Triagmos* assigned to the number three, which was especially favoured by the Pythagoreans, a predominant position in the world; furthermore the architect Hippodamus of Miletus, who drew up the plans of the new towns in the Piræus and in Rhodes and who as non-politician first outlined a theory of an ideal state. This state too is dominated by the number three; the divisions of classes, of land and the laws are threefold. Finally the idea of symmetry that dominates the studies of the famous sculptor and bronze-founder Polyclitus on the proportions of the human body contained in the work *The Canon* is clearly Pythagorean in origin. Thus we see that the influence which the earlier Pythagoreanism exerted on the motherland is not to be underestimated. But still more powerful and of far greater consequence was the influence which the later Pythagoreanism was to exercise on the development of later Greek thought through the agency of Plato.

III. THE ELEATICS AND HERACLITUS

12. *Xenophanes*

In contrast to the Pythagorean dualism Ionic thought persevered in its monistic character. But now a new problem arose from that of the primary substance which the Milesians had raised and tried to answer: in what way do the multiplicity and variety of the individual beings arise from the One which is the basis of everything? This difficulty which up till then had scarcely been touched upon, now demanded a solution. The problem of the One and the Many, of Being and Becoming, of Rest and Motion became the centre of the discussion, which was now carried on by the Eleatics and Heraclitus. Moreover it was inevitable that the epistemological questions indissolubly connected with the problem of change should now be raised.

The Eleatic school of philosophy was also an offshoot of Ionia in southern Italy. Xenophanes of Colophon (*c.* 570-475) left his native country at the age of about twenty-five when it came under Persian domination (546 B.C.). After a long life spent in travel which took him to Malta and Pharos,[1] Messana, Catania, and Syracuse, where at the artistic court of the king Hiero he perhaps made the acquaintance of the poets Simonides and Pindar, Æschylus and Epicharmus, he finally found a permanent home in Elea in southern Italy. He is perhaps the only Ionic philosopher who was not of noble birth; he had indeed to endure the mockery of king Hiero at his poverty, since he earned his living as a rhapsodist. Through this profession he himself became a poet. His strong sense of reality led him as an epic poet from the myth to history and he celebrated in two narrative poems the founding of Colophon and Elea. Perhaps we possess in certain chapters of Herodotus a condensation of the second poem. He observed with a keen eye the wonders of the various lands seen on his travels, the differences of customs and the peculiarities of nature. In the quarries of Syracuse, in Malta and Pharos he was struck by fossils of sea-animals and drew from these finds important conclusions about changes of the earth surface and the origin of life. But he also observed with a critical spirit the life, activity and mentality of his own people and indulging his satirical vein ridiculed in his *Silloi* (satirical poems) and occasionally in his elegies whatever appeared to him absurd. He attacked not only the excrescences of civilisation like the effeminate luxuriousness of his Ionic compatriots, but dared to lay his hands upon the most sacred authorities of the Greek people, Homer and Hesiod, because of their anthropomorphic representation of the Gods (*Fr.* 10-14) and further to criticise mercilessly the exaggerated importance which everywhere attached to athletic achievements (*Fr.* 2). Neither the Orphic-Pythagorean belief in transmigration (*Fr.* 7), nor the Bacchic frenzy of the worshippers of Dionysus (*Fr.* 17), nor the magician Epimenides escaped the mocking superiority of his clear mind and his strong self-contained character. He belied the "Dilettantism", which provoked the censure of Heraclitus (*Fr.* 40), by expounding a consistent, self-assured, philosophy of life and the world, which assured him a strong position from which he let loose with unerring aim the stinging shafts of criticism. Thus the historian became the philosopher of history, the ethnologist the philosopher of religion and the observer of nature the philosopher of nature. All this he regarded as a uniform whole; through the manifold of phenomena his eye perceived the spiritual unity of the Cosmos. His whole poetry was the expression of conviction and creed. Even in the elegies intended for light-hearted dinner-parties he attacked the "Prehistoric fables" and recommended a life of purity and piety and justice (*Fr.* 1). He gave expression to harmless joy of life (*Fr.* 22) and his contempt for meanness and avarice (*Fr.* 21). Finally in a poem *On Nature* he embodied his personal convictions on the nature of the world. The basic idea of this philosophy was the unity of everything, that is of the All-One. This All-One was at the same time the Deity, without beginning and without end, always similar to itself and hence unchangeable. This "One God" which is not beyond the world but organically inseparable from it, is quite different from the gods whom the people think in the way the poets have represented them. The "trampler of Homer" cannot do enough to divest his Deity of all human qualities. It is comparable neither in shape nor in thought to mortals. It remains motionless always in the same position and it is not in its nature to go from place to place. It is all eye, all ear and all thought; effortlessly it swings the All with the strength of its mind. This Deity is completely self-sufficient and in need of nothing. A multiplicity of gods, with superiority and subordination is unthinkable. How Xenophanes thought of the relation of this Deity to the world of appearances we do not know in detail: what is certain is that this relation was one of "immanence", so that we must designate his philosophy as pantheism. Nothing in our tradition indicates that he contended that apparent creation and destruction of individual objects is mere illusion. But his own words (*Fr.* 38, 36) show, that he distinguished between thought and sense-perception and recognised the relative character of the latter. He does not pledge himself to reach complete clearness about everything, but contents himself with reaching views which are "like reality". There is no certain knowledge but only belief supported by reasons and personal conviction (*Fr.* 34, 35).

With this reservation, Xenophanes sets forth his opinion to world and man with great exactness. His idea of the world is however very primitive. Although, like Anaximenes before him, he divests Iris of her mythical character and gave a natural explanation to the rainbow and the so-called St. Elmo's fire, which popular belief ascribed to the Dioscuri. Yet he imagined the stars as fiery clouds which glow at night like coals and are extinguished by day. The earth stretched downwards to infinity. On the grounds of his observation of fossils (*vide sup.*), he thought that it had originally been covered with water and that living creatures were created from the mud formed by earth and water.[2] The sea he regarded as the source not only of all water but of the winds as well.

Xenophanes has greater significance as an anthropologist. He conceived the idea of a mental progress in the development of mankind and while popular belief regarded the most important achievements of civilisation, such as agriculture and the cultivation of the vine and the discovery and use of fire and other contrivances as the gifts of benevolent gods, he was the first to recognise them as the personal creations of men. It was however in his treatment of religion that he showed the greatest penetration. In this, too, he saw the work of men; its various forms are determined by the peculiarities of the different peoples. He had already expressed the thought that "in his gods man depicts himself" and had given examples to illustrate it. His greatest achievement is that he was not led to atheism but purified the idea of deity from the last vestiges of human defects and thus cleared the way not only for a deeper conception of God, but also for a piety free from all superstition (such as for example divination), the substance of which is moral thought and moral conduct. This philosophy of religion, which is based on the idea of the unity of the world and the inseparability of God and Nature, remains the chief merit of Xenophanes. In details we miss, at least so far as the tradition allows us to see, the systematic working out of his thoughts. Nevertheless with his open-mindedness this man of progress in the sense of an enlightened rationalism, this philosopher who was the first to identify the divinity immanent in the world with unchangeable Being and the first to give thought the preference over the unreliability of sense-perception, appears clearly as the founder of a new tendency in Greek philosophy.

13. *Heraclitus*

The later development of the Eleatic philosophy, especially the metaphysics of Parmenides, is not only a continuation of the ideas of Xenophanes, but becomes fully comprehensible only if it is grasped as a reaction against the fundamental ideas of Heraclitus.

Heraclitus (*c.* 544-484) was born in Ephesus, which after the destruction of Miletus by the Persians (494 B.C.) was the most powerful city of Asia Minor and contained a world-famous shrine of Artemis, a monumental symbol of the fusion of Oriental and Greek culture. He was a member of the noblest family in which the royal office of sacrificial priest to the Eleusinian Demeter was hereditary. His attitude in public life was in accordance with the traditions of his house. A born aristocrat, he was alike an opposer of the tyranny which had long dominated his native city and of the democracy by the activities of which he felt so repelled that he withdrew into the solitude of the shrine of Artemis. Of serious and profound mind, filled with contempt for the activities and opinions of men, he found no satisfaction in the most admired sages of his time and pursued an independent line of inquiry. His results he embodied in his work (title unknown) without any detailed explanation, in pregnant, figurative and not seldom oracular aphorisms,[3] which are laconic to the point of obscurity. This method of exposition earned him the nick-name of the "Obscure", the first traces of which are found in Livy (cf. XXIII, 39). He himself thought that it was in accordance with the dignity of the subject and it gives us the true picture of his mind, which worked rather by intuition than in concepts and was more directed to the synthesis than the analysis of the manifold. The story is told that Socrates described the method to Euripides with the words: "What I understood is noble and I also believe what I did not understand; but to do that one would need to be a Delian diver".

Like Xenophanes, Heraclitus started from the observation of nature; he comprehended this as a uniform whole; as such it has neither come into being nor does it pass away. Xenophanes had found the essence of the world in the Deity; in the same way Heraclitus saw it in a spiritual principle—the Logos. But he remained nearer the position of the old Ionic Philosophers than the Eleatics, in that he regarded this world-reason as bound up with a definite material substrate, fire; and while the Deity of Xenophanes was throned in majestic repose and unchangeability, it was the unceasing change of things, the instability of all individual things that made so strong an impression upon Heraclitus, that he saw in this the general law of the universe and could only regard the world as something involved in incessant change and ever subject to new modifications. Everything flows and nothing is permanent: one can never step twice into the same river

(*Fr.* 91, cf. 12); we are and are not (*Fr.* 49a); everything passes into something else and is thus seen to be something that assumes different shapes and passes through the most varied states: that "from everything One is made and from One everything" (*Fr.* 10) "God is day and night, summer and winter, war and peace, repletion and hunger" (*Fr.* 67). The essence of all things is, according to Heraclitus, fire: "this world, which is the same for everyone, has been made by none of the gods or men; but it ever was and is and ever shall be an eternal, living Fire, kindled and extinguished measure for measure" (*Fr.* 30). The reason for this hypothesis lies in the last instance in the fact that fire seemed to the philosopher the substance which has least stability and least tolerates it in others. Hence he understood by his fire not merely the flames, but warmth generally. Hence he called it a rising vapour or breath. Things are evolved from fire by transformation into their substances and they return by the reverse process into it: "everything is exchanged for fire and fire for all things as merchandise for gold and gold for merchandise" (*Fr.* 90). But since this process of change is never still, there are never any permanent forms, but everything is continually in a process of transition from one state to its opposite and always contains in itself the contraries between which it is poised. "Strife" is the justice of the world and War, which is common to all, is the father and king of all things. What is at war with itself becomes united, what breaks up comes together again (*Fr.* 51) (cf. Byw. fr. 45; Plato *Soph.* 242E). It is a unity turned backwards just as in the lyre and the bow. Heraclitus censured Homer therefore for condemning discord. But he emphasized no less strongly the fact that the hidden harmony of nature always restores harmony from the contraries, that the divine law, the Like (*Fr.* 94), fate, wisdom, the universal reason, Zeus or the Deity rules everything, that the fundamental essence changes according to fixed laws into all things and returns from them into itself.

In its transformation the primary substance passes through three fundamental forms; from fire it becomes water, from water, earth; in the reverse direction from earth it changes into water and from water into fire.[4] The former is the downward path and the latter the upward path. That the same forces are at work in both directions is denoted by the sentence that "The upward and the downward path are one and the same". All things are continually subject to this process of change: but they appear to remain the same so long as they receive from one side the same amount of a particular substance as they lose on the other. A significant example of this change is offered by Heraclitus' proverbial utterance that the sun is renewed every day, in that the fire collected in the boat of the sun is extinguished every evening and during the night is formed anew from the vapours of the sea. The philosopher applies the same point of view (in common with Anaximander and Anaximenes) to the universe: just as the world arose from the primary fire, so when the world year has run its course, will it return by conflagration into it and after a fixed time will be formed anew so that the world is involved in an endless periodic change between the state of divided being and the union of all things in the primary fire. Attempts have been made to deny that Heraclitus held these doctrines; but this opinion is contradicted not only by the unanimous testimony of the ancients since Aristotle, but by Heraclitus' own words, and it can find no support in Plato (*Soph.*, 242Df).

The soul of men is a part of the divine fire, the purer this fire is the more perfect the soul. "The driest soul is the wisest and the best" (*Fr.* 118). Since however the soul-fire is likewise subject to continual transformation, it must recruit itself from the light and air outside us through the senses and the breath. When the soul leaves the body it is not extinguished but returns whence it came, to the world-fire. Heraclitus' physics however left no room for personal immortality and we should not be deceived by the symbolic expressions with reference to life and death which he borrowed from the language of the mysteries. On the other hand it was perfectly consistent when the philosopher who amid the change of individual existence recognised only the general law as permanent, placed a value upon apprehension by the reason directed to the universal, declared the eyes and ears of the ignorant to be "bad witnesses" (*Fr.* 107) and formulated this principle for practical conduct: "All human laws are nourished by a divine one" (*Fr.* 114); we must obey that one and extinguish wantonness more than a conflagration (*Fr.* 43). From one's trust in the divine order of the world springs the contentment which Heraclitus declared to be the highest good. He was convinced that a man's happiness depends on himself: a man's character is (i.e. determines) his lot (*Fr.* 119). The welfare of the community depends on lawfulness. The people must fight for its laws as for its walls (*Fr.* 44). But the aristocratic philosopher is of the opinion (*Fr.* 33, cf. 49) that the will of an individual can also be a law and he exercises the bitterest censure on the democracy which banished his friend Hermodorus (*Fr.* 121). In the same spirit of blunt independence he opposed the religious opinions and usages of the people in that he criticised in biting words not only the Dionysian orgies but also the idolatry and blood offerings of popular religion. For he was the first philosopher to recognise the symbolic character of religion and this made it possible for him to find a meaning in the popular cults (*Fr.* 15), the way to which seemed in some instances to be pointed out to him by language. Finally Heraclitus, like Xenophanes, was conscious of the limitations of human knowledge: he had certainly recognised the relativity of human ideas (*Fr.* 61, 82, 83) and he does not even except ethical values, which only have validity in the world of men and whose contradictions are resolved like all other things in the absolute world-harmony, in God (*Fr.* 102).

Heraclitus is the profoundest and most powerful of the pre-Socratic philosophers. His pantheism is in comparison with that of Xenophanes sharper, clearer and more precise. While in the latter the relation of God to the universe is vague in details, in Heraclitus it takes the form of an immanent spirit who creates nature, history, religion, law, and morality out of himself. The three fundamental ideas of this pantheism are unity, eternal change and the inviolability of the laws of the world-order.

14. *Parmenides*

Heraclitus' deliberate antithesis is Parmenides of Elea (*c.*
540-470) [5] a man of noble and rich family, who gave his native city an excellent constitution, but was persuaded by the
Pythagorean Ameinias, whom he honoured and revered even
after his death, to exchange an active political life for one of
philosophic retirement. If we find in him certain astronomical knowledge such as the identity of the morning and evening star and the illumination of the moon by the sun and
apparently also the spherical shape of the earth,[6] this he
owed to his relations with the Pythagoreans. Later he attached himself to Xenophanes. Like the latter he expounded
his doctrines in a poem. It begins with a chariot ride of the
poet to the "Goddess" who reveals to him the plain truth
and the deceptive beliefs of men. It falls accordingly into two
parts, of which the first expounds Truth, the second Deception. It was the writings of Heraclitus which impelled him
to make his theories public, and it is to Heraclitus that the
sharp attack in *Fr.* 6, 8f. expressly alludes. The idea from
which Parmenides took his starting point was that of Being
in contrast to Not-Being. He understood by Being not the
abstract concept of pure being but the "full", the space-
filling mass without any further specifications: Not-Being is
empty space (this was part of the Pythagorean doctrine).
"Only Being is, Not-Being is not and cannot be thought"
(*Fr.* 4, 6f). From this fundamental idea he derived all his
dogmas on the nature of Being. Being cannot have a beginning or cease to be; for it cannot be created from Not-Being
or reduced to Not-Being; it was never and never will be, but
is now, continuous and undivided. It is indivisible, since it is
what it is everywhere the same, and there is nothing by
which it could be divided. It is motionless and unchangeable,
everywhere similar to itself, comparable to a rounded sphere,
with equal extension on all sides from its centre. Thought is
not different from Being; for it is only thought of Being
(*Fr.* 8, 34ff). The only perception which is true is that
which shows us in everything an unchanging Being, namely
Reason; the senses, on the other hand, which present to us a

manifold of things, creation, destruction and change, that is a being of Not-Being, are the cause of all error.

Nevertheless Parmenides undertook in the second part of his poem to show how the world is to be explained from the ordinary man's point of view. In reality the only thing that exists is Being: the opinion of men places Not-Being beside it and thinks of everything as compounded of two elements, of which one corresponds to Being and the other to Not-Being; the light and fiery and night, the dark, heavy and cold, which Parmenides also called earth. The former according to Theophrastus, he described as the active and the latter as the passive principle, but added as a supplement the mystic form of the Goddess who controls everything. He undertook to show how the creation and arrangements of the world are to be explained on such presuppositions. Very little however has been preserved of these treatises, which included in their treatment the theories of other thinkers from Hesiod down to his own times. He described the structure of the world as consisting of a spherical earth and the different spheres which are partly dark, partly light and partly mixed, grouped around it and enclosed by the fixed vault of heaven. Like Anaximander and Xenophanes he believed that mankind had been formed from mud. Their ideas are ordered according to the material constitution of their bodies, each of the two elements recognising what is akin to itself. The character of the ideas depends on which of the two is predominant; they have therefore greater truth when the Warm (Being) is preponderant. As for the other gods, Parmenides is said to have given them an allegorical interpretation, just as Thagenes of Rhegium had done in his defence of Homer against the attacks of Xenophanes; Apollo is the sun, Hera the air, Zeus the warm.

Heraclitus and Parmenides both distrusted the evidence of the senses and sought to correct it through thought, but in precisely opposite ways. For Heraclitus, the senses give an illusion of a permanent being and he recognised the ever-changing substance of fire as the reality behind it. Parmenides saw however the deception of the senses in the apparent becoming and passing away, and recognised the unchangeable being behind it. This opposition is represented too in the philosophy of language which corresponds to their archaic thought. For Heraclitus, words as designation of things express their nature and are therefore a natural necessity, but for Parmenides they are arbitrary names and are therefore conventional. Both contrast words with the Word, the Logos, the unity of thought, being and speech. However misguided the attempt to make a pure logician out of the metaphysician Parmenides, nevertheless the Eleatic seized upon the weak points in the Heraclitus doctrines—the want of a basis which explains why the universal fire changes into other forms. He himself could find no reason for it, in fact he regarded it as impossible. Thus he arrived with Xenophanes at the conclusion of complete immutability of being and further his logical rejection of the world of sense which corresponds to its ethical repudiation in the Orphic-Pythagorean circles. Parmenides' rigid empty concept of being shows where a purely logical construction leads which denies all right to perception and experience. It was not without justification that Plato and Aristotle called the Eleatics the "interruptors of the course of the world" and the "unnatural scientists". Nevertheless the philosophy of Parmenides was of great significance for posterity. The fundamental metaphysical opposition of being and becoming, as Parmenides and Heraclitus expounded it, led to the compromise-systems of the 5th cent., of Empedocles, Anaxagoras, and the Atomists, who with Parmenides all denied to their basic substance an absolute becoming and passing away, but recognised in agreement with Heraclitus a relative changeableness, a combination and separation of these substances in individual beings.

Furthermore this extreme monist with this violent division of the human intellect into two opposing organs one of which is assigned a supremacy at the expense of the other, with his untenable rejection of the world of sense in favour of an abstract being only apprehended by thought, paved the way for the metaphysical dualism which found its most complete expression in the Platonic theory of ideas.

15. *Zeno and Melissus*

A third generation of Eleatic philosophers was represented
by Zeno and Melissus. Zeno of Elea, whose heroic end in
the struggle against a tyrant is renowned, was the favourite
disciple of Parmenides and was according to Plato (*Parm.*,
127B) twenty-five and according to Apollodorus forty years
younger than his master. In a prose work of his earlier years
he defended the doctrines of Parmenides in an indirect way
by the refutation of the ordinary conception of the world
with such acuteness that Aristotle (according to Diog., VIII,
57; IX, 25) called him the inventor of dialectic. Those of
his proofs with which we are acquainted are directed partly
against the assumption of a multiplicity of things and partly
against motion. His objections to multiplicity are: (1) that
if what is were many it must be both infinitely small and
infinitely great; the former because the units of which it is
composed must be indivisible and therefore without magnitude; the latter because each of its parts must have another
before it from which it is separated and this must likewise
have another, etc. (2) In the same way it must be both
finite and infinite in number; finite because there can be no
more things than there are; infinite because in order to be
many each pair of things must have a third between them
and likewise between this one and each of the two and so on
ad infinitum. (3) If everything is in a space it must itself be
the same space and also the space of this space. (4) There
remains to mention the assertion that if a bushel of corn
makes a noise when it is being shaken out each grain and
each part of a grain must produce some noise.[7] Still more famous and more significant are the four proofs against motion (Arist. phys. VI, 9 and his commentators). (1) In order
to cover a certain distance a body must first traverse the half
and before that the half of this half and so on; that is to say
it must in a finite time traverse an infinite number of spaces.
Thus the movement could not make a beginning. (2) The
same in another application (the so-called Achilles): Achilles
can never overtake the tortoise when it has any start of him;
since by the time he arrived at the spot A, the tortoise has

reached the second spot B, and when he is arrived at B it has gone to C and so on; hence the motion could never come to an end. (3) The flying arrow is at rest since it is at every moment in one and the same space; therefore it is at rest in every moment of its flight and therefore during the whole time. (4) Equal distances must at equal velocity be traversed in the same time. But a moving body passes by a second when this is moving in a contrary direction at the same velocity twice as quickly as when this is at rest. Thus the laws of motion contradict the facts. Later these proofs were used in a sceptical way. Zeno himself wished only to support the propositions of Parmenides; but by the method in which he pursued this end he gave a lasting impetus not only to the development of dialectic but also to the discussion of the problems inherent in the ideas of space, time and motion. The fallacies of his proofs and in particular the fundamental error, the confusion of the infinite divisibility of space and time with infinite dividedness, he certainly did not notice himself.

Melissus of Samos, the same person who in 441 B.C. as nauarch defeated the Athenian fleet, expounded in his work *On Nature* or *On Being* the Parmenidean doctrine of Being, which he defended, as it seems, among others against Empedocles and Leucippus. He proved with the same arguments as Parmenides the eternity and imperishability of being, but in divergence from him drew the inadmissible conclusion that it must also be spacially without beginning or end, that is to say infinite. He sought a further confirmation of his view in the denial of empty space. This he also used in an argument against the assumption of a multiplicity of things, for he was firm in his adherence to Parmenides' doctrine of the unity and undividedness of Being. With him he denied all motion and every change in the composition of things and the arrangement of their parts, since every change means the passing away of the existent and the creation of a new; as a consequence of that he also contested the division and mixture of substances. In his argument against space and motion he again made use of the unthinkableness of empty space, without which neither movement, nor condensation nor rarefaction is possible. Like Parmenides he rejected finally the evidence of the senses, against which he raised the objection that things often seem changed from their previous appearance, and that would not be possible if they really had been so constituted as they first appeared. It is no wonder that with regard to the gods he disclaimed all knowledge and declared it to be impossible, in agreement with Pythagoras who was roughly contemporary with him.

In the development of the Eleatic philosophy Xenophanes, with his critical tendency of mind and theological interests, appears as the predecessor of Parmenides. The latter formulated the profound but rigid central dogma of the school. Zeno and Melissus were its protagonists, who with the new art of their dialectic defended the conquests of the school against the attacks of adversaries, but not without danger of falling into the snare of mere polemics and thereby paving the way, much against their will, for the scepticism of the sophists which was eventually superseded by the Platonic-Aristotelian logic.

IV. THE COMPROMISE-SYSTEMS OF THE FIFTH CENTURY AND THE LAST OF THE PRE-SOCRATIC PHILOSOPHERS

16. *Empedocles*

An alliance of intellectualism and mysticism even closer than we find in Pythagoreanism was struck in the philosophy of Empedocles of Agrigentum (c. 495-435), who continued the dualistic tendency which had its origin in that town. He was a member of a distinguished family, and his grandfather of the same name had won an Olympic victory in horse-racing. He himself visited the Panhellenic colony of Thurii soon after its foundation in the year 444-443. He participated in the public life of his native city with such zeal that he was offered a king's crown but refused it. Finally he was forced to go into exile and died in the Peloponnese far from his home. A wealth of legend has sprung up around his death, the best known story being his supposed leap into

Ætna. The personality of Empedocles resembles that of Faust and is only to be understood if we recognise in his character the combination of a passion for scientific inquiry with a none the less passionate striving to raise himself above nature. With him it was not merely a question of knowledge of nature but of mastery of nature. His purpose was to discover what forces govern the natural world and to subject them to the service of his fellow-men. He resembles closely the miracle-workers and magicians, in that many superhuman feats were ascribed to him and his disciple Gorgias saw him at his "magic". He believed himself to be a higher being, for in the circle of birth, as physician, poet and leader of the people, he had reached the last and highest state from which there is a return to the blissful realm of the gods; but for the moment he still wandered like an immortal god among mortals (*Fr.* 112, 4, 23, 11), although like them he was a "wanderer gone astray" (*Fr.* 115, 13). They followed him in thousands when he passed through a city, prayed to him and asked him to show them the way that leads to salvation (*Fr.* 112). The knowledge of nature which he possessed he imparted to his disciple Pausanias as though it were a higher revelation (*Fr.* 5, 112) for which he demanded "faith" (*Fr.* 71, 1, 114, 3). To receive this knowledge and profit by it a man needs a pure and good mind (*Fr.* 4, 110). Perhaps following a precedent of the Pythagoreans he first communicated his doctrines to his disciples only under a vow of secrecy (*Fr.* 3). He expounded them in two poems, which far from being mutually contradictory are the products of one and the same mind, and were evidently meant after their publication to be regarded as a complete whole in three books (altogether 5000 verses).[8] Each of these works contains references to the other; in the purification poem the physics is presupposed, and in the physics we find the same pessimistic view of earthly existence as in the other work. Thus both poems form an inseparable whole, just like the philosophic system of Empedocles itself; only, in the one the stress is laid on nature and in the other on the things of the soul.

Empedocles' explanation of nature represents an attempt

to find a compromise between Heraclitus and Parmenides, between eternal change and eternal invariability. Parmenides is right; there is no such thing as an absolute becoming and passing away. But Heraclitus is also right; the individual things actually are in a continual process of change. What is called creation and destruction is in reality the mixture and separation of eternal and unchangeable basic substances (*Fr.* 8, 9).

These substances differ from one another qualitatively and are quantitatively divisible, not as atoms but as elements. Empedocles was the first to formulate this idea of an element. The name however is of later origin. Empedocles himself called them "the roots of everything". From Empedocles too originates the doctrine of the elements being four in number—fire, air, water and earth. None of these substances can be transformed into the others or combined with them to form new. Each mixture of the elements consists only in the mechanical mixture of small parts of them. Similarly each effect which substantially separated bodies produce on one another is due to the fact that small parts of the one fly off and penetrate the pores of the other. When the pores and effluences of two bodies correspond they attract each other as in the case of the magnet and iron.

But how is motion produced in these basic substances? That was a new question which arose from the problem of substance. Heraclitus had from the beginning included it in his "ever-living fire". Parmenides had denied it in a roundabout way. Empedocles now assumed two moving forces which bring about the mixture and separation of the elements; one a uniting force and the other a separating. He called the former Love, and the latter Hate.[9] These forces however do not always work in the same way. Just as Heraclitus caused his world to emerge periodically from the primary fire and to sink back again into it, Empedocles supposed that the elements, in a process of endless change, are brought by Love to unity and then separated by Hate. In the first of these states the world is a complete mixture of all substances and forms, a sphere which is described as a blissful god since all Hate is banished from it. The opposite pole is the complete separation of the elements. Between these extremes lie the world-states in which the individual beings come into being and pass away. In the formation of the present world Love, which was at first in the centre separated from Hate by the substances, set up a vortex into which the substances were gradually drawn; from this mixture air or ether was the first to be separated by the rotary motion and formed the vault of heaven; after this fire, which took up its position immediately beneath air; from the earth, water was pressed out by the rotation and from the water, air again (that is the lower atmospheric air) was evaporated. The heavens consist of two halves, a fiery and a dark which is sprinkled with particles of fire; the former is the day-heaven and the latter the night-heaven. Empedocles, in common with the Pythagoreans, regarded the sun as a mirror which collects and reflects the rays of the heavenly fire as the moon does those of the sun. The fact that the earth and the universe maintain themselves in their positions is due to the rapidity of the rotation.

According to Empedocles plants and animals arose from the earth. But just as the unification of the substances is only gradually brought about by Love, so in the creation of living beings he assumed a gradual progress towards more perfect creations. At first only separate limbs came forth from the earth; then these, when they met, were combined in monstrous shapes; and when the present animals and men were created, they too were at first shapeless masses which only with time received their structure. It is in itself not probable, nor is it affirmed by Aristotle, that Empedocles explained the efficient structure of organisms by the theory that only those of these chance creations which were fitted for life could have survived. Empedocles seems to have made a deep study of living creatures. He made conjectures about their procreation and development, the elementary composition of the bones and flesh, the process of breathing (which he supposed to take place partly through the skin) and other phenomena of this kind. He sought to explain the activities of the senses by his doctrine of pores[10] and effluences; in the case of sight the light which moves against the eye is met by the fire and water in the eye. He laid down the general principle of perception, that each element is recognised by its like in us (desire is caused in us by what is akin and dislike by what is repellant), and therefore that the nature of thought is governed by that of the body, in particular that of the blood which is the central seat of thought. But he did not allow this materialism to prevent him from subordinating sense-perception to reason, although he does not place them in such sharp contrast as Parmenides (p. 65f).

Above this realm of matter Empedocles believed a second and higher to exist, the realm of blessed spirits. In this belief Empedocles agreed with the Orphic-Pythagorean doctrine of transmigration, with the profanation of which he was accused (Diog. L., VIII, 35). These spirits are eternal and live in a blissful, divine community, from which however those are expelled who have sullied themselves with sin, perjury, or the enjoyment of a blood-offering. These must wander for "30,000 Horæ" through plant, animal and human bodies "wrapped in the strange cloak of the flesh" (Fr. 126). They live therefore in organic bodies and are the connecting link between the world of matter and that of the spirits. But since earthly existence is a punishment, the fall of the spirits on earth, the "slough of despond" is described in the most lurid colours (Fr. 118-124, 139). Of the lower forms of life, laurel trees and lions are the best dwelling places for souls (Fr. 127). The highest stage is formed by the bodies of priests, physicians and princes (Fr. 146). This doctrine naturally led to the prohibition of flesh food and blood-offerings (Fr. 136, 139), which were replaced by sacrificial cakes in animal form (Diog. L., VIII, 53), while it also precluded the eatings of beans and laurel berries (Fr. 140, 141). This system also seems to have rejected war as a product of hate; the golden age at least in which Love was queen knew nothing of war (Fr. 128). These are the conditions for the liberation of the spirits from evil and only in this way is it possible for him to share again the hearth and table of the other immortals (Fr. 147).

In the philosophic system of Empedocles we have a complete dualism; on one side the world of nature with the elements, on the other the spirits, both being combined in organic nature. The real life is the divine existence raised above the world of matter. Earthly existence is a punishment. But in spite of everything the Cosmos is interesting enough to occupy the whole strength of the mind for its investigation, although in this of course it requires the help of higher powers; for the human powers of knowing are limited (*Fr.* 2, 132). It is not clear in what way Empedocles imagined the relation of the spirit, especially in man, to the powers of thought which are localised in his blood. In any case thought is for him, like sense-perception, only a function of the body, which is composed of the elements. The assumption of a soul was therefore for him unnecessary. It is replaced by a dæmon; but he is a foreign guest in the realm of earth. Empedocles must have assumed that it was possible for this spirit to remember its previous life and earlier incarnations. He not only ascribed this power to Pythagoras in a high degree (*Fr.* 129), but also laid claim to it himself (*Fr.* 117). Perhaps the spirit regains the power when he has reached the highest stage in earthly existence and draws near again to his divine origin. There is no room in the world of Empedocles for the gods of popular belief this is "dark madness" (*Fr.* 132). The divinity he believed like Xenophanes to be exalted above all human form and idea. It is a holy spirit which pervades the world with its thought and whose law governs the complete All (*Fr.* 132-35). It almost seems that he believed the divinity to be identical with the Sphere (cf. *Fr.* 26-29 with 134).

Empedocles had enormous influence in after times. By his reduction of the material world to a limited number of elements and their combination in fixed mathematical proportions, he became the founder of modern chemistry, while his theory of elements was accepted until the beginning of the 18th century. His attempt to explain the creation of organic beings on a mechanistic basis places him with Anaximander among the precursors of Darwin. As a mystic he is one of the most curious and significant personalities of the Greek dualists and he continues to exercise on poetical minds a strong fascination. His pupil Gorgias inherited his gift of powerful expression and became the founder of Attic rhetorical prose.

17. *Anaxagoras*

The second of the above mentioned compromise-systems was put forward by Anaxagoras of Clazomenæ (500-428). But while the physics of Empedocles formed merely one though important part of his complete mystical system and is an attempt to explain merely one of the two worlds which together make up the universe as a whole, Anaxagoras, free from any trace of mysticism, followed the rational road of the old Ionic physicists.

Also a member of a noble and rich family, in distinction from the majority of his predecessors, he kept clear of politics and indeed neglected the administration of his estates to devote himself entirely to research. He was consciously and deliberately the first pure contemplative thinker, who saw in knowlege of the world the task and end of life and was fully convinced of its incidental ethical effects. His nature presented a happy combination of a capacity for knowledge founded on experience and observation with a power of speculation. What determined him to leave his native land we do not know; but we can recognise unmistakeably in his character a trait which is closely bound up with his philosophy—a striving to rise above the limitations of forms which had become merely historical. It was he who carried the Ionic philosophy to Athens, where he lived for practically thirty years (*c.* 460-430) on intimate terms with Pericles and his gifted wife Aspasia, who came from Miletus, with Euripides and other prominent men of the city, which after its victory over Persia set out to become the intellectual centre of Greece. Of course in contrast to the interest which the higher circles showed in philosophy, the mass of the people remained uncomprehending and distrustful of the new spirit of Ionic enlightenment. Consequently in the year 432 B.C. the priest of the Oracle, Diopeithes, carried a resolution in the assembly that "those people who do not accept the religion and who spread astronomical doctrines should be brought to trial" (Plut., *Per.* 32). When shortly before the outbreak of the Peloponnesian war the opposition against Pericles won power, Anaxagoras was one of the victims of this law. He left Athens and went to Lampsacus where he died a few years later in great honour. Of his prose work *On Nature*, which could be bought in Athens for a drachma (Plat. Ap., 26 D), important fragments have been preserved.

Anaxagoras agreed with Empedocles that a coming into being and ceasing to be in a strict sense and therefore any qualitative change of things is unthinkable. Therefore all coming into being consists only in a combination, and all ceasing to be in the separation of already existing substances, and each change of quality rests on a change of material composition. He could not however explain from the substance as such the motion through which combination and separation is brought about (the empty he denied with Parmenides and Melissus), still less the well ordered motion which has produced such a beautiful designed whole like the world.

The half material, half mythical forces of Love and Hate which Empedocles has used to explain this motion seemed inadequate to Anaxagoras. He thought it could only be the work of a being whose knowledge and power stands over everything, the work of a thinking, rational almighty being, of Mind or Nous. This power and reason can only be possessed by Nous when it is mixed with nothing else and is impeded by nothing else. Anaxagoras' leading idea, then, is the conception of mind in distinction from matter; and the most essential characteristic of this distinction he found in the fact that mind is absolutely simple and matter is completely composite. The former is "mixed with nothing", "exists for itself alone", "the finest and purest of all things"; it possesses complete knowledge of all things and the greatest strength. These expressions do not explicitly assert its incorporeality, but that is unmistakeably what Parmenides meant although the question of its personality was still far from the philosopher's mind. Its essential function consists in the separating of the mixed mass, so that its knowledge is nothing

more than a distinguishing. Matter on the other hand, before
Mind has worked upon it, exists as a mass in which nothing
is separated from anything else. Since everything is to be
evolved from this mass through mere separation of its components, it cannot be thought of as a homogeneous mass nor
as a mixture of such simple primary substances as the Em-
pedoclean elements. It consists rather, according to Anaxagoras, of a mixture of innumerable uncreated, imperishable
and unchangeable but not indivisible particles of peculiar
composition; particles of gold, flesh, bones, etc. Anaxagoras
calls his primary substances seeds or things. They are called
by later writers "homœomeries", the Aristotelian term. In
accordance with these hypotheses Anaxagoras began his cosmogony with a description of the state when all substances
were completely mixed. Their separation was brought about
when mind produced a rotary motion, at first at only one
point. The vortex spread out from this point, drew in more
and more parts of the endless mass and will draw in more
hereafter. We have no evidence that Anaxagoras supposed
mind to take a part in other stages of the process of world
creation. As a matter of fact, both Plato (*Phæd.*, 97 Bff) and
Aristotle (Metaph. A. 4, 985a, 18 and 7, 988 b 6) agree in
making the complaint that he did not know how to use his
newly discovered principle for a teleological explanation of
nature, but confined himself like his predecessors to the
blind action of material causes. The rotary motion first of all
separated the substances into two masses of which one contained the warm, dry, light and rare and the other the cold,
moist, dark and dense: the æther and the air (more accurately the vapour and the mist). As the motion continued the
separation of the substances progressed, but it never comes
to an end, for in every part are parts of everything and only
thus is it possible that a thing without any change of its
material constituents can take on a different appearance,
through the predominance of particular constituents. If snow
were not black (that is if it had not dark in it as well as
light) then the water into which it melts could not be black.
The thin and the warm were carried by the rotary motion
to the circumference and the thick and moist to the centre.

This formed the earth which Anaxagoras like the old Ionians imagined as a flat disc supported by the air. The stars were formed by red-hot masses of stone which were torn from the earth by the force of the rotation and hurled into the æther. They moved at first in a horizontal plane around the earth's disc; it is only since the earth has inclined downwards with its southern half that their paths intersect with the plane of the earth's surface. Anaxagoras imagined that the moon was similar to the earth and inhabited. The sun which is many times bigger than the Peloponnesus sheds the greater part of its light not only on the moon but also on all other stars. The earth which at first consisted of mud became dried by the warmth of the sun.

From the mud which was fertilised by germs contained in the air and the æther living beings were produced. What animates them is mind and this is the same in all, including plants; but they share it in varying degrees. In human beings sense-perception is also a function of mind. In the sense organs, which meet in the brain as their central organ (cf. Alcmaeon, p. 53), perception is produced not by the similar but the contrary. Anaxagoras had no doubt that the qualities of things which we perceive with the senses belong to the things themselves. He maintained however all the more emphatically that they give us much too incomplete information about the basic constituents of things. Hence only the reason affords us true knowledge; yet "the visible disclosed to him the view into the invisible" (*Fr.* 21a). He concluded from the composition of a meteoric stone which fell at Ægospotamæ in the year 467/66 the similar composition of the heavenly bodies and called the sun a glowing mass of stone, a remark which exposed him to the charge of atheism. He solved also the problem of the Nile inundation, which had long been a puzzle to the Greeks. He referred it to the melting of the snows in the Æthiopian mountains, an explanation which of course found no favour with Herodotus (II, 22). Because of his astronomical theories he maintained a critical attitude to popular religion. He rejected the belief in divination as well as every miraculous interference of the gods with the course of nature. He replaced the popular teleological idea of the world by a strict, causal, scientific explanation, so that the above-mentioned reproach of Plato and Aristotle is relevant only to the reverse side of a great merit of his method of investigation. Even a Pericles in a critical moment of Athenian history did not shrink from making a skilful use of Anaxagoras' scientific explanation in order to quell a panic caused in the crews of the fleet by an eclipse of the sun. It is at least not impossible that Anaxagoras gave a symbolical interpretation to the gods of popular belief and identified Zeus with his Nous and Athena with art; or that he attempted to extract ethical Ideas from Homer; but the evidence of course does not give sufficient grounds for believing him an orthodox worshipper of the gods.

If we regard the introduction of a mental principle in distinction from matter as Anaxagoras' chief service to philosophy and designate him the first dualist among the Greek philosophers, we must not overlook the fact that quite apart from his Nous being far from incorporeal this dualism is quite different from that of the Orphics, Pythagoreans, and Empedocles (also from Plato's). With the last it is a question of two fundamentally different and unequal worlds; the divine world of the spirits and the material world of earthly existence, afflicted with sickness, misery and death. No trace of this contempt for the corporeal world can be found in Anaxagoras. His gaze rests with equal wonderment on the paths of the stars as on the structure of human and animal bodies. His Nous, although it exists of itself and is mixed with nothing, is nevertheless, as the moving and controlling force, closely bound up with the whole Cosmos, and is active as soul and reason in human bodies. This metaphysics stands incontestably nearer the monism of the older Ionians than the Orphic-Pythagorean dualism.

18. *The Atomists*

The third compromise-system between the Heraclitan and Eleatic extreme views on becoming and being was atomism.

Leucippus was its founder. His birth-place is uncertain; Miletus, Abdera, and Elea are mentioned. Even Theophrastus who calls him an "associate of the philosophy of Parmenides" could find out nothing more definite about him, and in the Epicurean school his very historical existence was contested (Diog. L., X, 13). His lifetime must have coincided roughly with that of Empedocles and Anaxagoras. Two writings are attributed to him, *The Great World Order,* the fundamental work of the Atomistic school, from which we possess a short extract, and *On Mind* about the contents of which we have no certain knowledge. Both were later incorporated in the works of his great disciple Democritus, who completely overshadowed him. No differences can be established in the main doctrines of these two men, so that as early as Aristotle they are quoted together. For the whole of later times Democritus was the representative of the atomistic doctrines. He was born in Abdera (c. 460-370) and was according to his own statement, "young when Anaxagoras was old". He seems to have made the latter's acquaintance in Lampsacus shortly before his death and took up an attitude to his theories which varied at different times from sympathy to hostility. He undertook extensive travels which led him to Egypt, Babylonia, Persia and finally to Athens (*Fr.* 116). Democritus was a universal mind who embraced the whole of the philosophical knowledge of his time, and in this respect can be compared only with Aristotle. Thrasyllus, the court astrologer of the emperor Tiberius, as a complement to his edition of Plato, undertook the same service for Democritus. He divided his works into five groups and arranged them in fifteen tetralogies. They comprised ethics, physics, mathematics, music and technology. He called him on this account the "pentathlete". The chief metaphysical work was the *The Lesser World Order,* in which he attached to his cosmology a philosophy of civilisation. It is indeed the chief merit of Democritus that he included the realm of mental life in philosophy, doubtless under the influence of his great countryman Protagoras. By temperament one of the greatest idealists of all time, this materialist devoted his whole life to research and thought it a greater gain to discover a causal connection than to receive the crown of Persia (*Fr.* 118).

Democritus, like Parmenides, was convinced of the impossibility of an absolute creation or destruction, but he did not wish to deny the manifold of being, the motion, the coming into being and the ceasing to be of composite things; and since all this, as Parmenides had shown, was unthinkable without not-being, he declared that not-being is as good as being. Being, however, (according to Parmenides) is the space-filling, the full, not-being the empty. Accordingly Democritus declared the full and the empty to be the basic constituents of all things. But in order to explain phenomena from these postulates, he thought of the full as divided into innumerable particles, which on account of their smallness cannot be perceived separately. They are separated from one another by the empty, and are themselves indivisible because they completely fill their own space and have no empty in them. Hence they are called atoms or "dense bodies". These atoms have exactly the same composition as the being of Parmenides, although they are thought of as broken up into countless parts and set in an infinite empty space. They have neither come into being, nor can they cease to be; they are completely homogeneous in substance and are distinguished only by their shape and their size, and are capable of no qualitative change but only a change of position. Only to this can we refer the qualities and changes of things. Since all atoms are of the same substance their weight must correspond to their size. When however composite bodies of the same size are of different weight this can only be to the one's having more empty interspaces than the other. All coming into being of composite things consists in the combination of separate atoms and all ceasing to be in the separation of combined atoms. Similarly every kind of change can be referred partly to this and partly to the changes in the position and arrangement of the atoms. Things can only produce effects on others by the mechanical processes of impact and pressure; every effect from a distance (such as between a magnet and iron, light in the eye) is communicated by effluences. All qualities of things rest on the shape, size, position and arrangement of their atoms. Nevertheless there is an essential difference between them, which recalls Locke's later distinction between secondary and primary qualities. Some qualities such as weight, density, and hardness belong to the things themselves; others, the so-called sense qualities, which are ascribed to them merely express the way in which they affect the perceiving subject: by usage or convention (we call things) sweet, bitter, hot, cold, and (any) color, but atoms and the void (i.e. infinite empty space) are real (*Fr.* 125; cf. 9).

Whereas Empedocles and Anaxagoras had believed that forces were necessary to bring about motion of the primary substance—the former Love and Hate, the latter Mind—the atomists, like the old Ionic physicists, transferred motion to the primary substance itself. The atoms, thanks to their different size and weight, are from the beginning in a state of rotary motion. By this motion the similar atoms are on the one hand brought together, and on the other hand separate and isolated atom-complexes or worlds are formed by the conjunction of atoms of different shapes. Since the motion has no beginning and the mass of the atoms and empty space have no limits, there must have always been an infinite number of such worlds, which are in the most widely different states and have widely different forms. The world to which we belong is only one of such worlds. Democritus' conjectures on its creation, the formation of stars in the air, their gradual drying up and ignition etc., correspond to his general hypothesis. Democritus, like Anaximenes, imagined the earth as a round disc poised on the air and hollowed out in the middle in the form of a basin. By this hypothesis he sought to explain why the sun rises and sets at different times in different places. The stars, of which, however, the two greatest, the sun and the moon, only entered our system after their formation and before the inclination of the earth's axis took place, revolves around the earth sideways in a horizontal plane. Of the four elements, fire consists of small, smooth and round atoms, but in the other substances atoms of different kinds are mixed. Democritus seems to have devoted great attention to organic nature. Organic beings came

forth from the earth's mud. He seems to have made a particularly deep study of man. He attached therefore an account of civilisation to his cosmogony and zoogony. In it necessity appears as the main-spring of progress in the life of
man. Through necessity he learnt to combine with his own
species in the struggle against wild beasts. Need of understanding created language and so by the gradual invention
of technical devices, for which many animals provided him
with a model (*Fr.* 154) and which were greatly advanced
by the use of fire, man raised himself from a primitive, animal level of existence to a civilised life. We possess a condensation by Hecatæus of Abdera, which has been preserved
by Diodorus (1, 8), of Democritus' philosophy of civilisation, which bears a close resemblance to the myth of Protagoras in Plato (320 Cff). But although the structure of
the human body is a source of great wonderment to Democritus, he nevertheless placed all the greater value on the soul
and on mental life. He can however only explain the soul as
something physical. It consists of fine, smooth and round
atoms, that is of fire, which is distributed throughout the
whole body; its escape is partly prevented by inspiration and
its partial loss is made up by addition from the air. Particular activities of the soul have their seats in particular organs. After death the soul-atoms are dispersed (*Fr.* 297).
In spite of this, the soul is the noblest and most divine part
of man; in all other things there is as much reason and soul
as there is Warm. For example Democritus said that there
must be much reason and soul in air, for otherwise we
could not absorb this by breathing (Arist. *de respir.* 4). Perception consists in the changes produced in the soul by the
effluences which proceed from things and find their way
into us through the sense organs. Seeing for example is
brought about when the likenesses of the objects which are
emitted from these objects give a shape to the air which lies
before them and the air comes into contact with the effluences from our eyes. In this process each kind of atom is
comprehended by its like. Thinking too consists in a similar
change of the soul-body. It is correct when the soul is put
into the right temperature by the movements to which it is

subjected. This materialism however prevents Democritus as little as it did others (*cf.* remarks on Empedocles, p. 75) from drawing a sharp distinction between the values of perception and thought. The final elucidation of the true composition of things is to be expected only from the latter. But he realises just as well that we can only obtain knowledge of things by observation. The imperfection of sense-perception is perhaps what gives occasion for Democritus' complaints on the uncertainty and limitation of all knowledge. Hence we may not make a sceptic out of him; in fact he expressly opposed the scepticism of Protagoras.

Democritus is at the same time the founder of a thoroughly idealistic system of ethics. Just as thought is superior to sense perception, so reasonable knowledge of the good is superior to the impulses of the senses, and peace of soul, the harmonious tranquillity of the spirit, to pleasure and pain. In the logical working out of this idea Democritus arrived, without detriment to the eudæmonistic principle, which he shared with the whole of the ancient ethical theorists, at the moral autonomy of reason, in virtue of which nothing is so much to be avoided as an action of which one would be ashamed in one's own eyes (*Fr.* 264). These ideas, to which valuable statements on the meaning of the state must be added (*Fr.* 252, 250, 255, 259), Democritus embodied in several writings of which that *On Cheerfulness* was the most important. In later times isolated moral maxims seem to have been extracted and made into a collection like the *Principal Doctrines* of Epicurus. It is remarkable that Aristotle takes no notice of Democritus' ethics but makes this philosophic discipline start first with Socrates.

Democritus' views on the gods of popular belief seem strange to us although they actually fit well into his physical theories. Although he could not share in those beliefs as such, he nevertheless thought it necessary to explain them; and although he did not reject the view that extraordinary natural phenomena give reason for attributing them to the work of gods, or that the gods represent certain general ideas, his sensualism favoured another more realistic explanation. Just as popular belief peopled the spaces of the air with spirits, Democritus supposed that beings of human form inhabit this space; but they are superior to men in size and length of life and their influence is partly malevolent and partly benevolent. The images (p. 84) which they send out and appear to men in waking or sleep are believed to be gods. Democritus also tried to use his doctrine of images and effluences for a natural explanation of prophetic dreams and the influence of the evil eye. He also believed that natural omens of certain events could be read in the entrails of sacrificial victims. Democritus was long survived by his school in Abdera. No change was made in his fundamental doctrines, but in his later representatives a tendency towards scepticism made itself more and more apparent. The most important of them was Metrodorus of Chios, among whose disciples were Anaxarchus of Abdera, a contemporary and companion of Alexander the Great, and Nausiphanes. The latter however was also a pupil of the sceptic Pyrrho and for his part the teacher of Epicurus. Thus from the atomistic school connecting lines lead both to the Sceptic and Epicurean schools.

19. *The later physicists*

In the second half of the 5th cent. B.C. there took place in different parts of Greece a revival of the doctrines of the older Ionic physicists. But although these last representatives of the Ionic natural philosophy bear witness to the extent to which philosophical ideas had spread in Greece in the course of time, they nevertheless lack originality and exhibit an eclecticism which clearly betrays the weariness of philosophical speculation about the physical world. Like Thales, Hippon of Samos (according to others of Metapontum or Himera) adopted water as his primary substance. He supposed fire to be produced from water and attributed the formation of the world to the conquest of fire by water. He was supposed to be an atheist and was ridiculed as such in the *Allseers* of Cratinus and the *Clouds* of Aristophanes.

Of much greater significance and influence was Diogenes of Apollonia in Crete. He was perhaps a physician by profession, as far as we may conjecture from his penetrating, though of course still very primitive, account of the human vein-system. In deliberate opposition to the special position which Anaxagoras had assigned to mind, Diogenes returned to a strict monism. For without the supposition of a uniform basic substance the effect of different things on one another seemed to him inexplicable. This substance he found, like Anaximenes, in air and he regarded all things as changes brought about in air by rarefaction and condensation or cooling and warming. He ascribed the power of thought to this substance, probably in order to explain thus the finality of the existing world. The souls of all living beings too are made of air and their mental differences depend on their different degrees of warmth. If this air-substance leaves the body, death ensues. This doctrine, which was easily comprehensible even to the philosophic layman, enjoyed widespread popularity, as is shown not only by its mention in Euripides (*Troad.* 884ff; *Hell.,* 1014ff), Aristophanes (*Clouds,* 225ff, 264, 825ff) and even in Philemon in the 4th cent. B.C. (*Fr.* 91), but also by the remarkable fact that it was included in the epigram on the Athenians who fell at Potidæa in the year 431 B.C. as well as in numerous private tomb inscriptions.

The school of Heraclitus also continued to spread beyond its native territory until the beginning of the fourth century. Its combination with Pythagoreanism in the person of Hippasus has already been mentioned above (p. 54). In Athens Cratylus, the first teacher of Plato in philosophy, was its representative. Through the strictness with which he followed up the consequences of the Heraclitan doctrine of the flux for the theory of perception, he came to such a point that he dared to make no assertions whatsoever. He seems to have devoted himself particularly to the development of Heraclitus' philosophy of language, which Plato subjected to criticism in the dialogue named after him.

Finally two disciples of Anaxagoras must be mentioned here. Metrodorus of Lampsacus showed the worst possible taste in carrying to the extreme point the allegorical interpretation of Homer which had been undertaken by Theag-

:nes of Rhegium in the 6th century in reply to the attacks of
Xenophanes. He explained the Homeric heroes as constella-
tions and the Olympic hierarchy of gods as a symbol of the
human organism. Anaxagoras is also supposed to have put
forward such interpretations. Archelaus of Athens followed
more closely the lines of his master's natural philosophy, but
not without considerable divergences from him. He was on
terms of friendship with Cimon and Sophocles and is said to
have been the first teacher of Socrates. He abandoned the
division of mind and matter, and thought of mind as combined with matter from the beginning. He adopted air as
this substance from which the warm and the cold, that is
fire and water, are produced. The celestial bodies including
the earth and the atmosphere were then formed by condensation and rarefaction. Apparently Archelaus occupied himself with ethical questions and is supposed to have formulated the distinction between nature and convention. In that
case he is to be regarded as the forerunner of sophism.

The activities of these later physicists, among whom
Archelaus was the first Athenian philosopher and who what
ever their country of origin pursued their careers in Athens,
show that the centre of philosophical interest was moving
from the colonies in the east and west more and more to this
city in which Greek philosophy was to take deep root.

20. *The later Pythagoreans*

Aristotle makes natural philosophy come to an end with
Democritus. That is correct as far as Ionic philosophy is concerned. On the other hand a new centre of philosophic activity was created at Tarentum, where Pythagoreanism experienced a remarkable survival, which was to have important
consequences. These later Pythagoreans, of course, did not
succeed in realising the double ideal of a life ordered on a
religious, mystic basis in combination with intensive scientific research. A division took place in two directions: the
"acousmaticians" and the mathematicians. The first, who
were also called "pythagorists", held strictly to the rules of
life, and abstained from meat, fish, wine and beans. Their

observation of these rules led to their being ridiculed in the comedy. They lived on water, figs and vegetables, neglected their personal appearance, did not bathe and went barefoot, and wore a scanty cloak; they did not partake in the usual sacrifices and wandered as a sort of mendicant philosophers through the land. They glibly repeated the philosophical catchwords of their school and concocted a pseudo-scientific system which dispensed with all proof. Even if we discount the satirical exaggerations of the comedy, there nevertheless remains a caricature of the old, dignified Pythagoreanism, resembling the Cynical school.

The pure Pythagoreanism lived on in the other branch, that of the mathematicians. The connecting link between the old Crotonian and the later Tarentan generations is formed by Philolaus, who must have lived at Tarentum in his advanced old age (p. 53). One of his pupils is said to have been Eurytus who subscribed to an extraordinary number-symbolism. He made figures of men, animals and plants from small differently coloured pebbles and attributed a definite number to men, horses, etc. The representation of numbers by points arranged in geometrical figures (triangle, square, rectangle) which was customary among the Pythagoreans seems to be connected with this theory. We obtain a closer idea of their theories from an extract preserved in Diogenes L., VIII, 24 made by Alexander Polyhistorius from the writings of one of these men, perhaps Xenophilus of Chalcis, who died in Athens at the age of 105. This philosopher regarded the "monad" as the beginning of all things. From this the Dyad was produced and from it numbers, from the numbers points, from the points lines, from the lines surfaces and from the surfaces solids. The universe and the earth he thought to be spherical in form. He regarded the sun, moon and stars as divine beings endowed with soul. This picture of the world agrees with that in Plato's *Phædo* (see above p. 55). It is a remarkable fact that we find here too as later in Plato a tripartite division of the soul, although in rather a different form, namely into mind, heart, and reason, of which the first two are assigned to animals as well, but the reason to men alone. The world, th deity and bodily and spiritual health, that is the Good, consists in harmony.

The spiritual head of the later Pythagoreans was Archytas of Tarentum, who lived in the first half of the fourth century and was for a long time the regent and seven times commander-in-chief of his native city, which he governed in the light of the principles of the Pythagorean ethics (*Fr.* 3). According to the testimony of the seventh Platonic letter (338c ff) he was on terms of friendship with Plato and acted as intermediary in the latter's invitations to the Syracusan court. His humane treatment of slaves is particularly famous, as is the complete self-control which he showed down to the smallest word, a fact which is in accordance with his complete rejection of sensual pleasure. He was the author of numerous writings part of which were in dialogue form, of which some fragments have been preserved. He gave a new form to the old Pythagorean dualism in that he transformed it into a dynamic, energetic system and thus exerted epoch-making influence on mathematics, mechanics, acoustics, and astronomy. The substance of things consists in the concrete unity of form and matter. The moving primary force makes the matter of the elements into bodies. In the same way as he resolved matter into an everflowing and changing motion, he introduced into mathematics the geometry of motion by formulating the conception of the mathematical line as the path of a moving point. If therefore the nature of reality seemed to him to lie in motion, it is highly probable that the definition of the soul as "that which moves itself", which occurs in Plato's *Phædr.*, 245CD, and the view that the movement of the heavenly bodies is an expression of this self-motion is also to be ascribed to him. Finally he applied mathematics also to the solution of technical problems. He is supposed for example to have constructed a flying pigeon from wood.

We can also trace to the influence of Archytas the progress which is to be observed in the development of the astronomical theories of the Pythagoreans. Here belong the first attempts to explain astronomical phenomena from the motion of the earth around its axis instead of from rotation of the vault of heaven. This advance is attributed to the Pythagoreans, Hicetas and Ecphantus of Syracuse. A step still further was taken in the system (ascribed by the ancients to Philolaus) which assumed the existence of a central fire around which the ten spheres revolved: the sun, the moon, the earth, the five planets, the fixed stars and the anti-earth, which was invented to make up the number and which remains invisible to us because we live on the hemisphere which is turned away from it. That these astronomical theories cannot have been formulated long before the middle of the fourth century is proved by the circumstance that the whole Ionic physics down to Democritus knew nothing of them, that even in Plato's *Phædo*, that is in 380, the earth was imagined to be motionless in the centre of the world, and that only the latest writing of Plato, the *Laws*, betrays any knowledge of the apparently quite new theory of the continual motion of the earth, which was at least an hypothesis held by his pupil Heraclides Ponticus. The displacement of the earth from the centre of the universe prepared the ground on which Aristarchus of Samos (270 B.C.), the Copernicus of the ancients, could erect his heliocentric system as a "geometrical hypothesis" for the correctness of which the exact mathematical proof was produced by Seleucus of Seleucia in the year 150 B.C. These astronomical theories were only made possible by a corresponding advance in mathematics, to which belongs the discovery of the infinitesimal and the irrational, which can with probability also be ascribed to Archytas, while his pupil Eudoxus deduced from it further propositions. The foundation of stereometry, too, with the mathematical construction of the so-called five Platonic bodies by Plato's friend Theætetus, are doubtless connected directly or indirectly with these mathematical studies of the Pythagoreans. The revived Pythagorean order in Tarentum seems to have lived on until the end of the fourth century and individual Pythagoreans must have carried their doctrines to the motherland and formed communities there. Lysis and Philolaus seemed to have migrated to Thebes (above p. 51), Xenophilus to Athens (above p. 89) and Echecrates to Phlius. These and a few others are called "the last Pythagoreans" (Diog. L., VIII, 46), whose acquaintance Aristoxenus made before he joined the Peripatetic school. In Aristotle this younger generation is called "the socalled Pythagoreans", by which he apparently means to distinguish them from the older Pythagoreans. Over the later fate of the league until the revival of its doctrines in the neo-Pythagoreanism of the 1st cent. B.C. there rests an impenetrable darkness.

The great significance of Pythagoreanism lies in the dualism of its philosophical system, which seems at different times to be more or less toned down, but never completely given up; and secondly in its great astronomical and mathematical discoveries. Through both of these qualities it exerted a powerful influence on Plato and consequently on the whole of after times, when with the renaissance Copernicus, Giordano Bruno and Galileo resumed the traditions of its scientific theories.

V. THE SOPHISTS

21. *The origin and nature of Sophism*

Cicero (*Tusc.*, V, 4, 10) says of Socrates "he called down philosophy from heaven, settled it in cities, introduced it into houses and made it necessary for inquiries to be made on life and morals, good and evil"; that can be said with equal truth of Sophism, the intellectual movement of which Socrates appears in Plato as the opposer, although he shares with it the main object of his thought, namely man and human life. Hitherto the attention of the Greek philosophers had been concentrated on man's natural environment, the universe within which man came into consideration only as a part of the great whole, as an animal creature. The most varied attempts had been made to explain world-origin and world-events. All laid claim to correctness, without however a reconciliation of their opposing doctrines being possible. It is no wonder that the bold enthusiasm of the earlier philosophers was gradually replaced by a distrust of human powers of attaining knowledge of the ultimate basis of natural phenomena, and that a certain fatigue and reservation in speculation made itself felt; that the growing realisation of the uncertainty of sense-perception prepared the way for a fundamental scepticism. On the other hand man as an intellectual being and his own peculiar creation, civilisation, had hitherto attracted only an occasional fleeting glance from the philosophers. Xenophanes and Heraclitus had included religion and the latter also language in the scope of their inquiries. The Pythagoreans had discussed questions of ethics and politics, but more from a religious than a philosophical point of view. Meanwhile in Ionia, side by side with philosophy, a new kind of investigation had sprung up. With the growing extension of the Greek horizon they had made the acquaintance of foreign peoples, some of old and advanced culture like the Babylonians and the Egyptians, and, at the other end of the scale, of barbarian nations on a primitive level like the Scythians, Thracians and Lybians. The comparison of different customs and forms of life with those of their own people challenged reflection and criticism. It raised the question how all that had come about and the doubt whether one's own institutions were alone authoritative and valid for all time, and whether civilisation was the creation of benevolent gods or the work of man himself. Men like Hecatæus of Miletus, Xanthus of Sardes, Hellanicus of Mytilene and other "loxographers", as the predecessors of Herodotus are usually called after an expression of Thucydides (I, 21), had collected in their writings, which contained ethnological and geographical observations, a wealth of material and had occasionally adopted a critical attitude towards it. This was the beginning of Sophism, and it is no accident that its representatives mostly came from the periphery of the Greek world and that its oldest and most gifted master, Protagoras of Abdera, was a citizen of a town which was an advanced outpost of Ionic culture in the land of the Thracian barbarian. Sophism is then in the first place a philosophy of civilisation and is distinguished in its subject matter from the previous philosophy of nature. Its object is man as an individual and as a social being together with the culture created by him in language, religion, art, poetry, ethics, and politics. It asks the questions "Do all these institutions and ordinances from the worship of the gods down to the difference between free men and slaves, Hellenes and barbarians rest on nature and are they therefore sacred and inviolable or are they the creations of convention and therefore capable of change and improvement?"

Sophism differs from natural philosophy in its method as well as in its material. Of course even in the latter the empirical observation of nature, in particular of the heavens, also of animals, plants and minerals was by no means excluded, but since the final end was the formulation of a uniform principle for the explanation of the world, there was no other course open than that of speculation. The method of the old physicists was deductive in so far as they deduced the particular from their general principle. The sophists made no attempt to penetrate to the first causes of things. They took up their stand on experience and sought to amass the greatest amount of knowledge in all departments of life, from which they then drew certain conclusions, partly of a theoretical nature, like those on the possibility or impossibility of knowledge, on the beginning and progress of human civilisation, on the origin and structure of language; and partly of a practical nature such as on the appropriate and efficient arrangement of the life of the individual and society. Its method then was empirico-inductive.

The third main difference between previous philosophy and Sophism lies in the respective ends pursued by them. For the philosopher, the search for truth and knowledge was an end in itself and if he had disciples, which however was not an absolute necessity, he tried to turn them into philosophers too. His end was therefore purely theoretical. It was otherwise with the sophist: for him knowledge was only valuable in so far as it formed a means to the control of life. He cannot be thought of without pupils. His aim was not primarily to make sophists of them but he wished to give the layman a general education which they could use in life. His aim was therefore predominantly practical: the art and control of life.

The sophists attempted to realise their ends in two ways: in the first place by obtaining control of the education of the young and by giving popular science lectures and thus spreading philosophical education. They advertised formal courses of instruction, single lectures and series of lectures on particular subjects. The education of the young had hitherto consisted in gymnastics and the elementary facility in reading, counting and writing acquired from the grammatists, and a little reading in the poets and musical instruction. These meagre attainments were gradually felt to be inadequate for the evergrowing complications of life in the Greek democracies. Whoever wished to play a rôle in public life required not only a more extensive knowledge than had been hitherto usual, but above all a thorough formal training in thinking and speaking and practical instruction in pose and demeanour and methodical conduct in the most varied situations. The sophists pledged themselves to impart this training and when they said they would teach virtue, they understood under this term practical proficiency in living: efficiency in the conduct of life, both private and public (*Prot.*, 318, E). In this claim to teach proficiency in citizenship there was something revolutionary according to the ideas of the ethics of the old nobility. According to this excellence was the birth-right of the nobles and no one else. Here the sophists touched on the fundamental problem of pedagogics, whether natural endowment or education is decisive in the formation of the mind and character. The sophists who travelled from city to city as itinerant teachers and received high fees for their courses (especially the physicians, the plastic artists and the poets who wrote triumphal poems to order and also, at an earlier date, the Eleatic Zeno) were fully aware of the risk to which they exposed themselves when they took young people from the close circles of their families into their schools in order to initiate them into doctrines which were often enough in the sharpest contradiction to the old respected traditions. But the younger generation, which is ever eager to seize upon the new, received them with enthusiasm, and according to the evidence of their strongest opponents were not far from carrying their masters on their shoulders. They were incontestably the founders of systematic education of the young.

The sophistical education consisted in the introduction to particular sciences such as mathematics, astronomy and especially grammar, of which the sophists laid the foundations. One of the main parts of this was the interpretation of the poets (*Prot.*, 338E) from a logical, æsthetic and ethical point of view. The "logos", which was to the philosophers either the organ or the expression of knowledge, was used here as a weapon. For—and here was the great moral danger of the sophistical system of education—to the sophist it was not a question of determining the truth, but only of convincing one's hearers of what appeared advantageous in any particular case (e.g., for a plaintiff or a defendant); and the more difficult it was to refute the concrete arguments of one's opponent, the greater triumph it was for the orator and his art when it succeeded. These debates took a double form: either long speeches and counterspeeches, which treated the subject exhaustively or a dialogue in which short assertions and criticisms were made.

For adults the sophists held lectures on popular science which were sometimes given to an exclusive circle in the house of some well-to-do friend of the sophist and sometimes in public places. For the latter an admission fee was charged. They consisted partly in well prepared speeches tricked out with all the devices of rhetorical art, and partly in improvisations on a theme which the sophist asked his audience to suggest. It was of course natural that here the stylistic and rhetorical art was more prominent than scientific content and that a dilettantism of such lavish dimensions was not altogether above suspicion. Nevertheless the value of public discussion of religious, scientific, ethical and political questions should not be under-estimated and the echo which resounds to us a hundredfold from out of the pages of contemporary literature, particularly of tragedy and comedy, shows what applause they found. In addition to this the sophists took advantage of the great assemblies at the festivals of the Greeks in Olympia and other places to gain the ear of the representatives of every Greek nation; and since their life of travel had accustomed them to look beyond the narrow confines of the city state, they preached the doctrine of national unity and were the bearers and disseminators of a spirit of panhellenism. If sophism appears to us today as a single movement which is sharply distinguished from philosophy, that is due to the dividing line which both Plato and Aristotle drew between the two. Their contemporaries felt the difference much less strongly and had not even distinguishing terms for them. To them Anaxagoras, Protagoras, Socrates and even Plato were all sophists. For the word "philosopher" in its technical significance had as yet gained no currency.[11] Moreover the word "sophist" had not yet acquired the disparaging by-meaning of a hair-splitting twister of sense and word. That was the work of the petty successors of the great sophists, of the stamp of Euthydemus and Dionysodorus with their logical pettifoggery. The old sophists were honourable, highly respected men, who were not seldom entrusted by their native cities with diplomatic missions. Apart from their oral lectures they displayed considerable literary activity. We find in them the beginnings of the philosophic dialogue and they were the founders of artistic Attic prose. Whatever their origin and however far their travels might take them, they always found their way back to Athens, which one of them called the intellectual metropolis of Greece. It is far from easy to form a concept of "sophist" which will suit all these men. One of them, Prodicus, defined himself as something between a philosopher and a politician. They all had in common the character of itinerant teachers who instructed the young for payment. It was against this that Plato's ridicule was directed when he called them "shopkeepers with spiritual wares" (*Prot.*, 313C). Another common characteristic was their interest in human civilisation from a theoretical and practical point of view. They considered "philosophic rhetoric" as the most effective means to their ends (Philost., *Vit. soph.*, I, 480). Hence they can be termed anthropologists and teachers of the art of life. But the subjectivism and individualism which is attributed to the sophistical movement as such is by no means equally marked in them all, either in an epistemological or an ethical sense. In fact some of their doctrines contain a strong dogmatic element, while their ethical requirements show great variations. Their interest in particular branches of knowledge, such as mathematics and astronomy or linguistics differs widely in individuals and their political theories show strong differences which corresponded to their widely opposed conceptions of natural law. Finally rhetoric by no means occupies a predominant position in all alike. We must therefore distinguish in sophism, as in philosophy, various tendencies which take their rise from the individual representatives of the movement.

22. *The individual Sophists*

1. PROTAGORAS

The most gifted and original brain among the sophists was Protagoras of Abdera (*c.* 481-411). He must have first come to Athens about the middle of the century, where he lived in the circle of Pericles, who conferred upon him the honour of choosing him to draw up a constitution for the panhellenic colony of Thurii, which was founded in the year 444. We may mention here that, apart from him, Herodotus and Hippodamus of Miletus took part in the settlement of this colony. In the first years of the Peloponnesian war we find him again in Athens, where he lived through the deadly plague and observed with admiration the attitude of Pericles in the face of the death of his two sons (*Fr.* 9). About the time of the Sicilian expedition his work *On the Gods* involved him in a prosecution for blasphemy and he is supposed to have met his death by shipwreck on the crossing to Sicily. Among his numerous writings the most important of which bore the aggressive title *Truth, or the Rejection* (of Science and Philosophy), began with the monumental sentence "man is the measure of all things, of those that are that they are, of those that are not that they are not" (*Fr.* 1). That transfers the problem of knowledge from the object to the subject and thus made possible a real theory of knowledge. With "things" we have not only to think of concrete things but also of abstract qualities; and what is more not only of sensual qualities such as warm and cold, sweet and bitter, etc., but also of concepts like good and bad, beautiful and ugly, right and wrong. Less certain is in what sense we are to regard the expression "man"; whether in an individualistic sense, as is propounded by Plato in *Theæt.* (160 Cff), where he associates Protagoras' theory of knowledge with the Heraclitan doctrine of the flux, or, as later writers have conjectured, in a general sense, so that "man" is to be understood as species or finally in a collective sense, and the term refers to men as a group (nation, tribe). In any case Protagoras was not a representative of individualism in an ethical or political sense. That is shown not only by the apologia of his doctrines which Plato puts in the mouth of Socrates (*Theæt.* 165 Eff), in which the activity of the sophist is compared with that of the gardener and the physician, and the assertion is made that education can change a bad state of the soul into a better and can implant healthy and true feelings instead of bad and false ones, but also by the myth of the history of civilisation which is told by Protagoras in the dialogue named after him (322CD), according to which no human society can be formed without a feeling for morality and justice. There can be as little doubt that Protagoras regarded all morals and laws as only relatively valid, that is binding only on the human community which formulated them and only so long as that community holds them to be good. There is no absolute religion, no absolute morality and no absolute justice. In his work *On the Original State of Things,* which Plato (*Prot.,* 320ff) and Herodotus (III, 108; cf. *Prot.,* 321B) have used, he advanced the ingenious theory of a final purpose in nature which in the creation of living beings takes protective measures for the preservation of the species. Man is superior to animals not so much in physical as in mental powers. He has gradually worked himself up from an animal stage and has "invented" the necessary means for the preservation of his existence (clothing, housing, etc.); but above all by means of the divine spark of reason within him he has created language, religion and the state. Thus according to Protagoras man is by nature a social (i.e. of a *polis*) animal, but the constitution and laws of different people, like their languages, their religious ideas and their moral systems, are only conventional by usage. In full accordance with this is the agnosticism which he expressed in his work *On the Gods* (*Fr.* 4). As far as we can gather he attempted in this writing to show that the traditional forms of religion and culture are only usage or convention and perhaps he demonstrated the inadequacy of the current proofs for the existence of gods (cf. Xen., *Mem.* 1, 4, IV, 3). The *Contradictions* or *Opposing Arguments* (in two books) started perhaps with the sentence that two opposite ideas could be made of everything (Diog. L., IX, 51). Perhaps we have a feeble reflection of the arrangement of this book in the socalled *Dialexis,* written in the Doric dialect. Evidently the book was written on the eristical principle of statement and counterstatement. In this form the most varied subjects could be treated. That the ideas of right and wrong were among their number can be inferred from the parody of Aristophanes (*Clouds,* 1036ff) and from the peculiar but strongly exaggerated statement of Aristoxenus (Diog. L., III, 37; cf. 57) that this work "contained almost the whole of the *Republic* of Plato". The discussion of the advantages and disadvantages of the different forms of constitution in Herodotus (III, 80) is perhaps an echo of it. Protagoras is supposed to have expounded his principles of education in the work *On Personal Qualities.* We know only a few sentences from it: "Education needs natural gifts and practice"; "a man must begin to learn in his youth"; "education does not sprout in the soul unless a great depth is reached". Protagoras considered punishment necessary, but he admitted it only as a means of improvement and a deterrent and rejected the idea of vengeance (*Prot.,* 324, A, B). In a work *On Mathematics* he asserted that the propositions of geometry are only valid for ideal figures and not for reality, "since tangents do not touch the circle merely at one point" (*Fr.* 7). Finally Protagoras was also interested in linguistics and was the founder of the science of grammar among the Greeks. The terms for the three genders and tenses and the classification of the most important kinds of sentence are attributed to him. It is a mark of his rationalism that he attempted to subject language to law by refusing to ascribe feminine gender to the word helmet and formed a non-existent feminine form hen to the masculine cock.

In his lifetime Protagoras gathered a great following of young men about him. He influenced Democritus, his younger fellow countryman, in his theory of knowledge and philosophy of civilisation. His influence on the lay world was if anything greater: on statesmen, poets, historians and orators. Plato testifies (*Men.*, 91, E) that his fame long survived him.

2. PRODICUS

Rather younger than Protagoras was Prodicus of Iulis on the island of Ceos, the inhabitants of which were famed for their pessimistic view of life. Prodicus, too, seems to have shared the views and temperament of his countrymen. Plato represents him as an invalid and the pseudo-Platonic dialogue *Axiochos* (366Cff) describes his pessimistic views on the different ages of men, the most important professions and life itself as the "echoes" of his bodily infirmity. It is not altogether impossible that the theodicy in the *Suppliants* of Euripides (196ff) is directed against him. In any case reflections of this nature may have formed a part of his chief work *The Hours,* which of course contained also the antidote against pessimism, the beautiful myth of the choice of Heracles (Xen., *Mem.*, II, 1, 23ff). It was on account of this that the book found Plato's approbation (*Prot.*, 340 D; *Symp.* 177 B). He uttered a warning against a life of soft pleasure and admonished young men to follow the example of the hero in boldly surmounting the difficulties of life. Elsewhere he laid emphasis on the danger of the passions and the worthlessness of the goods most highly praised by the average man and of riches which according to the use made of them can become an evil as well as a good (ps—Plat. *Eryx* 397 C). It would not have been inconsistent with these principles if he had written "The praises of Poverty." We do not know the contents of his work *On Nature,* but we know an interesting theory of his about the origin of religion. At its most primitive stage he assumed a sort of fetichism, when men worshipped as gods the things which fed and were useful to them, such as the sun, moon, rivers, lakes, meadows, and fruits. He cited as an example of this the cult of the Nile in Egypt. This was followed by a second stage in which the inventors of the ways of life and arts, agriculture, cultivation of the vine, metal work, etc., were worshipped as the gods Demeter, Dionysus, Hephæstus, etc. (*Fr.* 5). These dangerous views on religion which led him to regard prayer as superfluous brought him into conflict with the Athenian authorities, and he is supposed to have been expelled from the school Lyceum for carrying on conversations on improper subjects with youths (*Eryx.*, 399 E). Prodicus, too, occupied himself with linguistic studies. He was the founder of the science of synonyms, which was at least a good exercise in the formulation and distinction of clear logical ideas. Although Plato usually treats him with irony, it nevertheless speaks well for him that Socrates occasionally recommended pupils to him (*Theæt.* 151 B) and that his native city repeatedly entrusted him with diplomatic missions (*Hipp. Maj.* 282 C).

3. HIPPIAS

Hippias of Elis came as an official ambassador more frequently to Sparta than Athens and apart from that travelled extensively in the rest of Greece, especially to Sicily and took a pleasure in delivering orations at Olympia. He possessed an extensive knowledge comprising mathematics, astronomy, grammar, and rhetoric, rhythmics and harmony, mythology, literature and history, so that we see in him the type of scholar who in Hellenistic times was engaged in "polyhistoria". At the same time he was a true sophist in that he felt an urgent necessity to communicate his knowledge to others. Like Socrates, he engaged people in conversation "even at the tables in the market place" and occupied himself with the history of the sciences, of philosophy (Diog. L., I, 24) and of mathematics. He seems to have made a contribution to the last science by his discovery of a curve which could be used to solve the problem of the trisection of an angle and the squaring of the circle, thereby taking the first step to the treatment of higher geometrical figures. He perfected the mnemonic system invented by Simonides of Ceos (*Dialex.* 9, 1ff), and seems to have had a talent for practical contrivances. He is supposed to have formulated the idea of self-satisfaction as the ethical end, not of course in the cynical sense of "freedom from needs" but as a striving after independence of other men, by making for oneself everything that one needs. Hippias, too, treated Homer from ethical and psychological points of view and saw definite character types in the most prominent heroes. In Achilles that of boldness, in Odysseus unscrupulous cunning, in Nestor mature wisdom. In his *Trojan Dialogue* he represents Nestor as imparting to Neoptolemus instruction on a life devoted to honourable activity. His studies in the history of civilisation must also have been very comprehensive. They included amongst other things a work *On the Names of Peoples*, a list of Olympic victors and a collection of all kinds of marvels. His main interest in these writings was the idea of convention. Whereas this appears in the Orphic mysticism (*Fr.* 105, 160K), in Heraclitus (*Fr.* 118), Pindar (*Fr.* 169, and in Plato, *Gorg.* 484B) as the universal moral law which as such is divine and the source of all human moralities and laws, Hippias follows in the footsteps of Protagoras and goes even further than he. He understands by convention law and usage in a conventional sense which he opposes to the unwritten laws of nature. He is convinced that convention often does violence to the demands of nature and regards it rather as a despot than, like Pindar, as a legal ruler. The conventional law is measured and corrected by natural law. He therefore looks beyond the narrow confines of the Greek city states to a free community of men with lofty aspirations. That is the beginning of the idea of world citizenship which at this time was already beginning to make itself felt. He seems to have attempted to bring about a closer approximation to the natural state by levelling out the social contrasts in favour of the weak. Nevertheless his doctrine of natural law was founded on a basis of ethnological observation, as we can see in the above-mentioned *Dialexis*.

4. GORGIAS AND HIS SCHOOL

Gorgias of Leontini (483-375) in his long life accompanied the varying fortunes of Greece from the Persian war until the times following the peace of the kings and its mental development from the prime of Æschylus and Pindar until the mature years of Plato, who dedicated his most significant dialogue to him. In the year 427 he came to Athens as ambassador of his native city to ask for its help against Syracuse. He stayed also for some time in Bœotia and Thessaly at the court of the Aleuades, gathering pupils about him wherever he went. He made use of his appearance in Olympi, Delphi and especially in Athens to spread the spirit of panhellenism, a mission which he bequeathed to his pupil Isocrates. He was at first a pupil of Empedocles and occupied himself with questions of natural science. It is possible that he published a work on optics. On the tomb of Isocrates he is represented as deep in the study of a globe of the heavens. Zeno's dialectic however led him to scepticism to which he gave the clearest expression in a work *On Not Being or Nature*. He established three propositions (1) that nothing exists (2) if anything existed it could not be known and (3) that if it could be known it could not be communicated to others. Although Gorgias in the second and third part of this work, of which we possess two extracts, touches on serious problems of epistemology and shows considerable shrewdness in pointing out that there are certain difficulties in distinguishing between ideas to which a reality corresponds and those to which none corresponds, and that the linguistic terms for things by no means coincide with these things, the whole work, and particularly the first part, gives the impression that the author wished to reduce the Eleatic philosophy to absurdity by means of its own dialectic. However this may be this work constitutes Gorgias' final renunciation of philosophy. From now on he devoted himself entirely to rhetoric and did not claim like the

other sophists to teach virtue, of which he adopted the popular view and distinguished between the virtue of man and
woman, adult and child, slave and free man. But as an epideictic orator and founder of artistic Attic prose he could not
altogether eliminate the philosopher in himself. He gave up
all pretensions of obtaining knowledge of the truth and contented himself with probability; but it was just his rhetorical art which he defined as mastery of the art of persuasion that led him to practical psychology and to a branch of
learning not yet discovered by philosophy. He was the
founder of æsthetics and especially of poetics. Both of the
model speeches which have been preserved and which formed
part of his handbook of rhetoric, the *Praise of Helen*
and the *Defence of Palamedes,* afford us a glimpse into
the nature of his thought. Gorgias is the discoverer of suggestion, which he handled with conscious and deliberate art.
He recognised in it a powerful instrument with which to
sway the minds of men and knew that it could be turned
to good or evil ends, which gave rise to its comparison with
medicine and poison (*Hel.,* 8-10, 13, 14). But besides serving
practical ends it could also be used for artistic purposes, and
it was here that Gorgias hit upon a second important idea—
that of illusion. Hesiod (*Theog.,* 27) and Solon (*Fr.* 26)
had been unable to distinguish between lies and artistic
composition: both came under the heading of falsehood.
Gorgias formulated the idea of justifiable deception, and not
only in an ethical sense (as e.g. *Dialex.* 3, 2), but in an
æsthetic sense. He called tragedy "a deception, which is better to cause than not to cause; to succumb to it shows
greater powers of artistic appreciation than not to". Tragedy,
too, is in his mind when he speaks of the psychological effects of poetry (*Hel.,* 9), among which appear pity and
fear. His comparison with the effects of purgatives on the
body (*Hel.,* 14) is closely akin to Aristotle's doctrine of the
purging of the passions by tragedy. Moreover it is probable
that Aristophanes in his famous contrast of the tragedy of
Æschylus and Euripides in the *Frogs* is indebted to certain
of Gorgias' ideas. Representational art, too, was treated by
Gorgias, and it seems to him under certain circumstances

to resemble tragedy in producing peculiar mixed feelings. Gorgias and his school like the other sophists were also interested in the history of human civilisation. Progress was caused by the inventions made in the course of time. He did not attribute these inventions to Prometheus like Æschylus, but for the greater part to Palamedes. It is in connection with this that he gave expression to the fine thought that intellectual activity has a good moral effect (*Pal.*, 30ff). This theory that the progress of civilisation is due to the discovery of all kinds of contrivances was also held by his disciple Polus (Plat., *Gorg.*, 448C; cf. 462B) and Critias (*Fr.* 2).

To the questions of truth and morality Gorgias had declined to give an answer. This is doubtless the reason why we find in his school two entirely opposed theories of natural law. One, which in Plato's Gorgias (482Eff) is put into the mouth of Callicles, is the doctrine of the right of the stronger. According to this theory morals and law are the work of the majority of weaker men, who thereby tame the stronger natures like beasts of prey and suggest to the young the idea of justice as the ostensible true justice. But both nature and history contradict this. The strong man will burst these bonds when he realises this deception and will make himself master of the weak. "Then the law of nature shines in its splendour". This theory of the unscrupulous will to power was held by Gorgias' pupil Meno (Xen., II, 6, 21), while another, Proxenus (6, 16ff), wished to win honour and power by lawful means. This theory which deliberately ignores Hesiod's distinction between the laws of the human and the animal worlds could find support in the writings of Gorgias himself. The *Praise of Helen* contains the following passage: "It is a law of nature that the strong shall not be hindered by the weak, but that the weak shall be ruled and led by the strong; that the strong shall go before and the weak shall follow after". Critias, too, was an adherent of this doctrine both in theory and practice. During his exile in Thessaly he came under the influence of Gorgias and saw in laws nothing but an instrument for taming the wild beast in man and an inadequate instrument at that. To this end some shrewd brain had "discovered" religion and sub-

dued men by a suggested fear of powerful and invisible beings who see and punish even crimes which are committed
in secret (*Fr.* 25). Those who see through the deception
are unaffected by it.

An exactly opposite use was made of the sophistical theory
of natural law by two other disciples of Gorgias. Lycophron, who went so far in his scepticism as to avoid the use
of the word "is" in a judgment sentence, declared that the
nobility was a hollow sham and that all men were equal
whether they had ancestors or not. It is in him too that we
find for the first time the doctrine of the social contract.
"The law is a contract, by which right is mutually guaranteed; but it cannot educate its citizens to be moral and just".
The relation of philosophy to the state was formulated still
more clearly by Alcidamas of Elæa; he regarded it as "a
siege-engine against law and usage, the hereditary kings of
states". How radical his opinions were we can gather from
the fact that he demanded the liberation of slaves in the
name of natural law: "God left all men free, nature has
made no man a slave". No doubt the movement for the
emancipation of women in the last third of the 5th cent.,
for which we have only the indirect evidence of Aristophanes
and Euripides, was also connected with this development in
the theory of natural law.

5. THE REMAINING SOPHISTS

Among the remaining sophists the following are worthy of
mention. Thrasymachus of Chalcedon, who was already
known in Athens in the year 427 and later in Larisa spoke
in defence of this city against the Macedonian king Archelaus' efforts at annexation, appears in Plato's *Republic* (I,
336B) as a brutal champion of the rights of the stronger.
He defines the just as the "advantage of the superior"
(338C) and seems to have been led to this opinion by his
despair of the justice of the divine universal power (*Fr.* 8).

It is of Antiphon of Athens, a sophist whom Plato never
deemed worthy of mention (but see Xen., *Mem.*, I, 6), that
we possess by far the most numerous fragments which have
been increased in recent times by finds in the papyri. Of his

two chief works one with the title *Truth* was unmistakably indebted to Protagoras and Parmenides. The author appears an eclectic who sometimes adopts the ideas of Xenophanes and Parmenides and sometimes those of Empedocles. He makes use of the contrast between *physics* and *nomos,* ascribes the state to a social contract and sees in morals and usage "bonds" of nature. In the most unambiguous terms he asserted that all men are equal and denounced the distinction between nobles and commons, Greeks and barbarians as itself a barbarism. His opinions go considerably beyond the principles laid down by Hippias (p. 103) and represent an uncompromising cosmopolitanism. In the second half of the chief work *On Concord* he gave expression to a pessimistic view of human life, and it seems that he gave descriptions of mythical peoples to serve as models of his theory of natural rights. He declared that education was the most important thing in life and anarchy the greatest evil. His *Art of Combatting Sorrow* created a new literary genre, the consolatory writing. He gave an undertaking to free anyone in need of consolation from sorrow by oral means. Rationalism could hardly be carried further than his systematisation of the means of combatting spiritual pain. Apart from this Antiphon rationalised divination too. From an ethical point of view he exhibits a remarkable combination of hedonistic and social principles. A peculiar position within sophism is occupied by Anonymus Iamblichi, that is the extracts from a sophistical work of the 5th cent. which are preserved in the Protrepticus of the neo-Platonist Iamblichus (ch. 20). The writer is politically a conservative. He knows of no distinction between *nomos* and *physics* but considers law and morality a necessary outcome of human nature. On this account he opposed the doctrine of the right of the stronger and regards the delineation of the superhuman type as no more than a fiction. Even if such a person did arise he would soon succumb to the systematic combination of law-abiding citizens.

Similar trains of thought are met in the speech against Aristogiton which had been preserved under the name of *Demosthenes* (XXV, 15-35, 85-91) which are perhaps to be traced back to a sophistical writing. We find here as well as in Antiphon and Lycophron the theory of the social contract. But this author regards *physics* as the individual nature which must adapt itself to the general ordinances of *nomos,* because in this the sovereign authority of the mind is embodied.

A condensation of the doctrines of Protagoras and Hippias is contained in the so-called *Dialexis* written in the Doric dialect. Its careless form indicates that it is a note book rather than a work intended for publication. At the same time it gives an idea of the lesser lights who attached themselves to the great masters of sophism. It was people of this kind, like the sophists Euthydemus and Dionysodorus ridiculed in Plato, who degraded sophism to paltry hair-splitting, logical quibbles and fallacies and brought this important movement into the ill-repute which came to be attached to the word "sophist".

23. *The influence of the Sophists*

The intellectual ferment which the sophistical movement caused can be judged from the hostility or sympathy of contemporary tragedy and comedy as well as from the testimony of its most powerful opponent Plato, who finally superseded them. It was on the lay world, to which its attention was primarily directed, that sophism exerted its most powerful influence. Sophocles' triumphal song on human civilisation in the *Antigone* and the breaking of the self-assured rationalist Creon on the unshakeable rocks of religious belief and sense of duty, his representation in the *Œdipus Tyrannus* of the might and truth of religion by the triumph of prophecy over the presumptuous wisdom of man, the picture in the Philoctetes of the unscrupulous egotism of the new type of despot in the person of the tortuous Odysseus—all these are unthinkable apart from sophism, as are the great controversies in the tragedies of Euripides on monarchy and democracy, theoretical and practical conduct of life and many other questions of the time, in the discussion of which the poet displays the brilliance of his dialectic art.

Historical writing, too, shows quite clearly, apart from the new linguistic and stylistic form, in content too the influence of sophism. Herodotus (III, 38, VII, 152; cf. *Dialex.* 2, 26) in his exposition of his ideas on the nature of *nomos* is following in the train of sophism. Thucydides was indebted to the same source for his realisation of the fundamental truth that the essence of politics and the moving force in history is power—a conception which is theoretically expounded in the Melian dialogue (V, 48; cf. I, 76, 2, II, 63, 2, IV, 61, 5, VI, 85, 1). In the historical writings of the fourth century which took their rise from Isocrates the emphasis laid on the significance of strong personalities is directly connected with sophism. Under the stimulation of sophism a mass of literature on specialist subjects was produced, of which those works were of importance to philosophy which contained political and æsthetic theories. In these departments they did much work that was ignored by Plato and resumed first by Aristotle. A particularly instructive example of the way in which sophism influenced individual sciences and contributed to their popularisation is the work on *The Art of Healing*, which has come down to us in the Hippocratean Corpus and was either written by a physician with a sophistical education or a sophist interested in medicine. Side by side with the influence of Ionic philosophy, which is revealed particularly in the Heraclitan ideas on diet, some contact with sophism is evident in one or two passages: in the works on *Air, Water, and Position* and *The Holy Disease*. It breathes the spirit of an enlightenment free from all superstitious illusions and intent only on the determination of empirical facts.

It remains the undying service of Sophism to philosophy that it turned Greek philosophy to the study of man himself and first laid the foundations of systematic education of the young. From now on rhetoric, greatly promoted by the oratorical school of Isocrates, the pupil of Gorgias, which was established in competition to the Platonic academy, remained an indispensable part of Greek education. It was precisely in this however that lay a great danger. Form threatened to overrun content and the art of persuasion to stifle the feeling for truth. Sophism had by its philosophic scepticism not merely thrown doubts on the possibility of science but by its relativistic theories and the thorough-going individualism of some of its members had shaken the existing authorities of religion, state and the family to their foundations. It had raised more problems than it had solved. Only now did it become necessary to establish the possibility of knowledge and the existence of a definite object of knowledge independent of the uncertainties of human opinion, and to find in the depths of man's own nature fixed ideals to guide him in his practical life. It was in this that Socrates and the men who found their inspiration in him recognised their task.

THE ATTIC PHILOSOPHY: SOCRATES AND THE SOCRATICS, PLATO, ARISTOTLE

24. *The new position and problem of philosophy and the development of the Socratic system*

Although Attica had up to now produced no philosopher of outstanding originality, Athens, through the leading part which it played in the Persian war, its growing prosperity and not least the poets who had raised its intellectual life to heights never attained before, had become the intellectual centre of Greece. Anyone who wished to gain a reputation as a thinker had to pass the test in Athens. Yet in the life of Athens and the Hellenes in general, with all their refinement of external form, there were gaps which began to become more and more apparent. The products of the whole world stood at the disposal of the Athenian citizen. New statues of the gods rose in their splendour, the immortal works of the finest artists. The people listened at the festival of Dionysus to the serious words and songs of tragedy and delighted in the sparkling wit and boisterous antics of comedy. Crowds thronged the lecture rooms of the sophists when they propounded their new wisdom clothed in the seductive cloak of beautiful language and invited young men to become their pupils. The Demos basked in serene consciousness of its power when they sat on the Pnyx and in the courts. All this was well, but there were people who had the impression that all this splendour was not good for the Athenians. They had become indolent, lazy, garrulous and avaricious. Actually one thing was lacking; the people received no moral education. Who was there to show the Hellene the path of righteousness, to teach him to distinguish between the values of different goods, to reveal the meaning and end of life? Religion was scarcely more than ritual; it had no sacred writings and could only give the vaguest guidance in moral conduct. The real teachers and educators of the people were its poets, who were at that time still conscious of their function, Homer being used most of all for this purpose. But they could do no more than give occasional hints and with their harrowing tales of human destiny touch the hearts of their hearers and move them to reflection. The waning authority of traditional religion under the attacks of the Ionic physicists and the sophists made this lack of moral education for the people all the more serious.

It was necessary to erect a completely new structure in place of the old. It was to this, the moral education of his fellow-citizens, that Socrates, the first Athenian philosopher, devoted his whole activity. But this demanded in its turn a knowledge of good and evil; and it was his efforts to attain this knowlege that prepared the ground for the discovery of those ideas which provided a new and more secure basis not only for ethics but for knowledge as a whole.

In the minor Socratic schools different sides of his doctrines were emphasised and developed or combined with older theories. Plato continued the work of his master with greater comprehensiveness and deeper understanding. But while Socrates in his complete pre-occupation with the things of this world resembles the Ionic monists and embodies the essential qualities of the Greek people, his philosophy is strengthened in Plato by the addition of Eleatic elements and combined with the dualistic mysticism of the Orphics and the Pythagoreans. It becomes a new system of idealistic character, which for the time being brought the dualistic

tendency in Greek philosophy into the ascendant. With Aristotle a reaction set in in favour of natural science, which had
been more or less despised by Socrates and Plato. He criticised the crude dualism of Platonic idealism, but retained its
basic ideas, although in a new form which seemed to comprehend the whole of reality, so that his philosophy represents the Socratic-Platonic philosophy of ideas in its most
consummate form. Apart from this Aristotle took up many
of the threads spun by the pre-Socratic physicists and treated
many questions of the mental sciences untouched either by
Socrates or Plato.

I. SOCRATES

25. *His life and personality*

Socrates was born in the year 470 B.C. (apparently on the
6th of Thargelion), or at the latest in the first month of the
following year.[1] His father Sophroniscus was a sculptor, his
mother Phænarete a midwife. His early education does not
seem to have exceeded either in measure or manner that
which was usual at that time. He learnt his father's art and
a group of statues at the entrance to the Acropolis, representing the three Graces, was ascribed to him. As a philosopher he was self-taught and it was only later writers who
represented him as the pupil of Archelaus in order to establish a connection with the older philosophers. He must have
at one time occupied himself with natural philosophy, for it
was his dissatisfaction with it that led him to abandon this
study. He had relations too with the sophists, attended their
lectures and occasionally even recommended pupils to them;
but urged on by a voice within him which he regarded as
divine and encouraged by a reply of the Delphic oracle, he
recognised that his mission in life was to rouse his fellow-
citizens from their thoughtlessness and lead them to reflect
on the meaning of life and their own highest good. To set
man in a wholesome inner unrest—that he thought was his
mission, his philosophy, his "divine service". Aristophanes
represents him as engaged in this activity as early as the year

423, and Plato before the beginning of the Peloponnesian war. He continued it until his death in the poorest of circumstances, with Xanthippe at his side, with complete self-denial, and without any reward. He allowed neither family cares nor state crises to distract him from his goal. A model of self-sufficiency, purity, integrity and virtue, yet full of human kindliness and social charm, cultured and witty, of unfailing good humour and imperturbable serenity, he became an object of veneration to men of the most diverse rank and character. A son of his people, he performed his duty fearlessly in war as in peace and took part in three campaigns (Potidæa between 432 and 429, at Delion 424 and at Amphipolis 422). On the other hand his principles kept him apart from politics. But when he was drawn against his will into the turmoil of public affairs, he did not flinch. As president of the assembly at the trial of the generals after Arginusæ (406 B.C.) he defied the raging mob and some years later refused at the risk of his life to obey the illegal orders of the oligarchic despots. His criticism of the democratic constitution, his habitual cross-examination of the people with whom he came into contact and the strong and self-conscious contrast which his whole nature presented with that of the average Athenian made him many enemies. We find indeed in his character many traits which made on his contemporaries the impression of oddness and eccentricity, of an "Atopia" which actually was never there. On the one hand a prosiness, a pedantry and indifference to outward appearances which accorded well with the Silenus-like form of the philosopher, but impinged harshly on the sensitiveness of Attic taste; on the other hand an absorption in his own thoughts which sometimes gave the impression of absent-mindedness and an emotional force so powerful that the vague feeling which even at an early age had frequently deterred him from taking certain steps seemed to him to be a "dæmonic" sign, an inner oracle with which he had been gifted, for he believed that in dreams, too, he received prophetic warnings. But all these characteristics, these peculiarities, had their origin in the energy with which Socrates withdrew from the world into himself so as to devote his undivided interest to the problems which arise from man's mental nature. His character shows a remarkable combination of critical shrewdness and a deep religious sense, of sober rationalism and mystical belief. Both these sides, however diametrically opposed they might have been, had their roots in one and the same thing—in the passionate longing which drove him in search of something absolute and unconditioned, which could be apprehended by the intellect and serve as a norm for moral conduct and which he believed to be also the wise and just power that governs universal events.

26. *The activity of Socrates: sources, aim, method*

Socrates himself left no writings behind him, so that those of his pupils, Plato and Xenophon, are the only trustworthy sources from which we can expect to derive any information about his philosophic views. Of later writers Aristotle is the only one who comes into consideration. His short and precise accounts of Socrates are valuable but contain in their essence nothing more than we already know from Plato and Xenophon. The latter pair of writers, however, impart widely different accounts of the Socratic philosophy. With Plato it is possible that he put his own doctrines in their entirety into the mouth of his teacher. With the unphilosophical Xenophon it is questionable whether his *Memorabilia,* which was written primarily for apologetic purposes, represents the Socratic doctrines unabbreviated in their true sense, and whether his conception of his duty as an historian was strict enough to prevent him from working much of his own into the speeches of Socrates.

The most recent research has shown more and more clearly that the most trustworthy sources for Socrates' own peculiar philosophy are almost exclusively Plato's *Apology,* his earliest dialogues and the speech of Alcibiades in the *Symposium* (215 E/222 B). Xenophon and Aristotle only come into consideration as far as they do not contradict Plato's account. But even the above mentioned groups of writings do not yield a completely uniform and coherent picture of the personality and activity of this remarkable man. There arises the difficult question: How could Socrates, with the purely intellectual "philosophy of ideas" which Aristotle ascribes to him and which he pursues in the Platonic dialogues, produce such effects, which Alcibiades declared to be unattained even by the most skilful orators and which are testified also by the Socratic, Æschines of Sphettus, in the remains of his dialogue *Alcibiades*—the deepest spiritual emotion, humiliation, shame, realisation of one's own failings and longing for improvement, passionate striving against the subordination of one's own ego to the compelling superiority of Socrates, unique personality combined with the irresistible conviction of the truth of his words, which penetrate the soul as the bite of a snake the flesh. It is utterly impossible that an effect of this kind which Socrates produced not only on Alcibiades but on numerous other young people can have been attained by merely instructing them in definition of ideas. The deepest cause lay in the fascinating personality of Socrates, in his power of "making others better" (218E). This was his end and aim: the moral improvement of mankind. This however could not be effected by moral sermons, but only by personal intercourse and setting men to work on themselves. The underlying idea here was the self-knowledge which the Delphic oracle enjoined. Thus he arrived at his remarkable method of examination, the so-called dialectic process to which he subjected the people with whom he came into contact, and at his "Maieutik" (*Theæt.* 149Ef) by means of which he sought to bring forth not so much the idea as the power for good, the better self in man. He felt himself spurred on in this work by his love; but what had he to offer to others? No complete formulated system which could be assimilated by the intellect; for he knew that he knew nothing. All that he could do was to set men in unrest and bring them into embarrassment. He often produced this result by pretending to receive instruction from others, whose mental inferiority was revealed in the course of the conversation. This procedure was keenly felt by those who suffered from it, his attitude being felt to be "ironical". In his conversations he was fond of starting from trivialities and truisms, pressing the most commonplace things into service to illustrate his theories— donkeys, smiths, cobblers and tanners, all of which, while seeming ridiculous to the uninitiated, hid a divine meaning which was always directed to the simple goal how to become good and honest. In every activity he insisted on technical proficiency and he too felt compelled to seek after understanding of the good. He would indeed have been no Greek if he had not sought to fathom the mystery of his own nature. Thus he was led to the "definitory question, what is the good?" To this question he never succeeded in finding a conclusive answer although he spent his life in the attempt. At the age of seventy he still confessed before his judges that he knew nothing.

27. The Socratic philosophy

Under these circumstances it is hardly possible to speak of a Socratic "system". Socrates laid no claim to authority; he was far more occupied in teaching men to think for themselves. He made no precise formulations of doctrine. It is on this account difficult to assign him a place in philosophy; yet his importance cannot be ignored. He was a "philosopher" in the original, modest sense of a man who, while recognising the limits of human knowledge, seeks after the truth. From a negative point of view it is certain that he rejected natural science. As positive achievements Aristotle ascribed to him the process of induction, definition and the founding of ethics. He is incapable of imagining even Socrates as anything but a systematic philosopher, which he was certainly not. Socrates had much in common with the Sophists; first a critical attitude towards everything that seemed to be founded merely on tradition; further the chief object of his thought—man as a knowing, active, social being; thirdly, that in his philosophic reflections he always started from experience. But he could not remain content with the subjectivity and relativity of the sophists. Behind morals he sought morality, behind prevailing law justice, in the history of existing states fixed principles for the communal life of man and behind the gods divinity. These were for him not theoretical, but practical problems which were comprehended in one question—how to live rightly. Its answer he considered to be the condition and the guarantee of happiness for man whose most important problem is care for his soul. Socrates naturally thought an answer to those questions impossible without some insight into the nature of good and evil. We have to bear in mind that these two Greek words had a double sense—a moral and a material sense—and just in the same way the expressions *eu* and *kakōs prattein* meant "to do good" and "to fare well", "to do evil" and "to fare ill".[2] Socrates was convinced that there is only one real misfortune—to do evil and only one real happiness—to do good. Since no one wishes to make himself unhappy or to do harm to himself, no one is voluntarily evil. He who knows what the good is will do good. By this "knowledge" he did not mean of course a purely theoretical knowledge which needed only to be learnt, but an unshakeable conviction based on the deepest insight into and realisation of what is really valuable in life, a conviction such as he himself possessed. The opposite of this "knowledge" of the good is therefore not error but self-deception. It is only in this sense that Socrates' basic ethical principles can be called an intellectual determinism. It follows from these principles that no one should under any circumstances do wrong, not even to his enemies, and that it is better to endure any kind of suffering, even death, than to commit a wrong. Hence the moral is something unconditioned and is the same in all its forms. But it is also a strength; the good man is stronger than the evil man and the latter can therefore do him no real harm, for the only real harm is spiritual and produced only by one's own wrong doing. It is implicit in this train of thought that no prospect of reward for virtue is held out; for doing good itself is Eudæmonia. It is the great thing about the Socratic ethics that it is turned towards this world. The question of a life after death he leaves open. His ethical system is unaffected by its denial or affirmation. Thus Socrates detached ethics from religion and established its autonomy. As a man of this temperament and these views he possessed in a high degree the quality which was called by one of the words brought into currency by the sophists, Autarkia. His self-sufficiency, however, in the sense of freedom from needs, bore a purely human character and had no trace of asceticism in it.

In politics Socrates had never except under compulsion shown any interest either theoretical or practical, although he remained until his last breath a loyal citizen in war and peace. He affirmed with the greatest emphasis that he had never considered politics as his vocation and that his position as a champion of justice would have kept him apart from it. That however did not prevent him from subjecting many institutions and the fundamental conceptions of the existing state to criticism. The majority principle of the democratic state and the selection of public officials by lot was contrary to his insistence on technical understanding and proficiency in every sphere of action, above all in such an important function as government. We have no evidence that he shared any of the political theories which were current in his time. When however a demand of the state brought him into conflict with his conscience, as happened in the end of his life, he did not doubt for a moment which he had to obey. "I will obey God rather than you", he explained to his judges.

However definite Socrates' belief in a divine government of the world appears, we know very little of his conception of that power. Those works of the Socratic literature which deal with the subject are all written in an apologetic vein and can hardly be objective in the question of Socrates' attitude to popular religion. It is a striking fact that the Platonic *Apology* avoids any detailed treatment of the subject, while it is quite impossible that the teleological views which Xenophon foists upon Socrates can have any bearing on the question. There was in Socrates just as little of the theologian as the social theorist. Plato's accounts make it seem probable that he did not altogether reject prophecy and we may well believe that he was capable of a prayer like that at the end of the Phaedrus. Although this is addressed to a particular god of popular religion, its content shows a spirit of refined piety. This is also indicated by the absolute trust in God which led him to see the divine will even in the wrongs that men did to him, a trust which he retained in the most difficult hour of his life.

28. *The death of Socrates*

When Socrates had carried on his work in Athens for a full generation he was impeached by Meletus, Anytas and Lycon on the counts that he corrupted the young by denying the national gods and attempted to introduce new divinities in their stead. Had he not disdained the traditional mode of defence before the court and had he made some concessions to the demands of his judges, he would have been doubtless acquitted. When he had been found guilty by a small majority,[3] in the following proceeding which was to decide his punishment he faced the court with unbending pride, so that the death penalty proposed by his accusers was carried with a greater majority than that by which he had been found guilty. In the thirty days of imprisonment which he had to endure until the return of the state ship from Delos he rejected proposals of escape as illegal and drank the hemlock cup with philosophical serenity. We may assume that personal enmity had been at work on his prosecution and condemnation, although the supposition which was earlier widely current that the sophists were concerned in it has long been shown to be false. The deepest cause of this prosecution and condemnation lay in the hostility of the majority of the Athenian people, especially the democratic party, towards the modern enlightenment. The trial of Socrates belongs to a whole series of cases which since the law of Diopeithes had been instituted against Aspasia, Anaxagoras, Protagoras and Diagoras of Melos for Asebeia. It was the rising of the instinct of the traditionally bound masses against a man of pre-eminent intellectual powers whom the comedy more than twenty years before had branded as the chief representative of all godless innovations. We have Plato's evidence that, but for the slur put upon him by the comedy, the accusation would never have been brought. But this attempt of the democracy which had been restored by

Thrasybulus to render harmless the movement of enlightenment in the person of Socrates was not only a transgression
of the law in the way the trial was conducted, for the philosopher had never committed any act punishable by law,
but it rested on a fatal illusion. The old times could never
be restored and least of all in this way. Socrates was all the
less to blame for the decline since he showed his contemporaries the only possible way to improve the existing state,
namely that of moral reform. His execution, from a legal
and moral point of view, was judicial murder and historically considered a gross anachronism. By a less uncompromising attitude he could in all probability have escaped his
sentence. On the other hand, his execution had precisely the
opposite effect to that which his enemies had hoped. It is of
course a later invention that the people of Athens themselves
reversed their own verdict by punishing his accusers; but
history has annulled it still more completely. The death of
Socrates was the greatest triumph of his cause, the crowning
success of his life, the apotheosis of philosophy and the philosopher.

II. THE MINOR SOCRATIC SCHOOLS

29. *Socrates and his followers*

Socrates, on his own testimony did not establish a school.
He had no philosophic system to impart and none which
others could develop. It was only possible to learn to "philos-
ophise" from him, that is, to meditate on the meaning and
end of life. His activity was so completely personal that it
admitted of no external imitation. His hope that disciples
would go forth from his circle to continue his work of ex-
amining men and stimulating their minds was never fulfilled. Yet he gave such a powerful impulse to philosophy
that until the end of the ancient world it never left the path
he pointed out, and from now on epistemology and ethics
occupied the centre of interest in a way that was fatal to
natural philosophy and science. Adherents and friends, of
course, he had in abundance, as we see from the mention of

their names in Plato. But only a few of them were possessed of real philosophic gifts. They were completely lacking in Xenophon (c. 430-354), who, in spite of all the veneration for the master he defended, shows in his Socratic writings such a lack of understanding for all that was essential in his personality and work that he has contributed most to the distortion of the true picture of Socrates. A more correct comprehension was shown by Æschines of Sphethos, of whom seven dialogues were extant in ancient times, but now unfortunately only a few valuable fragments are known. But he, too, was no creative thinker. The few who endeavoured to develop Socratic ideas combined them with elements from older philosophic systems into a new whole. As founders of philosophic schools we know, apart from Plato, four Socratics. Euclides founded the Megaric school with a peculiar combination of Eleatic doctrines with Socratic; Phædo the related Elean school; Antisthenes the Cynical school, under the influence of Sophism as represented by Gorgias, and Aristippus the Cyrenaic, under the influence of Protagoras.

30. *The Megarean and the Elean-Eretrian schools*

Euclides of Megara (c. 450-480) seems to have belonged to the oldest pupils of Socrates, whose society he cultivated at the risk of his life. He was present at the latter's death and after the execution the panic-stricken society of the Socratics found a refuge with him. It is possible that before becoming a convert of Socrates, he had become acquainted with the Eleatic philosophy. He remained faithful to its basic principles, the doctrine of the unity of being and ceasing to be, and of motion. But he called the One Being the Good which he identified with God, Mind, and Intelligence; virtue, too, he regarded as a unity. He refused to admit the reality of an opposite to the One Good. Thus his doctrine is Eleaticism ethicised under Socratic influence. It is highly improbable, that the Megarics evolved a philosophy of ideas similar to Plato's doctrines such as is discussed in the *Sophist* (246 B), owing to the incompatibility of a plurality of really existing ideas with the unchangeable All-One. In the poverty of positive ideas the Megarics devoted themselves particularly to the theory of knowledge, in which Euclides showed a partiality for the apagogic proof.

The Megaric philosophy in the hands of Euclides' successors, like Eleatic philosophy with Zeno, developed into a barren eristic, which took pleasure in the invention of clever but worthless fallacies. One of the most famous of these was *The Liar* of Eubulides of Miletus, who wrote against Aristotle and is supposed to have been the teacher of Demosthenes. A whole literature was written in connection with this problem, the Stoic Chrysippus alone being represented by six books. Other fallacies were *The Veiled Man* and the *Sorites* or the fallacy of the heap, which was intended to disprove the plurality of things on the lines of Zeno. Diodorus Cronus of Iasus in Caria showed similar ingenuity in showing the impossibility of motion and corporeal change. Nevertheless his discussion of the relation of possibility and reality in the so-called *The Master* (that is roughly "the irrefutable") is of interest. The most distinguished member of the school was Stilpo of Megara (*c.* 380-300), who lived for a time in Athens but brought the sentence of banishment on himself by his rationalistic attitude towards religion. He too made his contribution to Megarean dialectic by affirming that it was not permissible to apply to a subject a predicate different from itself. Apart from this he had a strong ethical vein; he placed mental goods above sensual and by carrying the principle of Autarkia to the point of Apathia, he prepared the way for the Stoic ethics founded by his pupil Zeno. Of Stilpo's pupil Alexinus, who was called Elenxinus on account of his love of disputation, we have only a fragment which parodies the proof of the Stoic Zeno for the rationality of the world.

The Elean-Eretrian school is so called after its two chief representatives, Phædo of Elis, and Menedemus of Eretria. Phædo had been liberated by Socrates from a life of the most abject slavery and was one of his favourite pupils. The scanty remains of his dialogues show that he regarded philosophy as a remedy against spiritual ills and as the guide to true freedom. Menedemus attached himself to Phædo's pupil Pleistanus and transplanted the school to Eretria. Like Socrates he wrote nothing. As far as we have any information about his teachings we know that they took the form of a definitely ethical intellectualism. In advanced age he died a voluntary death at the court of Antigonus Gonatas soon after 278 from grief at the fate of his native city.

31. *The earliest representatives of the Cynic school*

Antisthenes (445-365) regarded himself as the real spiritual heir of Socrates. He was born in Athens, but his mother being a Thracian slave, he was not a full citizen. He enjoyed the instruction of the sophist Gorgias and was himself already engaged in active teaching before he made the acquaintance of Socrates, whose devoted adherent he became from that time on. Plato, who, like Isocrates, was the whole of his life on strained terms with him, ridiculed him occasionally as "The late learning old man". In the gymnasium Kynosarges, the patron of which was Heracles, he founded his own school which received the name of "Cynic" either from the place where they met or from the mode of life which was led more by his pupil Diogenes than by Antisthenes himself. Among the writings of Antisthenes, which filled ten volumes, the most important were the *Heracles,* which glorified the Cynical ideal of life, self-reliance and physical endurance, toil and labour; the *Cyrus,* an educational romance (like Xenophon's work of the same name), in which love of mankind was enjoined upon his readers; the counterpart to this work, the dialogue *Alcibiades,* in which he denounced egoistical passion; the *Archelaus,* in which he attacked tyranny and the *Politicus* in which he did the same for democracy; finally, the polemic writing against Plato *Sathon,* that is "Bigtail," to which Plato wrote his *Euthydemus* in reply. Antisthenes was the first to use the form of the "Protreptikos" (inducement to philosophy).

What Antisthenes most admired and imitated in Socrates was his independence of character; on this account he attached no value to scientific investigation except in so far as it had some direct bearing on active life. Virtue, he said (Diog., VI, 11), was sufficient for happiness and for virtue nothing more was required than the strength of a Socrates: it was a matter of action and did not need much knowledge nor many words. He and his followers despised art and learning, mathematics and natural science. He followed Socrates in his insistence on definition but used it in such a way that it made all real science impossible. In passionate contradiction to Plato's theory of ideas, he regarded only individual things as having real existence and by that he meant doubtless, like the later Stoics, only the corporeal and sensually perceptible; in addition to this he demanded that to each thing only its own name should be applied and concluded from that (probably following Gorgias) that it is not permissible to apply to a subject a predicate different from itself. He rejected, therefore, definition by characteristics and held that the composite was nothing more than an enumeration of its constituents, while the simple could of course be explained by comparison with others, but could not be defined. He asserted, in agreement with Pythagoras, that a man could not contradict himself; for when he said different things, he was also speaking of different things. Thus he gave Socratic thought a completely sophistical twist.

It was a consequence of this lack of scientific basis that his ethics too took a very simple form. His main idea is expressed in the sentence, that only virtue is a good and sin an evil; all else is indifferent. Since the only good for a man is what is appropriate to him and this is nothing more than his mental and spiritual possessions; everything else, fortune, honour, freedom, health, life itself are in themselves not goods, nor are poverty, shame, slavery, illness and death in themselves evils; least of all should pleasure be regarded as a good and toil and labour as an evil; since the former, when it becomes a man's master, corrupts him, while the latter may teach him virtue. Antisthenes said that he would rather fall a victim to madness than desire. He chose as a model for himself and his pupils the laborious life of Heracles. Whereas Antisthenes in the above-mentioned (p. 125) quotation seems to turn from the Socratic strength to volantarism, with pure Greek intellectualism he regarded wisdom as the source of virtue and declared that it was one and could be taught, so that willpower coincides with wisdom and moral exercise with instruction. This virtue consists essentially in the revision of values, in freedom from madness and from the wrong estimation of goods which is made by the majority of men. This leads to true happiness which consists in independence and freedom from needs and passions. Antisthenes boasts (Xen., *Symp.* 4, 34ff) of the riches which his contentment with the absolutely indispensable affords him; nevertheless he possessed at least a dwelling however sorry it might be. It was only consistent when Cynismus repudiated this too together with the material foundations now indispensable to every civilisation, and preached the return to nature. Applying the opposition of nature and convention formulated by the Sophists they rejected completely the existing forms of communal life in favour of an extreme individualism. After this the Cynics led a life of formal mendicancy, without a house of their own, contenting themselves with the simplest food, and the scantiest clothing (the tribon). They made a principle of inuring themselves to privation, hardships, and insults; they showed their complete indifference to life by making a voluntary departure from it. As a rule they renounced family life, Diogenes proposing to replace it by communities of women and children; they attached no value to the opposition of freedom and slavery; for the wise man was free even as a slave, and a born master; for the wise man they considered civic life dispensable; for he was everywhere at home, a citizen of the world; their conception of the ideal state was a natural existence in which the whole of mankind lived together like a herd. Their disapproval of war was a natural corollary of this. In their behaviour they not only wilfully flouted tradition and respectability but outraged even the natural feelings of shame in order to show their indifference to public opinion. They treated the religious beliefs and cults of their people in a spirit of enlightenment; for in reality there was only one God, who was like nothing visible; only convention created the multitude of gods. Thus for the Cynics the only

true service lay in practising virtue, which makes the wise
the friend of the gods (that is the deity). Temples, on the
other hand, victims, prayers, vows, initiation and prophecies
were the objects of their unqualified condemnation. They
did not believe in survival after death while Antisthenes
gave a moral interpretation to Homeric and other myths.
The Cynics saw their special vocation in assistance of the
morally corrupt. As voluntary moral preachers and soul doc-
tors they undoubtedly did much good work. They denounced unmercifully the folly of mankind; they countered
overcultivation with a blunt, plebeian motherwit; to the effeminacy of their times they presented a will hard to the
point of roughness and met their fellow men in a spirit of
healthy contempt. Yet all this coarseness was merely external
and had its root in sympathy for the suffering of their fellow men and in that freedom of mind to which Diogenes
and Crates succeeded in attaining without sacrificing their
joviality or good humour.

The historian Theopompus declared Antisthenes to be the
most significant of all the Socratics; Plato recognised in him
and his pupils "a nature not unhonourable though unpleas-
ing", but his own pupil, Diogenes of Sinope (died *c.* 324),
thinking that his practice was not sufficiently in accordance
with his preaching, called him "a trumpet which hears nothing but itself". What he found lacking in his teacher was the
practical consequences of his theories. It was this that he
himself carried through with unswerving resolution. He had
no desire to be the doctor of diseased human society, but "a
savage dog". His chief work bore the title of *The Panther*.
The son of a banker and banished from his country, he
spent the greater part of his life in Athens and later in Cor-
inth, where in later times his grave before the Isthmean gate
was pointed out. He called himself with ostentation "The
dog", and the motto of his life was "I recoin current values"
(Diog., LVI, 20). He was fond of holding up the life of
animals as a model for mankind. He exerted his influence
less by his writings than example of his person, in which he
displayed his contempt for all culture. He affected less a
tone of moral indignation than that of an apt and biting wit.

Irony and sarcasm "this Socrates gone mad" handled with virtuosity. The anecdote which describes his meeting with Alexander is true at least so far in showing that in his self-assurance and feeling of independence he did not shrink from measuring himself with the lord of the earth.

A quite different and far more agreeable type of Cynic was represented by Crates of Thebes, the pupil of Diogenes. He was one of the wealthiest men of his city, to which he presented his whole fortune and chose the Cynic life of mendicancy, into which Hipparchia, the sister of his pupil Metrocles, followed him as his wife. His personality and career bear the stamp of the kindliness which won all hearts and opened all doors to him. He wrote only in a metrical form: parodies which show a kindly humour, especially the poem called *The Wallet* in which he described and praised the Cynical ideal of life, the happiness of poverty. His brother-in-law Metrocles of Maroneia was the creator of the witty anecdotes which form such a large part of the traditional accounts of Diogenes.

The further development of Cynicism will occupy us later.

32. *The Cyrenaic school*

Aristippus of Cyrene, who according to Diog., II, 83 was older than Æschines and so probably older than Plato (*c.* 435-355), seems to have become acquainted with the teachings of Protagoras while still in his native city; later he sought out Socrates in Athens and entered into close relations with him, without however renouncing his own habits or opinions on that account. After Socrates' death (at which he was not present) he himself came forward as a "Sophist", that is, a professional paid teacher, at first probably in Athens and probably in other places too; in this capacity he visited the Syracusan court, whether in the reign of the elder or the younger Dionysius or both is not certain. In Cyrene he founded a school, which is called the Cyrenaic or the Hedonistic school. To this his daughter belonged, who initiated her son Aristippus into the doctrines of his grandfather.

We are justified in concluding that the Cyrenaic teachings in their complete form had been already worked out by the elder Aristippus (in spite of Eus., *pr. Ev.* XIV, 18, 37) partly from the unity of the school and partly from the reference to their doctrines in Plato (*Phileb.*, 42Dff., 53C *Theæt.*, see below), Aristotle (*Eth.*, VII, 12ff.) and Speusippus, who according to Diog., IV, 5 wrote an *Aristippus*. In any case all indications go to show that of the writings attributed to Aristippus at least a part were authentic. Like Antisthenes, Aristippus measured the value of knowledge merely by its practical utility. He despised mathematics because it did not ask what was beneficial or harmful; physical investigation he considered to be without object or value; epistemological questions interested him only in so far as they provided a basis on which to establish his ethical system. Our perceptions, he said, following Protagoras (the development of whose doctrines represented in Plato's *Theætetus* 152Cff and 155Dff is probably his work), only give us information about our own sensations, but neither about the nature of things nor about the sensations of other men; for they are merely the momentary product of the collision of the respective movements of the perceived object and the perceiving subject. This provided a justification for deriving the laws of conduct only from subjective sensation. All sensation consists in movement; when this is gentle a feeling of pleasure is produced, when it is rough or tempestuous, we feel pain, but if only an imperceptible or no movement at all takes place then we experience neither pleasure nor pain. Aristippus believed that nature herself tells men that of these three conditions pleasure alone is desirable; that the good coincides with the pleasant, the bad with the unpleasant; pleasure is nothing more than sensation of a natural process in the body. Thus he arrived at the crowning principle of his ethics —the conviction that all our actions must be directed to obtaining the greatest possible amount of pleasure. By pleasure Aristippus did not understand mere tranquillity of mind, like Epicurus in later times (for that was merely absence of all sensation) but positive enjoyment; nor can happiness as a complete and comprehensive whole be the object of our lives, for only the present belongs to us, the future is uncertain and the past is gone.

It is indifferent what sort of things or actions it is which affords us pleasure; for each pleasure as such is good. Still the Cyrenaics did not wish to deny that there are differences of degree among enjoyments; nor did they overlook the fact that many of them are to be bought only at the cost of greater pain. Against such indulgences they warned their followers. And while bodily sensations of pleasure and pain are stronger and more primitive, they recognised that there are also sensations which do not arise from bodily states. They recognised, too, the necessity of judging correctly the relative values of different goods and enjoyments. This judgment we owe to wisdom or philosophy, which now becomes the art of living, a sort of "measuring art" of the goods of life, as the Platonic Socrates remarks in the *Protagoras*. It shows us how we have to use the goods of life, frees us from fancies and passions which disturb happiness, and enables us to utilise everything in the most fitting way for our well-being. It is therefore the first condition of all happiness.

In accordance with these principles Aristippus made it his aim in all his rules of life and his personal conduct (as far as traditional accounts allow us to judge) to enjoy life as much as possible, but under all circumstances to remain master of himself and his environment. He was not merely the adroit man-of-the-world, who is never at a loss when it is a question of discovering means of enjoyment, by fair means or foul, or finding an apt and witty turn to defend his conduct; he is the superior mind who knows how to adapt himself to every situation, to "appear in rags as well as in festive garments"; to get the best out of everything, and by limitation of his desires, by wisdom and self-control, to secure his cheerfulness and contentment. To other men he maintained his kindly and benevolent attitude. It seems that in his later life he tried to withdraw from civil life, so as not to prejudice his independence. For his great master he preserved feelings of the warmest veneration. The Socratic spirit, indeed, is unmistakable in the value which he placed upon wisdom and in the cheerfulness and the inner freedom which it secured him. But his whole theory of pleasure is essentially a contradiction of that spirit, just as his sceptical despair of positive knowledge was a denial of the goal in quest of which his master had given up his life.

This contradiction in the elements of the Cyrenaic school found expression in the changes which Aristippus' doctrines underwent at the beginning of the third century. Theodorus, the pupil of the younger Aristippus, called the "Atheist" on account of his repudiation of all belief in God, embraced the doctrines of the school and with ruthless logic pushed their hypotheses to their ultimate consequences. But in order to make the happiness of the wise man independent of externals, he found it not in individual acts of gratification but in a contented disposition of mind, where wisdom ruled. Anniceris did not wish to give up completely the theory of pleasure, but he introduced a considerable limitation by placing so high a value on friendship, gratitude, love of family and country, that the wise man would not shrink from sacrificing himself for them.

Hegesias, finally, had so lively a sense of the misery of life, that he was completely sceptical of attaining contentment by positive enjoyment, and declared happiness to be unattainable. He became a philosopher of pessimism. In his work *The Suicide of Abstinence* a man, prevented by his friends from dying a voluntary death by starvation, enumerates the hardships of life. His lectures in Alexandria had so many suicides as a consequence that he received the nickname of "counsellor of death" and Ptolemaeus II forbade their continuance. With this result Hedonism had found its own refutation. It underwent inevitable limitations in Epicureanism like Cynicism in the Stoa.

It is questionable whether Euhemerus, the friend of the Macedonian king Cassander (317-397), who is frequently mentioned with the atheist Theodorus, had any connection with the Cyrenaic school. His philosophy of religion which was embodied in a utopian romance believed the gods to have been originally men of great ability and power who demanded and received divine worship. How far Egyptian traditions and how far sophistical theories contributed to this peculiar theory of the origin of religion, cannot be established with any certainty.

III. PLATO AND THE ACADEMY

33. *Plato's life*

The most gifted pupil of Socrates was Plato the son of Ariston and Perictione of Athens (427-347 B.C.). Through both of his parents he belonged to the most distinguished families of Athens; his father traced his descent from Codrus, and his mother from a relative of Solon. On her side he was closely related to Charmides and Critias, who figure repeatedly in his dialogues and have given their names to two of them. Thus his boyhood and youth were passed in an aristocratic environment, in a house where interest in literature and philosophy was a matter of tradition. As the son of a rich family he probably served in the cavalry. According to Greek custom he engaged in gymnastics and is supposed to have received the nickname of Plato from the broadness of his chest, whereas previously he had been called Aristocles after his grandfather. A brilliant poetical and political career was expected of the highly gifted young man who at an early age composed lyrical and dramatical poems. His description in the *Republic* (VI, 493C-494E) of the talented young man brought up in a rich and distinguished circle who resists the inducements of his relatives and rejects the career which they propose in order to devote himself to philosophy is obviously autobiographical. For Plato the deciding event of his life was his acquaintance with Socrates which he made at the age of twenty and caused him to throw into the fire the tragedies which he was on the point of having produced. Before this he had studied the works of the older philosophers and had enjoyed the personal tuition of the Heraclitan Cratylus. It was his association with Socrates that rescued him from the quaking ground of this decadent Heraclitanism and brought him to firm earth. With him ne learned to direct his attention to the moral and here, too, he learned, as far that was necessary for a grand nephew of Critias, the short-comings of the Athenian democracy, for which of course Socrates had quite a different remedy than that sworn enemy of popular government—namely the technical competence of political leaders and moral education of the people. Plato's second experience which stirred his soul to its depths was the execution of his beloved master, an event which together with what had led up to it opened his eyes to the fact that the ailing and diseased state was no longer to be helped by mere change of constitution; only a completely new conception of politics in the sense of moral education of the people could bring about any improvement. Thus the thought might have slowly ripened within him of becoming himself the moral and social reformer of his people like Solon or Lycurgus. At first the execution of Socrates drove him abroad to Euclides in Megara. After his return to Athens he devoted nearly ten years to the writing of philosophical works which still moved along the lines of Socratic thought. It was perhaps at this time that he began his activity as a teacher, at first of course to a small circle. He seems to have been interrupted in this by the Corinthian war, during which he took part in a campaign, the same which is today still commemorated by the monument of Dexileus before the Dipylon. He must have felt the need of broadening his experience and deepening his mind by observation in the wide world. Like his ancestor Solon, Thales and Democritus, Hecatæus and Herodotus, he undertook travels which according to a widely current, but not entirely credible, tradition led him to the old wonderland of Egypt, to the famous mathematician Theodorus in Cyrene and certainly to the Pythagoreans of Tarentum. Here he seems to have made the acquaintance of Philolaus and certainly that of Archytas, in whom he found an ideal combination of philosophy, science and politics. The impressions which Plato received in his association with these later Pythagoreans were of the greatest importance for his further development and denote a turning point in his philosophical thought. It was the friendly relation of Archytas with Syracuse which secured him an introduction to the court of Dionysius I, which was at that time frequented by other Socratics such as Æschines and Aristippus. He may have had hopes of putting his political ideas into practice by winning an influence over that prince. But it soon became clear that the unscrupulous man of action and the ethical idealist did not harmonise. Plato however struck up an intimate friendship with Dionysius' brother-in-law which continued undisturbed until the latter's violent death. In Sicily he came to know and love the mimes of Sophron and the comedies of Epicharmus, which may have developed his talent for caricature. On his return journey Plato landed in Ægina which was at war with Athens. He was taken prisoner and brought to the slave market, but was ransomed by his friend the Cyrenaic Anniceris. The latter refused to accept the purchase money and for this sum Plato acquired a garden near the sanctuary of the hero Academus where he now (387) opened his school, the Academy. After the change of ruler in Sicily, Plato paid two more visits to the island, the first time (367) in the hope of winning the new prince Dionysius II over to his ideas, an attempt which again ended in disappointment. This apparently was the time when the introductions to the Laws were written, which Plato incorporated into his last work. The last journey was undertaken in the service of friendship. He intended to bring about the recall of Dio, who in the meantime had been banished from the court, and his reconciliation with Dionysius. From now on, and the more so after the murder of Dio, Plato gave up all hope of realising his political plans and lived only for his teaching and writing until his death in his eightieth year. Immediately after his death the legend sprang up which saw in him a son of Apollo.

34. *Plato as teacher and author*

We are always tempted to regard the dialogues as the principal part of Plato's activity, since it is from them that we derive our knowledge of his philosophy. But he leaves us no room for doubt that for him authorship was only of secondary importance, only a pleasant game, a noble amuse-

ment; the spoken word is living and animate, the written
only a shadowy imitation, a reminiscence of it. The dialogues, which in their form imitate the Socratic conversations, are therefore not mere philosophic expositions, but
works of literary art, and should not be put on the same
plane as the writings of the pre-Socratic philosophers. It is
noteworthy that Aristotle uses the Republic and the Laws
as sources for Plato's educational, sociological and political
views, but never quotes a dialogue as an authority for the
theory of ideas. For the main doctrines of Plato, the authorities were his lectures in the Academy and the discussions
connected with them. Of these only one, that *On The
Good*, which he delivered in his old age, is expressly mentioned in the ancient tradition.

For Plato, oral intercourse with his pupils was of first importance. The dialogues contained merely an extract from
this although in the later ones the tone of the lecture room
is more strongly marked. It was the Academy which provided the opportunity for this personal contact between master and pupil. It was organised apparently on the lines of the
Pythagorean order. Apart from this it was the first real
school of Greek philosophy, for no more than tentative beginnings had been made before. Master and pupils together
comprised a religious guild which was dedicated to the
Muses. The lectures and discussions began at an early hour
in the morning. The pupils lived in small houses scattered
about the garden of the Academy. In order to keep to his
hours, Plato himself constructed an alarm-clock which
emitted a whistling noise and thus summoned the pupils to
the lecture room. They met too, more informally at ban-
quets towards which they paid monthly contributions. The
most important thing was to join in philosophic study. By
this we must understand primarily the introduction to Plato's speculative philosophy and the epistemological, ethical
and political questions connected with it. Of the special sciences only mathematics and astronomy were pursued, while
interest in descriptive natural sciences like zoology and botany declined. A fragment of the comic poet Epicrates, who
wrote for the Attic stage from about 376 onwards, has been

preserved and represents Plato and his pupils as engaged in the classification of plants. Probably this activity was undertaken more as a preparation for dialectic exercises by way of the recognition of similar and dissimilar than as scientific research. The Academy was not attended exclusively by Athenians but also by numerous foreigners. It produced not only philosophers but also statesmen and generals. For it was becoming more and more the custom that the educated man should attend in his youth the schools of rhetoric and philosophy.[4]

The dialogues however form the only source of our knowledge of Plato's views on the after life. His activity as a writer extends over a period of about fifty years. It is contestable and scarcely probable that he had begun in the last years of Socrates. His complete works have been preserved. Apart from seven dialogues which in ancient times were rejected as spurious (of which the *Axiochos* and *Eryxias* are the most important), thirty-six works were regarded as genuine. These were arranged by Thrasyllus in nine tetralogies, the thirteen letters being counted as one book. Of these dialogues modern research has shown at least four to be spurious (the second *Alcibiades*, the *Hipparchus*, the *Erastæ*, and the *Theages*). Of the remaining thirty-two the following are extremely doubtful: the *Minos*, the *Cleitophon*, and the first *Alcibiades*, although the last was valued highly by the neo-Platonists and was actually used as an introduction to the study of Plato. Besides these the *Epinomis*, according to a statement of Diogenes Laertius (III, 37), was a work of Plato's pupil, Philippus of Opus, who also edited the laws on the lines laid down by Plato. Of the letters, the sixth, seventh, and eighth have most claim to authenticity. The longest and most important of all is the seventh addressed to the relatives of Dio, which gives us Plato's relations to the entanglements of the Syracusan court and affords us a glimpse into his philosophical development. Accordingly there remain twenty-seven works which are certainly genuine (apart from the letters), namely the *Apology* and twenty-six dialogues.

As would be expected from the long duration of his literary activity, Plato's writings show considerable differences in form and content. The character of each work is determined by the stage which his philosophical development had reached at the time of its composition, and by particular philosophic and artistic intentions which influenced the writer at the time, but which today are no longer always apparent. The dialogues showed two differences of form: some are diegmatic, that is narrated, dialogues, and the others are dramatic ialogues. The former offers the possibility of conversation around the narrated dialogue and an opportunity for the description of situations which is often carried out with great art and vividness. On the other hand the form of reference involves certain cumbrousnesses which Plato himself felt as irksome and led him eventually to give up this method of exposition (*Theæt.*, 143C). Since Plato, with few exceptions, made Socrates the leader of the conversation, he was compelled to make the action take place in the time of Socrates and to represent him as arguing with his contemporaries. Occasionally anachronisms occur which are indications for the time of composition. He sometimes criticised the philosophic theories of his own time, particularly those of Antisthenes and Aristippus, although he did not mention them by name. He generally uses the names of pre-Socratic philosophers. In the *Timæus* he discusses the theories of Democritus, whose name, remarkably enough, he does not mention. His most detailed studies he reserved for Heraclitus, the Eleatics, and the three most important sophists. Next to Socrates, it was Pythagoreanism that had most influence upon him. Plato's philosophy, therefore, as revealed by his writings, is not a finished and complete system, but shows a gradual development. From the years of maturity onwards, however, it appears in a finished form. With all regard for his mental development and the continuation of his work into advanced old age, the unity of his mind and the tendency of his thought is despite all changes as unmistakable in the writings of his youth as in those of his old age.

The concentrated efforts of a century of scholarship directed both to the contents and linguistic and stylistic form has finally succeeded in establishing a chronological order of the Platonic writings with such certainty that within the different groups only inconsiderable rearrangements are possible. Four periods can be distinguished in Plato's literary activity.

1. THE SOCRATIC PERIOD

In this period a special place is occupied by the *Apology,* which contains an account of Socrates' speech in defence of himself at his trial that is true in all essentials, but has been revised and touched up by Plato from a stylistic point of view. In close connection with the *Apology* stands the *Crito,* a Platonic defence of Socrates as a loyal citizen. In the dialogues of this period Plato still shows himself under the ban of Socratic intellectual determinism, the only change being that the Socratic insistence on expertness takes the form of a search after ideas. Thus the *Euthyphro,* the *Laches,* and the *Charmides* discuss the ideas of goodness and prudence, the *Protagoras* that of virtue and the question of its teachability. Like the last dialogue, the two *Hippias* (of which the *Minor* is a high spirited erotic trifle, while the *Major* seeks to grasp the idea of the beautiful)—open the war against the sophists, while the *Ion* is directed against the poets and rhapsodists. Most of these dialogues conclude without any definite result, which is in accordance with the Socratic principle of not-knowing; but they show Plato himself wholly absorbed in his search after truth. It is possible that the dialogue on justice in which Thrasymachus plays the chief part and which now forms the beginning of the *Republic* belongs to this period.

2. THE TRANSITION PERIOD

To this period may be ascribed the *Lysis,* which treats of friendship, a theme which is later worked out in the *Symposium:* further the *Cratylus* which is devoted to the philosophy of language and contains (428Dff) an unmistakable polemic against Antisthenes. Against him and the sophistic eristic in general, which Antisthenes followed in his theory of knowledge, the *Euthydemus* was directed, in which the logical fallacies of the later Sophists were ridiculed. The *Menexenus* we must regard merely as a light satirical trifle, which was directed against the epideictic rhetoric. It takes the form of a parody on the speech which was made at the public solemnity in honour of those fallen in battle and usually ended in a panegyric of Athens. The irony underlying this praise of the Athenian democracy passed unnoticed in later times and the speech was taken seriously and recited annually at this festival. The *Gorgias* may be placed at the end of this period, whether the date of its composition falls before or, as is more probable, after the first Sicilian journey. This forceful dialogue contains a deeply serious reckoning with the Sophistic rhetoric, in which the struggle is deepened to an opposition of two types of life; that of the practical politician who, on the principle of the right of the stronger propounded with great spirit by Callicles, has an eye only for outward success and his own advantage, and that of the philosopher, for whom justice, that is the morally good, is the absolute norm of conduct even if it should cost him his life. The Socratic theory of evil as error is here abandoned and philosophy appears as a remedy for souls polluted by earthly lusts and their corresponding sins. Although the dialogue moves within the frame of ideal dialectic, nevertheless the myth at the end on survival after death and the court of judgment in the other world shows the thread which connects the Socratic philosophy with the new view of life which Plato was evolving under the influence of Pythagoreanism. For the first time ethics receives here a transcendental basis, which is the most profound reason for the radical rejection of all purely worldly activities, not only of rhetoric and traditional politics but also poetry. The dialogue might well be called a renunciation of the world.

3. THE PERIOD OF MATURITY

To this period those dialogues are to be assigned which are devoted to the development of the theory of ideas, the first intimations of which are found in the Gorgias, and which reveal the adoption by Plato of the Orphic-Pythagorean dualism. The *Meno* takes up again the theme of the *Protagoras,* the teachability of virtue, and corrects the former attempt at a solution in the light of the new point of view. The Pythagorean theory of the soul is turned to account epistemologically as in the *Gorgias* it is ethically: learning is the recollection by the soul of the ideas perceived by it in its former existence. The use of an example from geometry to illustrate this *a priori* knowledge is an indication of Pythagorean influence. This philosophy of life reaches its zenith in the *Phædo,* where the doctrines of ideas and of the immortality of the soul are closely interwoven and the deprecatory attitude to the world is intensified to the point of hatred of life. True philosophy is "practice in dying and death". The *Symposium* with its pulsating vitality is only an apparent contrast. The theory of ideas is applied to the realm of the beautiful, but it is strongly emphasised that all earthly beauty is merely a shadow of "the beautiful in itself", to which the soul, the Eros, aspires. The *Republic,* too, which had been long in preparation and may have been completed in its present form in the year 374, although primarily occupied with this world and its problems, rests on the basis of the same metaphysical dualism as the *Phædo,* as is shown especially by the allegory of the cave at the beginning of the seventh book and the myth of the fate of the soul in the tenth. The ethical conclusions are the same as those reached in the *Gorgias.* The *Phædrus,* which according to an old but untenable testimony was long regarded as the first work of Plato, starts from a speech of Lysis on love and with an artistic transition proceeds to the discussion of the nature of Eros and the possibility of a philosophic rhetoric. It differs from the *Phædo* in sharing with the *Republic* the theory of the tripartition of the soul. This dialogue contains too a combination of the Orphic-Pythagorean theory of transmigration with the theory of ideas.

4. THE WORKS OF OLD AGE

These dialogues are characterised by a decline of the interest in the ontological in favour of the logical side of the theory of ideas, which Plato never abandoned even in his old age, but waged in its defence "the war of the giants about Being" (*Soph.*, 246E) against the opposition which gradually arose even within the Academy. A further characteristic is the approximation of the theory of ideas to the Pythagorean theory of numbers and finally a more penetrating study of this world, the Cosmos. First among these dialogues is the remarkable *Parmenides*,[5] in which Plato in the form of a conversation between the young Socrates and the head of the Eleatic school and his pupil Zeno defends himself against a series of criticisms of the theory of ideas and at the same time throws light on his relation to the doctrines of the Eleatics. This is followed by the *Theætetus,* of epistemological content, which in the course of a discussion on Protagoras' assertion that "man is the measure of all things" and the Heraclitan doctrine of the flux polemises against the logic of Antisthenes and the sensualism of Aristippus, and makes a series of unavailing attempts to define the idea of knowledge. This failure is perhaps meant to suggest to the reader that the only help in surmounting the difficulties touched upon is the theory of ideas, which, as we must suppose, is deliberately left unmentioned in this dialogue. Of the trilogy of dialogues planned by Plato, the *Sophist,* the *Statesman* and the *Philosopher* (*Soph.*, 253E; *Pol.* 257E), only the first two were completed. The *Sophist* is a continuation of the *Theætetus,* but the fact that the chief speaker is the Eleatic stranger points back to the *Parmenides.* The main purpose of the dialogue is the attack on the Sophists, Antisthenes being clearly regarded as their representative (251B). At the same time however the problem of the one and the many posed by the Eleatics is taken up and the theory of ideas undergoes a revision in the sense that the ideas approximate to the meaning of "generic concepts". The *Politicus,* the direct continuation of the *Sophist,* corresponds completely with the methodical structure and arrangement of the latter. It sees the true ruler, "the kingly man" in the "Knower", who alone possesses the true art of ruling. In so far as such a man does not need to bind himself to laws, which are imperfect because of their inelasticity, that is in a certain sense a recommendation of enlightened despotism.

The legal state, however, in its various forms is recognised as a makeshift. Thus their dialogue in its attention to circumstances of real life forms the bridge between the *Republic* and the work of Plato's old age, the *Laws*. The *Philebus* is connected with the preceding dialogues only by the short logico-dialectic section on the relation of the one to the many (14C-19A). Its chief subject is of an ethical nature—the relation of pleasure to good, a question which Plato had previously handled (in the *Protagoras,* the *Gorgias,* and the *Republic*) and which he now attempted to solve by the application of the Pythagorean opposites of the Limit and the Unlimited, with consideration of the contemporary theories of the Cynics, the Cyrenaics, and Eudoxus. The judgment passed upon art (music, tragedy, comedy, and even rhetoric) is less severe than that in the *Gorgias:* but the feelings awakened by them are not regarded as pure pleasure. Once again Plato planned a trilogy of dialogues which was to form a completion of the *Republic;* the *Timæus, Critias,* and *Hermocrates.* Only the *Timæus* was finished, Plato's only dialogue dealing with natural science. With its theory of creation, which he carried down to the first appearance of man and the animals, it was intended to form the substructure of the *Republic.* The chief character is the Pythagorean whose name the dialogue bears. Pythagorean influence indeed is everywhere evident in the cosmology, psychology, and the ethical ideas of the dialogue. The theory of ideas is restored. The whole of the investigations of natural science are in contrast to the reasoned truths of dialectic, and are emphatically declared to be mere probabilities. In the *Critias* the ideal agrarian state, projected into the earliest times of Athens, is contrasted with the imperialistic sea-power "Atlantis", which is conquered in a war with the former. In the third dialogue the Syracusan Hermocrates was to describe the degeneration from the original ideal state to the present and to show the way to betterment. In Plato's last work the *Laws,* the person of Socrates never appears and is replaced by a nameless Athenian who converses with the Cretan Clinias and the Spartan Megillus. A few traces betray the fact that the work was begun while he was still on good terms with Dionysius II. The theory of ideas remains unmentioned, but the basic ideas of the *Republic* are retained, not without however some remarkable concessions to the realities of life. Particularly valuable is the idea of a mixed constitution with elements from both monarchy and democracy. Plato's dualistic metaphysics reaches its culmination in the completely un-Greek assumption of an evil world-spirit. Side by side with profound and fruitful astronomical thoughts, such as the suggestion of the possibility of the heliocentric system, the phantastic idea of star-divinities is retained. The supremacy of religion in this legal state indeed goes so far that not only is poetry subjected to a rigid censorship, but incurable atheism is made a capital offence. Thus we see the defender of Socrates relapsing into an impatient and rigid dogmatism.

35. *Character, method and divisions of the Platonic system*

Although Plato's philosophy is nowhere transmitted as a systematic whole and in the dialogues we can only observe from afar its gradual growth and development, it is only in the form of a system that any account of it can be given. The justification for this is the incontestable fact that in the dialogues we see circles spreading wider and wider until they finally embrace the whole universe.

The Platonic philosophy is characterised by the fact that it unites in itself the different streams of previous philosophical development. This hybrid character was clearly recognised by the ancients themselves. But this should not be understood in the sense of a merely external and inorganic eclecticism, of which there can be no question in a man of Plato's creative power. In his critical examinations of the older philosophic systems he extended the circle of his inquiries more and more until he had created a new and original system of a universality which had never been achieved before except perhaps by Democritus. There were four philosophic tendencies which were of primary significance in the genesis of Platonism—Heraclitus, Socrates, the Pythagoreans and the Eleatics. To these the Atomists must be added although their influence is not to be compared with that of those just mentioned. Heraclitanism, with which Plato had become familiar before his acquaintance with Socrates, forms as it were the negative woof in the texture of Platonic philosophy in so far that its doctrine of the flux had in the lack of a fixed object questioned the possibility of knowledge. It was Plato's task to find and recapture this lost object of knowledge. The first help in this task was given him by Socrates with his search after the good and the supersensual. Conduct seemed to be determined by knowledge. But Plato's thought took a completely new turn after he had come into contact with Pythagoreanism. This introduced the dualism into both his metaphysics and his anthropology (psychology and ethics) which from now on remained dominant and enrolled him in the ranks of the philosophers who stood in opposition to the Ionic monism. Mathematics was the element which acted as intermediary between the sensual and the purely mental world, while astronomy fixed the attention on the visual world. Science and practical philosophy now received a transcendental basis. The question of what is essential, permanent and unchanging was bound to lead Plato to the doctrines of the Eleatics, especially those of Parmenides, who declared the world of sense to be mere appearance, and to the problem of the one and the many. From these three elements Socraticism, Pythagoreanism and Eleaticism, the central Platonic dogma of the ideas crystallised out, while Heraclitanism, as the negative foil of the world of ideas, was put to use in explaining the realm of matter, the not-being. Finally atomism contributed to the construction of Plato's physics and the later form of the dialectic. On the practical side of the Platonic philosophy, ethics, and politics, Socrates and Pythagoreanism were of decisive influence in bringing about an unmistakable leaning towards the aristocratic political system of Sparta, with a sharp division between rulers and ruled. Doubtless his experiences at the Syracusan court also contributed to the formation of his views. At any rate both were opposed to the extreme democracy which since Pericles' death had been supreme in

Athens. As a whole, Plato's philosophy is an idealistic system resting on a sharply defined dualism between mind and matter, God and the world, body and soul. It ascribes being in a true sense only to the mental and it sees in the material world only a faint imitation of the world of ideas and draws the practical conclusions of this doctrine with ruthless logic.

In the method of the Platonic philosophy the dominating feature is the search for knowledge by means of dialectic. Thought is always superior and more correct than sense-perception. This does not afford us knowledge but only opinion. It does not penetrate into the world of being but stops appearance. Mathematics provides a valuable preparation for dialectic thinking. Plato gradually succeeds in working down to the laws of thought and prepares the way for Aristotelian logic. In spite of this thorough-going intellectual method of knowledge an undercurrent of intuition makes itself apparent which leads more and more to the recognition of an irrational element in the nature of the mind and takes account of the importance of the instinctive, the forces which surge forth from the unconscious life of the soul. At first in the *Ion* Plato completely rejects this idea of the divine gift; in the *Meno* however he accepts it quite seriously as a possible cause of right opinion, and the proficiency which depends on it. In the *Phædrus* (244A, 268CD) it is recognised that "the greatest goods become ours through inspiration in virtue of a divine gift"; and in the *Symposium* it is Eros which gives the mind the wings with which it can rise into the realm of the beautiful and true. Moreover in the seventh letter (341C) we find the statements that the ultimate and most profound knowledge cannot be taught or committed to writing but can only be experienced by direct illumination. It accords well with this undercurrent of intuition that Plato frequently uses the form of the myth side by side with the ideal comprehension of knowledge in order to make clear the obscurities of his profoundest thoughts.

As far as the divisions of the Platonic system are concerned, the central place is occupied by the theory of ideas in its ontological, logical and teleological significance. The dualistic

principle of the two worlds finds its application in his anthropology as the relation of body and soul in the animal, and
especially the human world, in which the nature of the soul
is to be more carefully investigated in its various aspects and
functions. In ethics and politics, which is closely bound up
with it, the attention is according to the same dualistic principle completely fixed on the transcendental world. The same
is true of the æsthetics, that is the estimation of art in its
various forms. It was only late and reluctantly that Plato
brought the visible world, nature, into the scope of his consideration. In the *Timæus* he gives a sketch of his physics
with the reservation, however, that here we are not dealing
with real knowledge, but merely probability. His physics
consists of the application of the anthropological dualism to
the Cosmos. The philosophy of religion occupies no special
place in Plato's system, but both on its critical and positive
sides it runs through his whole thought and culminates in
the idea of the good which he identifies with God.

36. *Dialectic, or the theory of ideas*

Dialectic is primarily, as its name implies, the art of conduct-
ing a discussion, then the art of developing scientific knowledge by question and answer (*Rep.*, VII, 534E), and finally
the art of grasping conceptually that which is (*Phædr.*,
265D). Thus in Plato it becomes a theory of science, a
means of knowing the true reality of things. Socrates had
sought after the good, but never solved the problem. Plato
too at first occupied himself with ethical questions of the
separate virtues, a study which led him to recognise the
unity of the good. If then the good is an object of knowledge, it must be raised above the sphere of subjective opinion; it must be something definite, real and unchangeable.
That is equally true of the good and everything which is to
be an object of knowledge. In virtue of this the Heraclitan
world of coming into being and ceasing to be, with its eternal changeableness, cannot be an object of knowledge.
There must be another world which, like the capital being
of Parmenides, answers to the demands of permanence and

durability without which there can be no knowledge. The former is the world of sense-perception, the latter the world of thought. Thought fixes its attention not on what is peculiar in things but on the general, that which is common to all things which belong to a "kind" of being. Thus it is not the particular in each separate thing that is lasting and essential but that which it has in common with other things of its kind. This common quality, which since Aristotle we call the concept, was termed by Plato the idea. "We suppose an idea to exist when we give the same name to many separate things" (*Rep.*, X, 596A). It was in mathematics that the significance which he attached to the form of things was to be seen most clearly. The form of a square, for example, is fixed once and for all, however many individual examples of the figure may exist. All these individual figures are only squares in so far as the square form is present in them or they participate in it. Everything else about them is insignificant for the idea of the square. The empirical figures of geometry belong of course to the world of sense. Thus mathematics occupies a middle position between the world of sense and the world of reality. Hence for Plato the nonsensual nature of things is the only true reality, which is to be distinguished from their sensual phenomena. The ideas are for him not mere things of thought, as Antisthenes considered them to be, but realities. There are ideas of everything possible: not merely of things, but of qualities too, and relations and activities; not only of natural things, but of the products of art, and not only of valuable things but of bad and worthless things. The ideas form a world which exists of itself, is eternal and unchanging and can only be comprehended by thought. In this pure and independent existence they have their abode in a "super-celestial" place, where the soul in its pre-existence has perceived them. All learning and knowledge consists in the recollection by the soul of the ideas when it perceives the things of sense. The earthly sensually perceptible things are mere shadowy images of the bright world of ideas, a view which finds clear and emphatic expression in the famous simile of the cave at the beginning of the seventh book of the *Republic*.

In the Platonic philosophy the ideas have a threefold significance—ontological, teleological and logical. Ontologically they represent real being, the thing in itself. Each thing is what it is only through the presence of the idea in it or through its participation in the idea. Thus the ideas as the one stand in opposition to the many; they are changeable, it remains always the same. The ideas have furthermore a teleological or paradeigmatic significance. All becoming, including human conduct, has its end and aim in a being. These ends can only be in the realisation of that in which thought recognises the unchanging, primary patterns of things. As such the ideas are like the ideal image in the head of the artist, to which he endeavours to give a material form. To this extent the ideas have also the meaning of causes and moving forces which make the things of the world what they are. In their logical aspect the ideas enable us to bring order into the chaos of individual beings, to recognise the similar and distinguish the dissimilar and to apprehend the one in many. These three aspects are by no means of equal importance in Plato. In his later works their logical side gradually takes precedence, without however the other two, and in particular the ontological, ever being abandoned.

This is connected with a series of problems which arose in the course of time, partly in his critical examinations of the other philosophic movements. The course of his development does not lead from the concept to the idea but from the idea more and more to the concept. The first of these problems is that of the absolute existence of the ideas, which offered no difficulties when they were concerned merely with moral ideas, but was bound to lead to a duplication of the world when ideas of all things were postulated (*Parm.*, 130-B-D). This is the difficulty which Aristotle in his criticism of the theory of ideas called the problem of the third man. When two particular things owe their similarity to an idea, to what must we ascribe the similarity between the idea and the two particulars? This leads to a *regressus in infinitum*. Furthermore if the ideas are separate from things, how can the latter at the same time participate in them? The second problem is that of the one and the many. When the idea in the paradeigmatic sense of an ethical ideal, through its extension to all things, becomes untenable and comes to have merely the meaning of "the general", the question arises: How can one idea be in the many things which participate in it? (*Parm.*, 132A). With this is connected the third problem of the nature of *methexis*. This is only possible when both one can be many and many one (*Parm.*, 129B). Finally the extension of the theory of ideas to all things brings the problem of appearance and reality into a new light. Whereas in the period when he was concerned with ethics, the things which were known *a priori* were the peculiar province of the theory of ideas, it was now a question of the relation of sensually perceptible things to the ideas and the relations of sense perception to knowledge. The following dialogue is devoted to surmounting the difficulties that arose in the *Parmenides*. In the *Theætetus*, which ignores the theory of ideas and makes no mention either of recollection or the idea of the good, which in the *Republic* (VI, 507B, 508E, 509B) is the basis of all being and knowledge, the consideration of empirical objects caused Plato to make a change in his method of approach. This new method by which Plato sought to apprehend mentally the totality of things and which he used for the first time in the *Sophist* together with the new dialogue form is "diæresis" or the analysis of ideas. With this dialectical method of analysis and synthesis which ends finally in the combination of several predicates in a subject idea—in opposition to Antisthenes who held that only identical judgments were possible—the theory of ideas takes on more and more a logical and epistemological character. Plato now applies it to the problem of sense-perception, which did not come into consideration in the treatment of ethical objects, and with this form of his theory that no object can be scientifically apprehended otherwise than by thought, he became the founder of science. In this super-ordination and subordination of concepts which the diæretic method makes possible, the apex of the pyramid is formed by Being, the concept which comprises and includes all other kinds. Plato of course never regarded Being as a mere concept. This is what determines the metaphysical content of this new form of the theory of ideas. He succeeded in bridging the gulf between the super-sensual world of the ideas and the world of sense in establishing a new relation between the two without which knowlege of reality would be impossible.

In the last phase of Plato's philosophy his dialectic underwent a further modification. Just as the change from the Socratic views to a metaphysical dualism points to a definite influence by Pythagoreanism, this influence was renewed in his old age. He now sought to combine the chief dogma of the Pythagoreans, that the nature of things is number, with his own theory of ideas. The *Philebus,* in which the Pythagorean opposites, the Limit and the Unlimited, the One and the Many, already appear, forms the transition to this final form of the Platonic metaphysics. Plato now defines the ideas as numbers. Differing however from the Pythagoreans in that the latter regarded being as an imitation of numbers, while Plato made use of the relation of *methexis.* He now sought for the origin of the ideas and found it in the One as the origin, to which the Dyad with the double function of multiplication and division, doubling and halving, is opposed. Number is the limit, multiplicity is unlimitedness; it is also called "the great and the small" because this has no upper or lower limit. Here the One appears as the whole Cosmos, the division of which ends in the indivisible, the indivisible type or form. This is the point of contact between Plato and his antithesis Democritus, whose theories are examined in the *Timæus.* The main problem of this late Platonic philosophy is the question how the sensual world is to be evolved from the ideas or numbers. This is discussed on Platonic lines in the *Epinomis* (990Cff). This question too forms the content of the writing *On the Good* which has been lost. The idea of the good, too shared in this last transformation of the Platonic philosophy. In the *Republic* (VI, 504Eff; VII, 517Bff), it was compared to the sun as the ultimate source of all being and knowledge and at the same time the final goal of the world (*Phædr.,* 99Dff); knowledge of it is the "greatest science" (*Rep.,* VI, 505E). Now this highest idea and its knowledge take on a mathematical character. It is the one, the monad, the ultimate basis of all being; arithmetic becomes the "greatest and first science", the knowledge "of the whole production and power of the straight and the crooked with reference to the natural becoming of being" (*Epin.*, 990C). Mind is identified with one, science with two, opinion with three and perception with four. To these principles of knowledge the elements of the object of knowledge, the individual object (that is, the world) correspond: point, line, surface and solid. To this must be added the idea of the combination of the mental and the corporeal, which leads to the idea of the world as a graduated structure. This idea of the good was identified by Plato both in its earlier and later forms with God.

37. *Plato's anthropology*

For Socrates man was the most important thing in the world. The same is true of Plato, who considers him both as an individual and a social being. In man too it was the "supersensual", the soul, which engaged Socrates' attention. He simply assumed its existence and left open the question of its possible survival after the death of the body. His unshakeable conviction that the care of the soul was man's highest task and that the body ought to serve the needs of the soul was unaffected by any answer to that problem. It is otherwise with Plato. He shared indeed his master's belief in the supreme importance of the soul; but he wished to prove the correctness of this belief. To this end he gave it a metaphysical basis which he borrowed from the Orphic-Pythagorean mysticism and combined with the theory of ideas. It is certainly no accident that we find the first traces of it in the *Gorgias*. At the time of its formulation Plato's change from the Socratic views to his cosmic and anthropological dualism must have been completed. The new conception finds its comprehensive exposition in the *Phædo*. From now on Plato adhered to the theory not merely of the immortality but, what alone is logically correct, of the eternality of the soul. The soul is both pre-existent and post-existent. Plato adopted the Orphic-Pythagorean theory of transmigration and endeavoured to support it by philosophical proofs, such as that of the simplicity and consequent indestructibility of the soul and that of the recollection of the ideas perceived by the soul in its previous existence. Especially important is the sharply defined dualism which distinguishes two kinds of beings—the unseen and eternal, to which the soul belongs, and the visible and transient, to which the body belongs. Body and soul therefore enter into a temporary combination. It depends on the moral conduct of the soul how often and in what form it will be re-born. In the next world, however, a judgment awaits it which will decide its future fate according to its conduct during its earthly existence—an idea which, as Plato specially emphasises, is for him no myth but "a reasonable truth".

While in the *Phædo* special emphasis is laid in the simplicity of the soul, the *Republic* contains the doctrine of the tripartition of the soul into the reasonable, the courageous, which includes feeling and will, and the desires. What is peculiar and essential to the soul is mind or reason. The second part supports this with all its strength, a view which is illustrated in the *Phædrus* by the metaphor of the two horses driven by reason, one of which strives upwards to the realm of ideas, while the other endeavours to pull the team into the realm of the earthly. The *Phædrus* (245Cff) adds the further proof for the eternality of the soul that what moves itself must be without beginning and imperishable. In the *Timæus* (69Cf) only the reasonable part of the soul, which is localised in the head, is held to be immortal, while courage and the sensual desires, which reside respectively in the chest and the belly, are reckoned to the unreasonable and transient parts of the soul. Plato presents us with no complete psychology in the modern sense of the word, although scattered observations are numerous enough, such as those on the erotic feelings and their gratification, which in animals sometimes involves self-sacrifice; those on egotism and sympathy or on pleasure and pain. Plato never discusses how the three parts of the soul are to be reconciled with the unity of consciousness. The will, to which the Greek with his decided intellectualism attached a minor importance and

for which his language contains no single term, stands in
Plato on the border line between the courage and desire.
Plato adhered all his life to the conviction that no one voluntarily does evil, but endeavoured in curious way to establish freedom of the will. Just as Kant ascribed it to the intelligible character, whose work the empirical is, Plato, in
the myth of the choice of life, transferred the free action of
the soul to its previous existence. Its fate for good or evil is
settled by the decision reached here; the blame is his who
makes the choice, but God is blameless. The myth at the end
of the *Republic* provides a completion to the metaphysics
of the soul contained in his other dialogues by placing the
entrance of the souls into the earthly realm under a general
law. Whereas according to Orphic theory only guilty souls
are banished into the world of matter, in the *Republic* (614-
DE) they descend "pure" from heaven, although of course
the majority pollute themselves by earthly sins. Only the real
philosopher will succeed in bringing his life's journey to a
happy end (619E). This crude dualistic psychology, according to which the body is nothing more than a "vehicle" of
the soul and actually a hindrance to the free development of
its powers (*Phæd.* 66AB), is closely bound up not only with
Plato's whole metaphysics, but is also in virtue of the theory
of recollection inseparable from his epistemology, and is the
ultimate basis of his views on ethics, politics and æsthetics.

38. *Plato's ethics*

In his so-called Socratic period Plato in his search for the
good was led to the recognition of its unity, so that the
names of the different virtues appeared to him to be merely
so many terms for one and the same moral attitude. At the
same time he subscribed to an epistemological determinism
which made man's conduct dependent on his knowledge of
moral values. From this point of view evil appears as error
which can be removed by instruction. This is what is usually understood by Plato's theory of the teachability of virtue.

This theory, which he held up to the time of the composition of the *Protagoras,* is silently dropped in the *Gorgias.*

Here evil is no longer error, but a disease of the soul which must be healed by a science corresponding to medicine. This is no other than philosophy. The means which it uses for curing the diseases of the soul is now no longer instruction but punishment. There is no greater misfortune for a man than to commit a wrong and go unpunished; for then he is deprived of the only possibility of improvement. The cause of this change of doctrine is his adoption of the dualistic psychology of the Pythagoreans, which finds expression in the myth at the end of the dialogue.

It is only a transitory concession to popular ideas and unimportant for Plato's main ideas when in the *Meno* he admits that correct notions can lead to virtue, that is only to a preliminary stage of real virtue in the sense of the philosopher. The theory of ethical temperaments, too, elaborated in the *Republic* (IV, 441Cf) is of minor significance. It assumed four basic virtues: wisdom, courage, prudence and justice, the function of the last being to preserve the correct proportions between the first three, which correspond to the three parts of the soul. From the *Gorgias* onwards Plato's ethics remained strictly dualistic in the sense that the corporeal with its earthly needs and lusts is the cause of all misery and evil, that all earthly goods including life are worthless, and in particular circumstances are even hindrances to the development of the soul towards the good, that is resemblance to God, which in the other world is the only criterium; for the soul in its true nature belongs to the supersensual world and can find its true, full bliss only in exaltation to that world and in return to its origin. The Orphic-Pythagorean conception of the body as the prison and tomb of the soul, as an evil by which it is defiled, finds its most powerful expression in the *Phædo,* where "correct philosophy" is defined as "practice in dying and death" and "striving after death". It is only by systematic efforts during this life and finally in death to detach itself from the earthly companion which has been forced upon it that the soul can attain to its original purity and knowledge of the truth. Fundamentally these remained Plato's views during the whole of his life, although they are not always expressed with the same explicitness. The visible world may well be a copy of the perfect and eternal ideas; it nevertheless remains a blurred and imperfect copy. Earthly beauty however, as in the *Symposium,* may become the impulse which stimulates the soul to soar on the wings of Eros to knowledge of the beautiful in itself.

In spite of this, Plato's theory of values, conditioned as it was by his un-Greek dualistic metaphysics, brought him into a position of antagonism to the essential and basic values of Greek culture. Plato was one of the rare characters who in their conviction of immortality of the soul are in deep earnest. It was inevitable that the goods of this life should pale before the glory of eternity. His low estimation of earthly life and all bodily things was completely un-Greek. The introduction of gymnastics in the *Republic* should not deceive us on this point. It was intended in the first place to promote the harmonious development of the soul, to harden the body and increase its power of resistance against the desires and passions of the senses (III, 411E, 403Dff). Un-Greek again is his rejection of all politics in the traditional sense. The great Athenian statesmen and the measures they took in defence of their country are condemned as "farce and nonsense". No less un-Greek is the judgment passed on poetry, which is rejected except in so far as it serves religious and ethical ends, and is applied to the Homeric epos as well as tragedy and comedy after a long inner struggle. A considerable part of music and of all "mimetic" art comes under his ban, since it is directed only to amusement, that is to pleasure instead of directing people to the good. Representative art is included in his condemnation; they fashion only shadows of shadows and are as far removed from the truth as poetry. The faults which Plato finds in these mimetic arts are in the first place the worthlessness of their subject matter, the world of sense, and secondly, the fact that they arouse impulses, feelings and passions which it is precisely the task of reason to repress. Plato is of course too much of a Greek to find a place for asceticism in his philosophy or to fall into the cynical abnegation of culture, a tendency of

which he manifestly disapproves. But his efforts to put civilisation on a moral basis are in full earnest. It was in pursuance of this end that he was led to reject those things which
civilisation commonly holds to be good.

On the positive side Plato's ultimate aim is the possession
of the good or happiness. This consists however precisely in
doing good, which as such is accompanied by a feeling of
pleasure. That is the state of harmony in the soul, an inner
intellectual and moral order which corresponds to the order
in the external world. It is the beauty and health of the soul,
the supremacy of the divine part in man over the lower impulses. The whole moral constitution of a man when it is as
it should be is called by Plato justice. He draws a picture of
the ideal just man who does not doubt the rightness of his
principles even if he has to suffer the death of a criminal by
crucifixion while the malefactor for his part triumphs.

The Platonic ethics like the Socratic is based absolutely
on the autonomy of reason and is thus far completely independent of religion, that is at least of the religion which
was current at that time. It actually corrects religion after
the fashion of Xenophanes and Heraclitus by purging the
ideas of the gods of their impure anthropopathic elements.
Yet Plato's ethics is based on a religion—his own. This consists of a philosophic monotheism, which identifies God with
the idea of the good, belief in providence with the conviction
that the world is work of reason and a copy of the world
of ideas, and sees its worship of God in virtue and knowledge. The good is for Plato something absolute and in this
sense he answers Protagoras' dictum, that man is the
measure of all things, with his own "God is for us the measure of all things". It is the highest mission of a man's life to
strive with all his strength to become similar to the perfection that is God. In his last works he attacks atheism in its
various forms and puts forward a complete theodicy. His
religious beliefs became more conservative as he grew older.
He regarded the stars as visible gods and ascribed to the
popular gods a certain educational value. It is not without regret that we find the author of the *Apology* demanding in

his old age the death penalty for incurable atheists. Religion for him became finally a means for the moral education of the people.

39. Plato's theory of the state

For the Greek ethics and politics were closely bound up with each other. As long as the Polis existed it was quite impossible to think of the individual as separate from the community. Even the subjectivist Protagoras has no doubt that man is impelled by a natural instinct towards the formation of communities. The constitutions that had been developed in the course of time had indeed effected both in democratic and oligarchic states a far-reaching emancipation of the individual, so that the unscrupulous despot in the latter and the undisciplined masses of the former presented examples of two extremes. Plato had experienced both in his own native city, as he himself describes. The execution of Socrates finally brought him to the conviction that no improvement could be made in the state by mere changes of constitution in the traditional manner, but that the evil could only be remedied by a moral regeneration of the state. An indication of the direction which this had to take was given him by Pythagoreanism. In the *Gorgias* we see him in deliberate opposition to the empirical state. The state should not be founded on the lust for power on the part of individuals or even particular classes. Its aim should be to educate its citizens up to the good. Thus Plato's *Republic* is dominated by the idea of the good, which finds its expression in "justice", that is the correct regulation of the spiritual and physical needs of the individual and the human community. It is because of this, too, that the *Republic* has a metaphysical anchor-stone corresponding to his sharp dualistic distinction between body and soul, earthly and eternal, the first of the two components being the means and the second the end. The simile of the cave at the beginning of the seventh book and the myth of the soul at the end of the tenth book go to prove this. It is only by keeping his gaze constantly fixed on the transcendental eternal world that Plato derives his strength for the radical reforms with which at more than one point he applies the axe to the roots of the Greek world.

The metaphysical foundations of the Platonic state are revealed in its structure. The three classes into which the citizen body is divided correspond to his theory of the three parts of the soul. To the intellectual part of the soul the class of the philosophical educated rulers corresponds; to the courageous the warrior class of the guardians, to the sensual, lustful part the class of the peasants and merchants. This third class is not treated in any more detailed way, for it is only the object of government. Thus Plato's state is essentially an aristocracy, although of course an aristocracy of the intellect. Nothing indeed seemed to Plato more false than an absolute equality in the distribution of political rights. It is not an arithmetical (that is mechanical) but a geometrical equality (that is one graduated according to the capability of the citizens) that should be the dominating principle in the distribution of rights. Nor is mere philanthropy a quality which makes a governor nor again the shrewd psychology of the sophist, who knows the habits and desires of the "great beast" and knows how to handle it accordingly. It is only knowledge of the good and its application to popular education that suffice for this. It follows from this that the main problem is the rearing of qualified rulers, so that the main topic of the work is the education of the two upper classes. The third class is permitted to retain its private property and family. The rulers and the guardians however have to surrender both. Their children are begotten from healthy men and women under the supervision of the State, so as to ensure the production of a noble race capable of great achievements. The children are to be brought up communally in state establishments. In the twentieth year the first process of weeding out takes place. After this they have to undergo a period of military and physical training which lasts for two or three years. Then follows a course of preparation in mathematics, astronomy and harmony. In the thirtieth year a further selection is made and those who pass the test are introduced to dialectic, to which five years are devoted. Finally they are engaged in practical work in leading positions in the army and administration. Only when they have reached their fiftieth year are the problems of government entrusted to them. The girls take equal part in gymnastics and mental education. A strict watch is kept over the whole mental and moral life of the citizens. The whole state takes the form of a religious community; it might almost be called a church in which religion, art and science are fused into an inseparable whole. Details of worship are to be referred to the judgment of the Delphic Apollo. Poetry and music however are subjected to a strict censorship and are only permitted to compose hymns to the gods or songs in praise of noble men. Neither Homer nor tragedy nor comedy find a place in Plato's state. Art too has to conform to severe and simple forms. Everything has to be subordinated to the end of realising the idea of the good. To that end not only are the greatest creations of Greek art and poetry but even marriage and family life sacrificed. Of any personal rights or regard for the individual (except in so far as it is useful to the community) the *Republic* contains no mention. Even the activity of the rulers is called a sacrifice made for the state which will find its reward in the next world. Plato recognised no difference of people nor the different political forms which such a difference calls for, nor again any historical development. In unambiguous words Plato endows his state with absolute validity. It is as fixed and changeless as the world of ideas itself. It rises as a bright ideal above the dark background of historical constitutions, which are subjected to a severe and pertinent criticism. It is an integral part of the Platonic system, which sees in the sensual and individual side of human existence not a means to the realisation of an ideal but an obstacle in the way of true knowledge and perfect morality.

We can see how dear the realisation of his political ideas was to Plato not only from his repeated journeys to the Syracusan court, where he long based his hope on Dionysius II and afterwards on Dio, but also from the revision which his ideas underwent in two works of his old age. In the *Republic* (IX, 580B) Plato had already compared the tyrant with the truly kingly man. This idea of a perfect monarchy he elaborated later in the *Politicus,* in which he replaced the philosophic ruler by the monarch, the political expert who is bound by no laws but knows and ordains what is best for the state, puts the right men in the right places and like a skilled weaver understands how to bind all threads of the political machine into an artistic whole. Besides this ideal of an enlightened despotism, however, Plato recognises the constitutional state as a makeshift.[6] He distinguishes three forms of this: monarchy, aristocracy and democracy, with which tyranny, oligarchy and mob-rule are contrasted. The ideas which are here propounded lead on the one hand to the *Politics* of Aristotle and on the other to Plato's last work, the *Laws.* In this Plato gives up many of his radical proposals—the communism of women and children, the surrender of private property and even the rule of the philosopher. They are replaced by a state council modelled on the Pythagorean Synedries, a collegium of guardians of the law, which should watch carefully over marriages, household life and the upkeep of a definite number of allotments (5040) into which the land is once and for all divided,[7] while transferable property up to four times the minimum on which a family can exist is given free. Trade, manufacture, and agriculture are to be put in the hands of metœcs and slaves. In the third book, after a rapid survey of the development of civilisation and the state, he propounds the fertile idea of a constitution composed of elements taken from all three fundamental political forms. But in spite of these concessions to the realities of terrestrial life, which are treated in considerable detail, Plato still holds firmly to his basic political idea that the state is an institution for preparing the soul for its eternal life. The idea of a state founded on reason is indeed carried even further and becomes almost a theocracy, dialectic being replaced by an elaborate system of religious education. The doctrine of transmigration is retained and art and poetry are subjected to moral and religious ends. His contempt indeed for all that is earthly goes so far that he declares that human things are not worth serious consideration. The best thing for man is to be "a plaything of God". Whereas Plato had earlier found the

source of error and evil in the corporeality which is in conflict with the supersensual nature of the soul, in the *Laws*
this dualism is superseded by the introduction—unmistakably under oriental and more precisely parsistic influence—
of an evil world-soul, to which both evils, active and passive,
are ascribed. To this terrible power Plato attributed the
atheism which shook the foundations of state religion. It
was this senile belief and mistaken anxiety for the spiritual
welfare of his fellow men that led Plato to propose measures
for removing by execution those who despite instruction per-
sisted in their error. With this appeal to force against reason, freedom of thought came under the ban of the state and
philosophy was transformed into dogmatism.

40. *Plato's physics*

Socrates had from the first turned his back on natural science. Plato, too, was the less disposed to devote any attention
to this study because for him the only world accessible to
true knowledge and thought was of a supersensual, mental
nature, while of nature, the realm of the corporeal, there
could be only an untrustworthy vague idea transmitted
to us through the senses. All his efforts and thoughts had
been directed to educating mankind into an understanding
of the supersensual, mental world of the ideas which could
provide the only basis for human society. His philosophic
system formed a self-contained whole even though nature
was considered inferior copy of the world of ideas which possessed no reality in a full sense and was consequently not to
be apprehended by thought. In his advanced old age, however, he finally turned his attention to the phenomenal world
in the *Timæus,* his only scientific dialogue. He must have
had definite grounds for doing so, although of course we can
do no more than conjecture what these were. Plato himself
gives some indications of one of these reasons in the name of
the Pythagorean from whom the work derives its title. It
was through Pythagoreanism that he obtained his knowledge
of two sciences which were appropriate to his idealistic system and at the same time formed a link between the world

of the mind and the world of matter. Mathematics taught what was eternal in the earthly and perceived the supersensual in the material, while astronomy turned the gaze from the earth and directed it into the depths of the universe to those mysterious celestial bodies which move of themselves and seemed to be animate and visible gods, whose movements are ordered by number and measure and can be comprehended by the thinking mind. Mathematics of course was only "a ferment in Plato's mysticism" and the star gods strictly speaking belonged to the heavenly world. Nevertheless here was sufficient reason for turning Plato's attention to the Cosmos, the divine order of which was a model for man. Furthermore, a new view of the world had meanwhile come to the fore and had gained a currency which caused Plato serious misgivings. This was atomism, a materialistic philosophy which saw in everything mere mechanical processes and the power of blind necessity. This conception, the essential atheism of which was diametrically opposed to his own idealism, Plato felt bound to challenge.[8] It was now necessary for him, equipped with the scientific knowledge of his time, including medicine, which was equally worthy of attention, to attempt to expound his ideas of the relation between the visible world and his world of ideas, just as Parmenides had once followed his "Truth", which contradicted the world of the senses, by an account of the world of appearance based on the attempts of others.

There is no better way of bringing out the relation of Plato's *Timæus* to the rest of his philosophy than by a comparison with the two parts of Parmenides' didactic poem. Plato's theory of knowledge leaves no possible place for any empirical "knowledge"; that would be a contradiction in itself. For this nothing is more indicative than Plato's rejection of scientific experiments, whether as an inadequate method of arriving at knowledge or, what is particularly significant, as a presumptuous prying of man into the divine order of nature. He therefore leaves not the slightest doubt in the discussions of the *Timæus* that we are dealing not with real knowledge in his sense, but with seeming knowledge, probable judgments, which are obtained not by connected logical deduction but by unreliable conclusions. It is indeed nothing but a "game and a recreation". It is necessary therefore for a correct understanding of Plato's physics to bear in mind that he does not move one finger's breadth from his dualistic conception of the world or from this theory of two worlds. It was precisely in the bridging of the gulf between the transcendental world of the ideas and the phenomenal world of the senses that the great difficulty lay which the Platonists were from first to last at great pains to overcome. Each idea is one, but the things which fall under it are indefinite in number; each idea is eternal and unchangeable, the things have come into being, are transient and in a state of perpetual change; the idea is purely and entirely what it is, the things are never so; the idea has complete being, the things hover between being and not-being, just as opinion, of which they are the objects, lies between knowing and not-knowing. This imperfection of sensual existence he believes can be explained only by the fact that it consists only partly of the idea, while the other part is derived from a different principle. The idea is the source of all that is real and perfect in it. The nature of the second principle is to be found in what distinguishes the sensible phenomenon from the ideal. It is conceived only as something infinite, everchanging, not-being and unknowable. This second principle is materia, for which Plato does not use the expression which became current after Aristotle—matter. He compares it with the material upon which a craftsman works.[9] This is the third thing which together with the idea and the particulars of sense we have to postulate in order to explain the origin of the particular. It is described as the shapeless, the invisible, the all-receiving, as the mother and refuge of what has become, as its nurse, as the "plastic" mass,[10] which underlies the whole of nature and is moved and shaped by everything which enters into it. It is finally described as "a sort of space" and as that in which becoming takes place. But this does not mean that Plato understood absolute space by his materia. It is rather the extended substance that fills space, and is quite formless and without qualities. He denies it any form of being, but not its existence; nor does he describe it as a nothing, like empty space. He only contrasts it as the everchanging with the permanent unchanging being of the ideas. The materia before the creation of the world was in a state of irregular motion. By a natural necessity the invisibly small particles of matter came together according to their kind and formed in separate regions the four elements: water, earth, air and fire. This original state of the world in Plato's account corresponds to Democritus' theory of creation. We must however never lose sight of the fact, that for the Abderites the material atoms made up the sum of real being, whereas Plato considered them to be merely co-causes in world creation. The ideas are the real world. In Democritus, furthermore, natural law is the only moving force, while Plato makes this merely an instrument of the creative divine mind.

In order to establish the relation between the world of ideas and materia and to form an ordered world, the Cosmos, from its chaotic surging, matter must be shaped by mind. To illustrate this idea Plato makes use of the mythical form of the creator. This does not involve a creation *ex nihilo,* an idea which was entirely unacceptable to the Greek mind, but merely the reduction of the primitive state of chaos into an ordered and designed Cosmos. For Plato the soul as the self-moving is the beginning of all motion and the principle of life in the organism. He now applies this idea to the universe. The first problem of the Demiurgus is therefore the creation of a world-soul. This he makes after the pattern of living creatures from a mixture of their constituents. It is itself invisible, but takes part in thought and the harmony of eternal ideas. It occupies a middle position between the ideas and the corporeal world and connects the two, and in virtue of its own motion it moves the world Out of this materia the Demiurgus created the whole structure of the world after the patterns of the world of ideas All organic nature is his work, all relations of number and measure and all the regularity in its existence. He gave living creatures the shape that was best fitted to their several ends. All reason and knowledge in the universe and in the particular have their origin in him.

The fundamental nature of the visible world consists in its being constructed "by means of forms and numbers". We see this in Plato's treatment of the four elements. Applying the science of stereometry founded by his friend Theætetus he assigns to the elements four of the five regular solids as basic forms. The cube corresponds to earth, the pyramid to fire, the octahedron to air and the icosahedron to water. The fifth the dedocahedron, the form which stands next to the sphere, was used by god in designing the universe as a whole. These stereometric figures are reduced further to surfaces, the surfaces to lines and the lines to points or atom-lines.[11] By this conversion of the atoms into small geometrical figures the transition of elements into one another was made possible. This law-obeying mechanism with its processes of combination and separation, rarefaction and condensation, warming and cooling play the part of "concomitant causes", in the creation of the world while the real creative force is the reason which works towards an end. It is in this teleological conception of nature that Plato differs completely from the causal mechanistic explanation of the world put foward by Democritus. In the *Timæus*, too, Plato makes a remarkable use of the doctrine of transmigration. He assumes a progressively deteriorating series of creation, women being made from men and the different animal species from the highest to the lowest being created from human beings. In his discussion of the human body Plato has incorporated a wealth of medical detail into the dialogue. This betrays his acquaintance with Pythagorean physicians like Alcmæon of Croton and the Hippocratean and Sicilian schools of medicine, to which Philistion of Locri, who lived at the court of Dionysius II, belonged. The highest animate beings are the stars, especially the planets, whose spheres revolve around the terrestrial globe which is at rest in the centre of the spherical universe. When all stars have returned again to their original positions a great world-year of 10,000 years is completed. Thus the whole universe is a great living creature comprising mortal and immortal beings, a visible God, a copy of the God compre-

hended by thought, big, beautiful, magnificent and perfect
of its kind.

These views are presupposed in the *Laws*, with the exception of the two modifications mentioned before—the removal of the earth from the centre of the world and the introduction of an evil world-soul. The comparison of the
world with a living creature should not mislead us into regarding Plato's world-system as a monistic pantheism. Every
living creature presents for him a combination of two principles, a spiritual and a corporeal, a conception which is thoroughly dualistic. In the *Timæus*, too, Plato holds fast to the
transcendence of the ideas and the soul, which are similar
to them in nature; but in so far as living creatures and
their highest form, man, are a combination of the same
constituents as the universe, namely the eternal spiritual
and the transient corporeal, the microcosm is a replica of the
macrocosm.

41. *The influence of Platonism*

The influence of the Platonic philosophy on world-history is
hardly to be over-estimated. At first it lived on in different
forms in the Academy and—of course with considerable
changes of form and essential detail—in the philosophy of
Aristotle and the Peripatetic school. Here however the dualism which gave it its peculiar strength and influence,
with its contrast of mind and matter, body and the soul,
god and the world, lost in prominence, to be revived only in
the Jewish-Hellenistic philosophy, with particular curtail-
ments in Posidonius, in neo-Pythagoreanism and neo-Platonism. Plato had made this dualistic mysticism, which he
had borrowed from the exclusive circles of the Orphics and
the closed corporation of the Pythagorean order, into the
dominant principle in philosophy, and had raised it from a
religious belief to scientific theory, from an anthropological
dogma to a philosophic system embracing the whole Cosmos.
It was this principle more than the scientific content of his
system that carried Platonism outside the philosophic schools

into the lay world. It was now inevitable that in any subsequent discussion of immortality Plato should play an important part. His philosophy became a strong pillar of Christian dogma. It suffices to mention merely the name of Augustine. In the mediæval scholasticism the controversy of the realists and the nominalists renewed the old antagonism of Plato and Antisthenes and his difference with Aristotle on the relation of ideas to things. Furthermore the perception of the ideas as expounded first of all in the seventh Platonic letter was held by the neo-Platonists and the mediæval mystics to be the highest illumination of the mind. From the Renaissance onwards, however, which with the founding of the Platonic Academy in Florence by Marsilius Ficinus again resumed the tradition of Platonism, it was more the scientific ideas of Plato which fertilised the minds of thinkers: the astronomy of Pythagoras and Plato influenced Copernicus and Galileo; Plato's ideal state inspired Thomas More to the composition of his *Utopia,* Bacon to that of his *Nova Atlantis,* and Campanella to his *State of the Sun.* Finally Plato's epistemology and his metaphysics has influenced the whole of modern philosophy in a positive or a negative way; in fact all idealistic and spiritualistic systems are to be traced more or less directly to him. Thus Plato occupies a position in the history of philosophy as Raphael has depicted him in the middle of his "School of Athens"—as the prophetic thinker, who with raised hand points upwards to the supersensual world of the mind and the eternal abode of the soul.

42. *The old Academy*

The doctrines of the Academy continued to move along the old Pythagorean lines laid down by Plato, although with many variations of detail. He bequeathed the headship of the school to his sister's son Speusippus (347-336). Speusippus attached more importance to sense-perception than Plato, provided only, as he shows in his work on Similarities that the observations were made in a scientific way. In his main work on the Pythagorean numbers, which he based apparently on writings attributed to Philolaus, he replaced the ideas by mathematical numbers, which he regarded as separate from things. He distinguished ten substances which represented the ten grades of being (1) the absolute One; (2) the absolute Many (corresponding to the Pythagorean contrast of form and matter, the Limit and the Unlimited); (3) Number (especially the number three as being the sum of 1 and 2 and consequently the smallest "many"); (4) the geometrical spacial dimensions (point, line, surface and solid); (5) the cosmic bodies perceived by the senses (that is the five elements in the form of the regular stereometrical solids); (6) animate beings (plants, animals, human beings, dæmons, star-gods, the invisible God); (7) Thought (corresponding to the unoriginated prime number 7, the seven planets and the seven Greek vowels); (8) instinct or desire; (9) motion (with nine sub-species); (10) the Good, perfection in a state of rest. The prime numbers are thus at the same time the eternal principles of things and their stages of development. Speusippus was of the opinion that what is best and most beautiful lies not in the beginning but what comes forth from the beginning. The highest perfection, the art-form as it were, of cosmic figures, he considered to be the number ten, which dominated the Pythagorean table of opposites and the so-called Philolaic world system. The world is eternal and Plato's account of creation, as set out in the *Timæus,* was intended merely to serve didactic ends, just as one draws a mathematical figure. To the immortality of the soul even in its inferior parts he gave his full assent. Happiness depends on morality, which itself consists in a natural way of life. He did not admit pleasure as a good and attached a utilitarian value to wealth and health. With the help of far-fetched etymologies he interpreted the popular gods as physical forces and brought upon himself the charge of atheism.

After Speusippus, Xenocrates of Chalcedon became the head of the school for a quarter of a century (339-314). He was a man of pure and honourable character, but of melancholic temperament, a copious author and without a doubt the chief representative of the Academic school, which he

led for twenty-five years. It seems that he was the first to
make explicitly the division of philosophy into its three main
parts—dialectics, physics and ethics. He drew his theory of
the fundamentals of all things from the Pythagoreans. These
are the One, or the not-straight, and the indeterminate Dyad,
or the straight, the former being the "father" and the latter
the "mother" of the gods. The One he identified with *Nous*
or Zeus. Their first offspring is the ideas which are at the
same time mathematical numbers. For the deduction of dimensions from the numbers he used the hypothesis of tiny,
indivisible lines, a theory against which the work preserved
under Aristotle's name, the *On Indivisible Lines* is directed.
The world-soul is produced by the addition of the Self and
the Other to number. This Xenocrates defined (on the basis
of the *Timæus*) as a self-moved number. He regarded
(probably under the influence of Aristotle) the creation of
the soul as not having taken place in time. The world, according to Xenocrates, is divided into the sub-lunar world,
the heavens and the world above the heavens. All three parts
he considered to be filled with dæmonic forces both good
and evil, a theory which gave a considerable impetus to the
fatal process of dæmonisation of ancient religion. The elements, to which he added æther, are composed of minute
bodies. From everything everything can be made—an idea
which hovered temptingly before the minds of the mediæval alchemists in their search for the philosophers' stone.
Like Speusippus he held that the irrational parts of the soul,
and perhaps animal souls too, survived after death. He depre-
cated flesh foods on the grounds that through them the un-
reason of animals could gain an influence over the eater. He
embodied his ethical theories in numberous writings. What
we know of them shows that he remained loyal to the spirit
of Plato's moral teachings. Happiness consists in the possession of virtue and the means which conduce to it. He made
a more definite distinction between practical and scientific
wisdom. The latter alone, he agreed with Aristotle, constitutes real wisdom. Scarcely a single original thought is to be
found in the work of Xenocrates' successor, Polemo of Athens (314-269). He laid chief emphasis on ethics. He de-

clared that the highest good is morality, which he defined as a natural way of life—an idea which the Stoic Zeno is said to have taken over from him. Like his master he included abstinence from flesh in his code. He was on terms of intimate friendship with the slightly younger Crates, who after the former's death became for a short time (until 268) head of the Academy. Apart from these school heads a few other persons of significance were members of the Academy.

Philippus of Opus was, to judge by the pseudo-Platonic *Epinomis,* which is most probably his work, more mathematician than philosopher. In his opinion the highest knowledge is afforded by astronomy and mathematics. Wisdom consists in knowledge of them. All true piety depends on wisdom and right ideas of the heavenly gods. He follows Plato in rejecting the gods of mythology, but he attaches all the more importance to the dæmons, of which he recognises three classes, as intermediaries in our relations with the gods. He has however a low opinion of human life and earthly things, and he adopts the evil world-soul of the *Laws* (896E-898D). Apart from virtue it is by means of mathematics and astronomy that we are raised above the misery of earthly existence and assured of an eventual return to heaven. The famous Eudoxus of Cnidus (according to Apollodorus, *c.* 497-355) was also a mathematician and deviated still more from the teachings of Plato, whose lectures he attended as well as those of Archytas. He not only considered that things contain the ideas in the form of a material mixture, but followed Aristippus in holding that pleasure is the highest good and endeavoured to give this theory a logical basis (Arist., *Eth. N.,* 1101, b, 27ff., 1172, b, 9ff.). This was probably what led Plato to the new examination of the theory of pleasure contained in the *Philebus.* Heraclides of Pontus who about the year 339 B.C. opened a school of his own in his native city, borrowed from the Pythagorean Ecphantus not only the assumption of minute primary bodies out of which the divine spirit constructed the world, but also the theory of the diurnal revolution of the earth, to which he added the assumption that Mercury and Venus revolve around the sun. He considered the soul to be composed of æthereal matter. We are reminded, too, of the Pythagoreans by the credulity which this learned and imaginative but uncritical writer showed in his numerous dialogues towards magic and prophecy.

Greater fame was achieved by Crantor of Soloe in Cilicia (c. 330-270), who was a pupil of Xenocrates and a friend of Arcesilaus. He wrote the first commentary to Plato's *Timæus,* but aroused greater admiration by his treatise on grief. It occupied a prominent place in the series of consolatory writings which extends from the time of the sophists until the "Five books on the consolation of philosophy" composed by the Roman Senator Bœthius (A.D. 524). The work of Crantor was used by Cicero and the author of the consolatory writing addressed to Apollonius which has been preserved among the works of Plutarch. In this work Crantor attacked the Stoic doctrine of Apathia and included pain, both bodily and spiritual, among the god-ordained necessities of human life. He resembled Plato, the Pythagoreans, and the Orphics in regarding life as a punishment, and in so far as we humans are equally responsible for the misery of life. We should be glad that the dead have escaped from the troubles of life. These ideas seem to have been illustrated with copious quotations from the poets, like the pseudo-Platonic dialogue *Axiochus.* It is possible too that the story of Silenus and his revelation that the best thing is not to be born at all and the next best to die soon, found a place in his work.

Thus the Academy remained faithful to the dualistic conception of the world and humanity in the form which Plato had developed from Pythagoreanism until Arcesilaus gave an essentially different character to the doctrines of the school.

IV. ARISTOTLE AND THE PERIPATETIC SCHOOL

43. *Aristotle's life*

Aristotle of Stageira (384-322) was the son of Nicomachus, the physician-in-waiting of the Macedonian king Amyntas.

After the custom of the Asclepiads the boy was at an early age instructed by his father in the scientific principles of his art, so that from his first years his mind was turned towards empirical investigation. After the death of his parents the boy's education was continued under the guidance of his guardian Proxenus. In his eighteenth year he came to Athens and entered the Academy, where he remained for twenty years until the death of Plato. In the shadow of his pre-eminent mind Aristotle grew to manhood. The impression which he received was so deep and tenacious that it left ineffaceable traces in his thought. It was long before his own mind could shake itself free from Plato's influence and develop along its own lines. Of a completely different type and turned towards the reality perceived by the senses, his mind doubtless received a valuable completion by his introduction to the world of the supersensual, but it was to some degree turned aside from the natural path of its development. All his life his personal attitude to Plato, although at a later date he criticised the theory of his master, made considerable alterations in them and in some respects even completely rejected them, was one of reverence and devotion, which finds its expression in the so-called altar-elegy, in which he calls him a man "whom bad men have not even the right to praise and who showed in his life and teachings how to be happy and good at the same time".

After Plato's death Aristotle left Athens, doubtless because he had become too independent to submit to Speusippus, whose theories differed fundamentally from his own. His departure however did not signify any break with the Academy. Accompanied by Xenocrates, he founded a branch of the Academy in Assus in the Troas, which Hermias, the ruler of Atarneus, had presented to the Platonists Erastus and Coriscus, and taught there for three years. It was here that Plato's pupils succeeded in doing what he himself had attempted and failed in Sicily—in gaining the frienship of a ruling prince and influencing him politically and ethically. Hermias gave Aristotle his niece and adopted daughter Pythias in marriage and they had a daughter of the same name. It was here too that Theophrastus became his pupil and persuaded him to settle at Mitylene, a town not far from Theophrastus' native city Eresus (343). In the next year he was invited to Pella by Philip of Macedon to supervise the education of his son Alexander. This appointment was doubtless due to the agency of Hermias, who had concluded an alliance with Philip in anticipation of the war which was threatening between Macedon and Persia. When the betrayal of this alliance to the Persian court in the year 341 brought about the fall of Hermias and his sentence to death by cruxifixion, he sent from prison as his last greeting to Aristotle the message "that he had done nothing that was unprincipled or unworthy of philosophy". Aristotle in return dedicated to him an epigram which was inscribed on the cenotaph in Delphi and a hymn to virtue, to die and suffer for which the Hellenes thought enviable. Aristotle attended Alexander until the latter's expedition into Asia. His writing *On Monarchy*, probably in the manner of Isocrates' *Nicocles*, was dedicated to Alexander on his ascension to the throne. The king repaid his debt to his teacher by rebuilding the latter's native city, which had been destroyed by Philip. Long after Alexander had begun his conquest of the world, Aristotle could dare (perhaps in the treatise *Alexander, or Colonisation*) to warn the king against the equal treatment of Hellenes and barbarians, an idea which he was beginning to regard favourably. It was only after the execution of Aristotle's nephew Callisthenes, who was suspected of participation in a conspiracy against Alexander, that their relations lost in cordiality (327). This however caused no wavering in his conviction of the rightness of the Macedonian politics. He corresponded with the state chancellor Antipater and indeed was on such intimate terms with him that in his will he appointed him executor. Meanwhile Aristotle had in the year 335 settled at Athens and founded his own school in the eastern part of the city, in the Lyceum before the gate of Diochares. This school received the name of Peripatetic either from the cloisters or from the fact that the members discussed scientific matters while walking up and down. The school was founded under Macedonian patronage. It was, like the Academy, a "Thiasus" dedicated to the

Muses, but under Aristotle's direction it grew into a huge
scientific organisation with a large library, numerous staff of
teachers and a regular system of lectures, to which Aristotle's own pedagogic writings owe their origin. Here among
his numerous pupils he continued his work until shortly before his death. After the death of Alexander, however, and
the rise of the nationalist party under Demosthenes, the Lyceum was regarded with suspicion on account of its friendship with Macedon. A charge of "Asebia" was brought
against Aristotle, who then withdrew to Chalcis in Eubœa.
Here he lived on an estate of his dead mother and a few
months later succumbed to an illness of the stomach (322
B.C.) His will, which has been preserved (Diog. L. V.,
11ff.), reveals his thoughtfulness in providing for the members of his family and household. It remains a witness to his
restrained, but true humanity.

44. *The philosophic development and the works of Aristotle*

Neither in his character nor philosophy does Aristotle show
the unchangeable rigidity with which he had until recently
been credited. This false view had its origin in the one-
sidedness with which of the two great groups of his writings
only the pedagogical works had been used as source for his
philosophy, while the other works, which are chronologically
earlier, written in the dialogue form and intended for a
wider circle of readers were neglected. The pedagogical
works, which originally formed merely the basis of Aristotle's lectures in the Lyceum and were in various states of
completion, were first made known to the public in the edition of Andronicus of Rhodes (*c*. 60-50 B.C.). From this
edition the whole of later antiquity drew its material, while
the works which were published by Aristotle himself and
the fluent style of which was praised among others by Cicero were thrown more and more into the background. Of
these we possess only fragments. They were mostly scientific discussions in dialogue form in which Aristotle himself
occasionally appeared as leader of the conversation. The long

speeches and counterspeeches filled several books, a prœ-
mium serving as an introduction. They differed considerably
from Plato's dialogues, although they had a common feature
in the occasional introduction of myths. Thus the Platonic
simile of the cave undergoes a characteristic transformation.
The remains reveal at first a close connection with Plato and
then the gradual liberation of Aristotle's own thought. The
comparison of their contents enables us to distinguish older
and later strata and to discover the preliminary sketches
within the pedagogical works. The total number of Aristotelian works is estimated by Hermippus of Alexandria (*c.*
200 B.C.) at 400, and by the Peripatetic Ptolemæus (1-2
cent. B.C.) at one thousand books.

The method just indicated has succeeded in distinguishing
three periods in the life of Aristotle, which are characterised
not only by changes in his external circumstances, but also
by changes in his philosophic views, until the final maturity
of his own peculiar philosophy. These periods are (1) the
Platonic period, when he attended the Academy, (2) the
Transition period, when he was engaged in independent
teaching in Assus, Mitylene and later at the Macedonian
court, (3) the time of his second stay in Athens as the head
of the Lyceum.

1. THE PERIOD OF THE ACADEMY, 367-347

To the second half of this period, that is when he had
reached years of manhood, belong two treatises which still
have a strong Platonic colouring—the dialogue *Eudemus,* or
On the Soul, and the *Protrepticus.* The first received its
name from a friend Eudemus of Cyprus, who fell before
Syracuse in 354, while fighting on the side of Dio, and was
composed shortly after his death. It corresponds to Plato's
Phædo. Aristotle shows himself in his metaphysics still completely dominated by the influence of Plato. He shares the
doctrine of recollection and the perception of the ideas in
pre-existence. Bodiless existence he believes to be most appropriate to its nature (*Fr.* 41). The consequent pessimistic
view of life finds expression in the story of Midas and Silenus and the latter's declaration. that "not to be born is the

best thing and death better than life" (*Fr.* 44). On the other
hand his refutation of the proposition that the soul is a harmony shows a progress beyond Plato. It is based on the
argument that harmony is a quality and the soul a substance
and that the two belong therefore to different categories
(*Fr.* 45). It is clear that this fundamental idea of the Aristotelian logic has already been discovered.

The *Protrepticus* was not a dialogue but a monitory epistle addressed to the Prince Themison of Cyprus, just as Isocrates had done to Nicocles, with the intention of gaining a
political influence over him (*Fr.* 50). Large fragments of it
are preserved in the *Protrepticus* of the neo-Platonist Iamblichus. The work culminates in a description of philosophic
Eudæmonia. It still stands on the basis of the Platonic dualism and holds fast to the transcendence of the ideas. Politics
and ethics provide absolute norms which are based on philosophic knowledge of true existence (*Fr.* 52). The Orphic-
Pythagorean doctrine of the body as the tomb of the soul
and the consequent low valuation of all earthly goods including corporeal life are adopted in their most extreme
form (*Fr.* 59, 60, 61). It exerted a far-reaching influence on
Cynic and Stoic philosophy and through the mediation of
Cicero's *Hortensius* converted Augustine to religion and
Christianity.

2. THE TRANSITION PERIOD, 347-335

In this period, which starts with his activity as a teacher in
Assus, Aristotle began to break loose from Platonism and to
adopt a critical attitude towards the views of the Academy
and to modify the theories taught in that school. The pro-
gramme as it were of this new phase of his thought is contained in the dialogue, in which he introduces himself as
leader of the discussion. It consisted of three books: one historical, one critical and the last speculative. The first contained an historical survey of the development of philosophy
starting from the old proverbial wisdom of the Orphic theology and especially oriental, Egyptian and Persian religions
(*Fr.* 3, 6, 7). He brings forward the theory of the periodical
recurrence of philosophical systems and places Zarathustra

6,000 years before Plato, so that a new æon seems to begin with the latter, who stands in the middle of the world-period of 12,000 years. The second book contained a criticism of the theory of ideas which, as the later works of Plato from the *Parmenides* onwards show, had been the subject of lively discussion even in the stronghold of the Academy itself, while the friends in Assus seem to have been rather sceptical about it. Aristotle however defends himself against the reproach of disputatiousness (*Fr.* 8, 9). In the third book Aristotle developed his own world-system and philosophy of religion. This seems to have depended to some extent on Plato's astral theology; but it contains, too, the basic idea of Aristotle's metaphysics—that of an unmoved mover of the universe. Just as in Kant, Aristotle's purely intellectual idea of God seems to have had a double source—spiritual experiences and the spectacle of the heavens with its stars. Here he already declares his belief in the divinity of the Cosmos and the mind.

To this period belongs the first sketch of the *Metaphysics*, the first metaphysics, which comprised the first, second and last books of the *Metaphysics* in their present form. In this work his criticism of the theory of the ideas is distinguished from his later treatment of this central dogma of the Platonic system (*M.* 4-5), by the fact that Aristotle speaks in the first person plural and thus counts himself among the Platonists, whereas in the later treatises this form of speech is completely absent. Aristotle however was even at that time convinced that Platonism could be saved only at the price of dualism (that is the separation of the ideas from things). Apart from that, this early metaphysics contained an attack on the theories by Speusippus and Xenocrates in the treatise now surviving as *M.* 9-10 (from 1086a onwards). This was later replaced by the more complete and finished treatment of the same subject in *M.* 1-9 (as far as 1085b).

An early ethics corresponding to this early metaphysics is also to be assigned to this transition period. This is the Eudemean Ethics, which hitherto has been regarded as a work of Eudemus of Rhodes. It is a lecture which he held in Assus, with the exception of the three books IV-VI, which coincide with the *Nicomachean Ethics,* V-VII. It occupied a middle position between the latter and the *Protrepticus,* the theonomic morals of which it still retains. The dominating ideas, that good sense, that is philosophical strength of mind, which in transcendental intuition (contemplation) recognises God as the highest good and the unconditioned norm, and regulates moral conduct in the light of this. What good sense is to scientific life virtue is to practical. From enjoyment only a life of pleasure can ensue, but correctly understood it forms with good sense and virtue a constituent of philosophic Eudæmonia. The connection with the late Platonic ethics of the *Philebus* and the *Laws* is quite apparent.

It was in Assus, too, that the early politics was completed. It was begun in the time of his first stay in Athens. This would be still clearer if the books *On Justice* and *On the Statesman* had been preserved. Nevertheless a fragment of the latter books proves that Aristotle regarded the Good as the kernel of political theory. To this early politics belong Books II and III, VII and VIII of the *Politics* as they now stand. They contain the ideal of a State and the criticism of previous utopias including Plato's *Republic.* The norm for the ideal state is provided by the conception of nature which includes the being and the yet-to-be of the Platonic metaphysics. The three fundamental forms of constitution and their perversions were also contained in it. Aristotle sacrifices the ideal state of Plato in order to avoid the rejection of the real state. The early politics consisted too of lectures in which the *Protrepticus* and the *Eudemean Ethics* were utilised.

Finally the basic theories of his physics and cosmology belong to this period. The first book of the *Metaphysics,* which was written soon after Plato's death, refers repeatedly to passages on the *Physics.* The first two books of the *Physics,* therefore, with the basic idea of matter and form, potentiality and actuality and the theory of motion must have been already written. The same is true of the treatise *On the Heavens* in which (I, 9, 10) considerable portions from the dialogue *On Philosophy* are embodied. At this stage the theory of the æther as the fifth element must have been firmly

established, and also the cosmology with its recognition of
the monad, the eternity and spacial finiteness of the world.
These attempts at constructive theory are accompanied by a
criticism of the Platonic theory of the natural world. The
treatise *On Creation and Destruction* is closely connected
with that *On the Heavens*.

3. HIS ACTIVITY IN THE LYCEUM, 335-322

To these last thirteen years of Aristotle's life belongs his
wonderful organisation of detailed research into nature and
history, which he carried on with the help of his pupils. It
embraced the whole knowledge of that time and to a great
extent first made that knowledge possible. At the same time
he gave lectures in the school he had founded, which formed
the basis of the pedagogical writings which have been preserved. These works belong to the last period, except for
those parts which are to be attributed to the two previous
periods, especially the second in which Aristotle had laid
down the principles of his philosophic system. They were
not however published by him, although he may have begun
to arrange them. After his death they remained the property
of his school, where they circulated among the members.
They were first given to the general public by Andronicus
(see above p. 175). He seems to have collected everything to
which he had access. It is possible that he included the mass
of writings which after the death of Theophrastus were acquired by Neleus, the son of Coriscus (p. 173), who lived at
Scepsis in the Troad. Here they were discovered in a cellar
by Apellicon, brought to Rome by Sulla and published by
Tyrannio and Andronicus. The study of Aristotle received a
new impetus from the publication of his pedagogical works
which is reflected in the numerous commentaries written
upon them. The enthusiastic study of the new works however gradually killed the interest in the earlier exoteric writings which gradually fell into oblivion. This fact explains
the confused and unequal state in which the pedagogic
works have come down to us. They may be divided into the
following groups:

1. *Logical works* (first combined in Byzantine times un-

der the collective title "Organon"): *Categories,* that is Assertions on Being and the forms of existence (things, qualities, etc.); in their present form not by Aristotle, although he is responsible for their contents; *On Interpretations* (on proposition and judgment), the authenticity of which was contested even in ancient times; the two, *Analytics, Prior* and *Posterior* (each two books), of which the first treats of inference and the second the process of proof; the *Topics* (eight books), which deal with dialectic, that is the proof of probability; connected with this is the *Sophistici Elenchi,* on sophistical fallacies.

2. *Metaphysical works.* The so-called *Metaphysics* in its present form does not present a uniform whole, but is a collection of lectures of different dates. This explains why the same problems are treated in several different forms. The title which is usually derived from the position which the work occupied in the Aristotelian Corpus ("after the *Physics*") was probably due to a Peripatetic who lived before the time of Andronicus and indicates its contents all the more accurately in that Aristotle, in contrast with Plato, builds his metaphysics on his physics. He himself calls it the *First Philosophy,* that is the science of the first principles of the world and the "science which we search after". In the present collection the following strata are to be distinguished. ABM 9-10 and N belong to the oldest constituents. The books A-I form a compact mass with the exception of α (ἔλαττον) and Δ; α which was ascribed even in ancient times to Pasicles of Rhodes consists probably of the notes which this pupil took of a lecture which (according to p. 995a, 14ff.) gave an introduction not to metaphysics but to physics; Δ appears in the index of Hermippus (in Diog. L. V, 23) as a work *On Expressions Used with Several Meanings* (that is, on expressions which are used in several meanings). Of the remaining eight books of this part, A gives the general foundation of the theory of principles together with an historical survey of previous theories; B is the book of problems which poses fifteen questions, of which some are answered in Γ. E distinguishes "the first philosophy" from the other sciences, while the first chapter belongs to the older introduc-

tion (A-E1); chapters E2-4 form the connection between this and the books Z-Θ, which were inserted at a later date and form the kernel of the metaphysics. They treat the theories of substance (ZH), potentiality and actuality, which provide the starting points in I for the discussion of the one and the many and the opposite. K1-8 is an abbreviated repetition of the contents of ΒΓΕ; the chapters 9-12, which are concerned with motion and the infinite, are an extract (probably not by Aristotle) from several books of the physics. Δ is an isolated lecture, a metaphysics "in nuce", of which the critical and theological conclusion with the quotation from Homer (Il. II, 204) is directed against the dualism of the Academicians. M and N attack the theories of ideas and numbers of the Academy, M4-5, repeating the criticism of Plato's central dogma made in A9 (p. 177) while M9 is a repetition of M1. The main difference between the older and the later parts of the *Metaphysics* consists in the fact that in the former metaphysics appears as the theory of the supersensual while the latter are occupied in the endeavour to extend its scope and to make it into a theory of being, comprising the whole of the world including that of sensual perception.

3. *Works on Natural Science.* Among these the most important is the physics in eight books, of which the seventh seems to emanate from notes by Aristotle but was a later insertion. The books treat the problem of motion. Of these Θ, which itself quotes the *Physics,* is of later origin and leads on to the *Metaphysics.* A and B were written shortly after Plato's death (p. 178). The four books *On the Heavens* stand in close connection with the *Physics.* They deal with the form and motion of the heavenly bodies and the eternity of the universe. The two books *On Creation and Decay* are concerned with absolute coming into being and passing away. The *Metereology* is considerably later. It consists of four books, of which the last is an independent treatise and perhaps an early work of Strato of Lampsacus. The work *On the World* is Stoic in character and was not written by Aristotle. To this period, too, belong the zoological works of which the most important is his so-called "Ani-

mal Stories", a comparative anatomy and physiology in ten books, of which the last is post-Aristotelian and is perhaps to be ascribed to Strato. A work of similar content *Anatomical Studies,* in seven books, which was illustrated with drawings, has been lost. The introduction to *On the Parts of Animals* (four books) criticises the mechanical methods of classification adopted by Speusippus and Plato in the Academy. The *On the Gait of Animals* and *On the Movement of Animals* (each one book) belong here too. Of these, the latter work investigates the mechanics of animal movement and brings it into relation with the problem of motion in the universe, while in the *On the Descent of Animals* (five books) the problem of heredity is discussed. The five books *On the Soul* deal not only with the human soul, but include the whole of the organic, human, animal and plant world in the scope of their inquiry. The methods, too, in which investigation was carried on were not speculative but empirical. With this work "on the soul" a number of smaller treatises are to be classed which are usually referred to under the collective title *Parva Naturalia.* They deal with perception and perceptions, memory and recollection, sleep and waking, dreams, prophetic powers in sleep, long and short life, death, life, and breathing. On the other hand, the treatise *On Breathing* shows clearly the influence of the school of the Coan physician Praxagoras and his great pupil Erasistratus (3rd cent. B.C.), while the last (9th) chapter owes a great deal to the Stoic Chrysippus. The *Problems* no doubt emanate from genuine Aristotelian notes; they are however the work of various younger members of the school. The following works are spurious: *On Physiognomy, On Heeding Miracles, On Plants, On Colors, On Indivisible Lines, Mechanics.*

4. *Works on Ethics and Politics.* Three different versions of the *Ethics* have been preserved under Aristotle's name. Of these the Eudemean belongs to the time of his stay in Assus. The so-called *Great Ethics,* which however is actually the shortest of the three works, seems to go back to a lecture which originally adhered closely to Plato and was later revised by a pupil. To this version, Aristotle himself

seems to have made several additions which indicate a later date of composition. The chief work is the *Nicomachean Ethics* which belongs to the last period. It consists of ten books and probably owes its name to the fact that they were edited after Aristotle's death by his son Nicomachus. Owing to this early publication they occupy a special place in Aristotle's pedagogical writings.—Of the *Politics* the second, third, seventh and eighth books were written while he was at Assus, while the fourth-sixth are to be attributed to his second stay at Athens, as the mention of the murder of Philip of Macedon goes to prove. The collection of the constitutions of one hundred and fifty-eight different states, of which that of Athens was restored to us by a papyrus found in the year 1891, was undertaken as a preparation for the main part of the *Politics,* which deals with the nature and conditions of existence of the non-monarchical constitutions. The work was probably carried out between the years 329-28 and 327-26.[12] The only remaining work of a political nature which belongs to this period is the lost writing in dialogue form dedicated to Alexander, *Alexander, or About Colonists.* The two books *Economics* are spurious.

5. *Works on Æthetics, History and Literature.* Among these the *Rhetoric* (three books) and the *Poetics* are to be reckoned. The latter work is unfortunately not complete and was at an earlier date preceded by a dialogue, *On the Poets.* Apart from these, the antiquarian researches must be mentioned by which Aristotle endeavoured to provide a chronological basis for his histories of politics and literature. These include the collections of Didascalia, the records of dramatic performances in Athens, and the compilation of the list of victors at the Olympic and Pythian games. An inscription found at Delphi, which must have been set up about the year 335-34, expresses thanks to Aristotle and his nephew for this work. With the help of his pupils Aristotle now undertook to lay the foundation of the history of the different sciences. Under his direction Theophrastus wrote the history of natural philosophy, Eudemus of Rhodes that of mathematics and astronomy and Meno that of medicine. He was in constant touch with the medical schools of Cnidus and

Cos and above all with the representatives of the "pneumatic" tendency in medicine, which had its centre in the Sicilian school of Philistion and Diocles. Finally, when we find him engaged on a work on the Homeric problem, on the collection of *Barbaric Customs* and a treatise *Pleas of the City-States on Territorial Rights*, we realise the variety and scope of his activities. We see in Aristotle the creator of philology in its widest sense, a study which was later transferred by Demetrius of Phalerus to its new centre at Alexandria. With this kind of empirical and historical research Aristotle had travelled far from his starting point and his master Plato, and has gathered up again the threads spun by the sophists, whom Plato had so vehemently opposed. His universal mind embraced with equal power speculative philosophy and empirical research. He was the founder of philosophy as we understand it and its greatest exponent in his own time.

45. *The Aristotelian Philosophy*

INTRODUCTORY

Historically speaking Aristotle is through Plato the discipular grandson of Socrates. But the relation of the series Socrates-Plato-Aristotle is essentially different from, for example, that of the series Zeno-Cleanthes-Chrysippus. In the latter case the doctrines of the founder of the school appear with few unessential modifications in his successors. In the former, however, we have three original geniuses, who each created his own philosophy, so that what was taken over from the teacher is overshadowed by the pupil's own creative ideas. The contrast is most obvious between Plato and Aristotle—the Athenian a born poet and an imaginative and speculative mind, with a tendency to mysticism enforced by the influence of Pythagoreanism; the Stagirite a man of sober disposition relying on the facts of experience and a powerful scientific organiser. Thus, while Aristotle takes his departure from Plato, and with him and Socrates doubts the possibility of knowing without deriving the general from the particular, that is without the formation of concepts, he nevertheless breaks completely with the basic idea of the Platonic philosophy—the belief in a world of ideas comprising in itself the only true realities and separated from the world of sense. That is the Platonic dualism. Plato would allow the world of sensual perception no real being. For Aristotle, however, this is the real object of investigation. Conceptual thought, together with sensual perception, on which he places a much higher value, is only the means whereby we obtain knowledge of this world. His thought is analytical, his point of departure the given reality, which he endeavoured to penetrate to its ultimate basis. Thus although he took over from Plato the concept of form, he uses it in quite a different way: the form is for him immanent in things, the cause which expresses itself in them and gives them their shape. It is at once concept and thing, both real and ideal cause. His philosophy is indeed, like that of Socrates and Plato, intended to be a conceptual science; the particular is to be traced back to general concepts and to be explained by deduction from those concepts. Aristotle brought this process to the highest perfection both on its dialectic—inductive and its logical—demonstrative side. He carried it through with rigid scientific strictness, excluding the poetical and mythical ornament with which, in imitation of Plato, he had not scorned to embellish his early works. His presentation, too, is remarkable for its brevity and clearness of its expression and the richness of its philosophical terminology. In this respect his work surpasses that of Plato while remaining at least in the extant writings inferior in artistic merit. But the philosopher who could think of the forms not as existing for themselves alone in separation from things, but merely as the inner nature of particular things, combined with this ideal philosophy a clear and precise realisation of the necessity of the most comprehensive experiential knowledge such as we find in none of his predecessors except perhaps Democritus. He was not merely a "scholar" but also an observer of the first class. The breadth and variety of his historical knowledge, particularly the works of the earlier philosophers, was equalled by the extent of his knowledge of the natural world and his penetrating researches, although of course, it is not to be expected that his achievements in this field could challenge comparison with the results obtained with the help of modern methods and instruments.

Thus Aristotle, despite the analytical character of his thought, and although the term system is still foreign to him, appears in virtue of the universality of his inquiries as a "systematic". His philosophy in its complete form can hardly have been presented in its entirety in any other way than as a system. It is however difficult to apply Aristotle's own ideas on the divisions of philosophy to the contents of his writings. He distinguishes three sciences: theoretical, practical and poetical; furthermore the first is subdivided into physics, mathematics and the "first philosophy" (*Metaphysics,* cf. p. 163), which is also called theology, while the practical philosophy falls under two headings, ethics and politics, although to the whole he gives the name Politics. It seems to us to be most practical to make the distinction of logic, metaphysics, physics and ethics the basis of our account of the Aristotelian philosophy, and to make the necessary additions to these main divisions at the end.

46. *The Aristotelian logic*

Aristotle's Logic rests on the basis of Socrates' and Plato's work in this direction. He made it into a separate science which he called "Analytics," that is, the introduction to the art of investigation, and treated it as a scientific methodology. Scientific knowledge in a narrow sense consists, in his opinion, in the deduction of the particular from the general, of the conditioned from its causes. But the chronological development of knowledge takes the opposite course. While the soul in its thinking capacity contains within itself the possibility of all knowledge and in so far all knowledge of possibility, it attains nevertheless only gradually to actual knowledge. What is in itself the better known and more certain, is not so for us (*Anal. Post.* I, 71b, 33ff.; *Phys.* I, 184a, 16). We must abstract general ideas from particular observations and progress in an ascending scale from perception through memory to experience and hence from experience to knowledge (*Anal. Post.* II, 19; *Metaph.* A, 1, etc.). It is because of the significance of experience for knowledge that Aristotle defends the truth of sensual perception. The senses as such are never deceptive. All error springs rather from the false relation and combination of what they tell us. The Aristotelian Logic therefore, besides the conduct of proof, includes (in the second *Analytics*) induction in the scope of its inquiry. He precedes both however (in the *Prior Analytics*) by the theory of inference which is their common form. It is only in connection with the theory of inference that Aristotle discusses even concept and judgment.

An inference is "a statement, in which something new is derived from certain hypotheses" (*Anal. Pr.* I, 24b, 18). These hypotheses find their expression in the premises, that is in the propositions (both are given the name of *protasis* by Aristotle). A proposition, however, consists either of an affirmative or negative statement and is accordingly composed of two concepts, a subject and predicate (the copula being still assigned to the predicate). Aristotle however treats the concepts only in conjunction with the theory of definition and his metaphysical inquiries. In the propositions or judgments he thinks only of categorical judgments, which he divides according to their quality (as it is now called) into affirmative and negative, according to their quantity into general, particular and indefinite (explicative proposition into general, particular and singular), and according to their modality into assertions on existence, necessity and mere possibility. He distinguishes further between the two kinds of opposition, the contradictory and the contrary (cf. p. 190). He shows which judgments may be reversed simply and which only with an alteration of their quantity. He remarks finally that it is only from the combination of concepts in the judgment that the contrast of false and true arises. This part of the logic however is mainly occupied with the theory of inference. Aristotle was the first to discover in inference the basic form in which all thought moves and progresses and to give it the name which it now bears. The syllogistic laid down in the first *Analytics* contains an exhaustive account of categorical inferences in their three figures, of which the second and third owe their validity to their deduction from the first. It does not deal with the hypothetical or the disjunctive.

The proofs are composed of inferences. The problem of every proof is the deduction of the conditioned from its grounds in which (see p. 187) knowledge as such consists. The hypotheses of a proof must therefore consist of necessary propositions of general validity. A proof is only complete when what has to be proved has been deduced from its first hypothesis through all intermediate stages. Such a deduction would not be possible if the hypotheses from which it is derived must in their turn be deduced from something further and so on *ad infinitum:* or if an infinite number of middle stages lie between the hypotheses and what must be deduced from them. All mediate knowledge therefore presupposes an immediate, which more precisely is of a double nature. Both the general principles from which the proof starts and the facts to which these principles are applied must be known to us without proof. Just as the facts are known to us directly through perception, so Aristotle recognises in the reason a power of immediate, direct and consequently error-free knowledge of the most general principles. Aristotle did not consider the problem whether these principles are merely formal or whether ideas of definite content (like that of God) can be known in this way. The highest and most incontestable of all thoughts he calls the proposition of contradiction. This he formulates in several different ways, both in its logical and metaphysical application. But in order to provide a scientific basis for these convictions, too, proof is in this case replaced by induction, which confirms a general statement by showing its actual validity in all the particular cases to which it refers. But a complete observation of every particular case is, as Aristotle cannot hide from himself, impossible. He looks about for a simplification of the indirect method and finds it in the procedure followed by Socrates. He takes as the basis of his induction those hypotheses which from the number or authority of their supporters would seem to have been derived from experience, and endeavours to reach correct determinations by dialectic comparison and testing of these hypotheses. He makes profound and masterly application of this method in the *Aporæ* which usually formed the beginning of any inquiry which he undertook. Although his observation may lack accuracy and completeness and his use of other's data the criticism which we are accustomed to require today, in this respect, too, he achieved all that could be reasonably expected considering the state and resources of scientific research in his time.

Definition rests partly on proof and partly on immediate knowledge which receives confirmation through induction. All our concepts denote something general, a necessary and constant property of the things of a particular class. The concept in the narrower sense in which it is an object of definition denotes the nature of the things, their form as distinct from their substance, that which makes them what they are. If such a concept expresses what is common to many things of a different kind, it is called a generic concept. If the distinctive properties of the species are added to those of the genus, the species is defined. If this is more exactly defined by further characteristics and this process is continued as long as possible, we arrive at the lowest concept of species which can no longer be divided into subspecies but splits up into particular things. These are what determine the concept of each thing (*Anal. Post.* II, 13). A definition should therefore not only contain a complete list of the characteristics which enable us to deduce the object from a generic concept, but the enumeration of these characteristics should follow the correct order, which corresponds to the gradual progress from the general to the particular; the essential method of definition is exhaustive and logically progressive division. Everything that falls under a generic concept is identical with respect to that genus; everything that falls under the concept of a species is identical with respect to that species. The two extremes within the same genus are contrarily opposed, while two concepts are said to be contradictory when one is the simple negation of the other (A, non A), cf. p. 188. (Aristotle probably overlooked the fact that this opposition can exist only between proposition and not between uncombined concepts because he did not yet recognise the copula as an intrinsic constituent of the judgment together with the subject and predicate.) To these kinds of opposition he added, however, that of the concepts of relation and that of possession and deprival.

Now all our concepts fall under one or more of the chief kinds of assertion or categories, which denote the chief points of view from which things may be regarded, while they themselves have no higher concept above them as a common generic concept. Aristotle enumerates ten of these categories—substance, quantity, quality, relation, where, when, position, possession, activity and passivity.

He was convinced of the completeness of his work in this department. But no definite principle can be discovered in his deduction, while the categories of possession and position are only mentioned in the *Categories* and the *Topics* and are omitted in all later enumerations. The remaining categories, too, are not all of equal significance. The first four are the most important and among them that of substance takes first place, the others being deduced from this. It is this category which, according to Aristotle, forms the essential subject of the "first philosophy", the so-called Metaphysics.

47. *Aristotle's metaphysics*

This science is devoted to the investigation of first causes, of Being as such, the eternal incorporeal and motionless which is the cause of all movement and form in the world. It is, therefore, the most valuable and comprehensive of all sciences. The problem is threefold and gathers round the three questions of the particular and the universal, form and matter, the mover and the moved.

1. THE PARTICULAR AND THE UNIVERSAL

Plato regarded only the ideas, the universal which forms the content of our concept, as the original and real. The ideas, therefore, he believed to exist for themselves alone and independent of the particular things. This theory was rejected by Aristotle. In the *Metaphysics* A9, M4-10, he submits the theory of ideas and the suppositions implicit in it to a minute examination. His criticism is despite some injustices and misunderstandings destructive of the theory. His most telling points are that the general is nothing substantial, that properties cannot be outside the things of which they are the properties, that the ideas lack a moving force, without which they cannot be the causes of phenomena. He for his part can only regard the particular as real in the full sense, as substance; for this name can only be applied to something which is neither predicated of something else nor an accidental property of something else. This is only true of the particular thing. All universal concepts on the other hand express merely particular qualities of substances and generic ideas merely denote the common nature of particular substances. They can indeed be called unreal and derived substances but they may not be regarded as something subsisting outside the things themselves; they are not a one outside the many, but a one from the many. It is, of course, a contradiction to attribute a higher reality to form, which is always a universal, in comparison to that which is a compound of form and matter (*vid. infra*) and at the same time to assert (p. 185) that only the universal is the object of knowledge which is in itself the prior and better known. The results of this contradiction are to be observed throughout the whole Aristotelian system.

2. FORM AND MATTER

Despite his attack on the independence and transcendence of the Platonic ideas, Aristotle by no means wished to give up the leading thoughts of this theory. His own definitions of form and matter are indeed only an attempt to embody these thoughts in a more tenable theory than Plato's. He says with Plato that only the necessary and unchangeable can be the object of knowledge. All sensible things are accidental and changeable. They can both be and not be (they are possible [able] both to be and not to be). Only the nonsensible which is thought in our concepts can be as unchangeable as the concepts themselves. Still more important, however, for Aristotle is the consideration that all change presupposes an unchangeable and every becoming something that has not become; more precisely its nature is twofold. The substrate, which becomes something and upon which the change takes place; and the qualities in the communications of which to the substrate this change consists. Aristotle used the word matter in a new sense to denote his substrate. To the qualities he applied the name which was current for the Platonic ideas, the form. (Other terms, p. 190, 1). Since the aim of becoming has been reached when matter has assumed its form, the form of a thing is the reality of it and form in general is reality or the real. Since, on the other hand, matter as such is not yet what it later becomes but must have the power of becoming this, it is potentiality or the potential. If we think of matter without form we obtain the "first matter", which being undefined is called the (qualitatively), unlimited, the common substrate of all definite substance which, however, in as much as it is the merely potential, never exists nor has existed in itself. The forms, however, are not to be regarded as mere modifications or even as creations of a most universal form. Each of them, insofar as it is a definite form, is eternal and immortal like the Platonic ideas, but they differ from these in not being outside the things, and since the world is eternal, they never have been. The form is not merely the concept and the essence of each thing but also its final end and the force which realises this end. Its different relations are usually divided between different subjects. On account of this Aristotle frequently enumerates four kinds of causes—the material, the formal, the moving and the final cause. The last three, however, are in virtue of their nature and in particular cases (such as the relation of the soul to the body and of God to the world) merged into one. Primary is only the distinction between form and matter, which is present throughout the world; where something stands to something else as the more perfect, the defining and effecting, the former is called the form or the real, and the latter the potential or matter. Actually, however, matter acquires in Aristotle a significance far above the concept of mere possibility.

From it are derived natural necessity and chance which limit and interfere in the working of nature and the plans of men. All incompleteness in nature rests on the nature of matter, which determines, too, such fundamental distinctions as that of heaven and earth, male and female. It is due to the resistance of matter to form that nature can only gradually rise from lower forms to higher. Only in matter can Aristotle find an explanation of the fact that the lowest subspecies split up into a multitude of individuals. It is unmistakable that matter becomes thereby a second principle endowed with its own power and distinct from form. However great the advantages which this theory of form and matter and the newly created pair of concepts, potentiality and reality, offers the philosopher in his explanation of phenomena, it contains one serious confusion of thought (cf. p. 192). The being is at different times identified with the particular and with the form, while the materia is conceived sometimes in an abstract and sometimes in a concrete sense. It is, nevertheless, a merit of Aristotle's interpretation of the world that through the distinction between potential and actual being, one of which is converted into the other by motion, and especially through the important concept of the entelechy the ground was cleared for the idea of evolution and the mathematical type of ontology and concept which Plato represents was replaced by a biological type.

3. THE MOVER AND THE MOVED

The relation of form to matter yields the idea of motion or, what is the same, change, to which everything in the world that contains matter is subject. Motion is actually nothing more than the realisation of the potential as such. The impulse to this realisation can only be given by something which already is what the moved is to become through its motion. Each motion therefore presupposes two things: a moving element and a moved. If a being moves itself, these two factors must be divided between different elements in it, such as body and soul in man. The moving element can only be the actual, the form, the moved only the potential, matter. The former operates on the latter in that it impels it to move towards a definite form or reality, for matter has from its very nature (in so far as every predisposition involves a demand for its activity), a desire for the form as something good and divine (*Phys.* I, 192a, 16; II, 192b, 18; *Met.* Λ, 1072b, 3). Where form and matter come into contact motion must necessarily always arise; and since not only form and matter, but the relation between them on which motion depends must be eternal (for both its beginning and disappearance could only be brought about by motion); since, too, time and the world, neither of which can be thought of apart from motion, are without beginning or end (cf. § 48. init.), motion can never have begun nor can it ever cease. The ultimate cause of this motion can only lie in an unmoved; for if all motion is due to the action of a mover on the moved and presupposes a mover different from the moved, the latter presupposes in its turn a mover different from itself. This necessity recurs as long as we have no mover which is not itself moved. If, therefore, there were no unmoved mover, there could be no first mover and hence no motion at all, still less a motion without a beginning. If, however, the first mover is unmoved, it must be immaterial, form without matter, pure actuality; for wherever there is matter there is a possibility of change, of progress from the potential to the actual and motion. Only the incorporeal is changeless and unmoved; and as form is perfect being and matter imperfect, the first mover must be absolutely perfect, that in which the scale of being reaches its highest point. Moreover since the world is a uniform whole working towards the definite end, and the motion of the world-sphere is uniform and constant, the first mover can only be one, the final cause itself. But pure incorporeal being can only be mind or thought. The ultimate basis of all motion lies, therefore, in the deity as the pure, perfect and inexhaustible mind. The activity of this mind can only consist in thought, for every other activity has its object outside itself, which is unthinkable for the activity of the perfect self-sufficient being. This thought can never be in the state of mere potentiality; it is rather an unceasing activity of thought. The object of its thought can only be itself, for the value of thought is determined by its contents and the most valuable and perfect is only the divine mind itself. Hence the thought of God is "thought of thought". His happiness consists in this unchangeable self-contemplation. He acts upon the world not by passing beyond himself and directing his thought and will to it, but by his mere existence. The absolutely perfect being, the highest good, is also the end to which all things move and strive. On him the uniform order, the cohesion and life of the world depends. Aristotle did not assume the action of the divine will on the world or any creative activity or interference of the deity in the course of the world. The relation of God, the mind which thinks of itself, to the world, as Aristotle conceived it, is best expressed by the term "energism".

48. *Aristotle's physics*

ITS STANDPOINT AND GENERAL PRINCIPLES

Whereas the "first philosophy" deals with the unmoved and incorporeal, the subject of the physics is the moved and corporeal, more precisely that which has the cause of its motion in itself. "Nature" is the cause of motion and rest in that in which motion and rest are original qualities (*Phys.* II, 192b, 20). The precise nature of this source, however, and its relation to God remain unclear. Aristotle's system, indeed, gives him no justification for his frequent treatment of nature as a real power operating in the world.

Aristotle understands by motion (*vide,* p. 194) in general every change, every realisation of a potential. In this sense he enumerates four kinds of motion, the substantial—coming into being and passing away; the quantitative—increase and decrease; the qualitative—transformation (the passage of one substance into another); and the spacial (change of place). He assigns however only the last three to motion in a narrow sense, while the concept of change includes all four. All other species of change are determined by spacial motion. Aristotle examines (*Phys.* III, IV) more minutely than any of his predecessors the concepts relating in the first instance to this species of motion. He shows that the unlimited cannot be actually, but merely potentially, present in the infinite multiplicability of the numbers and the infinite divisibility of magnitudes. He defines the space of a thing, which however is not sharply distinguished from its place, as the boundary of the body which immediately surrounds the thing, while time is "the number of motion in respect of before and after". He concludes from this that outside the world there is no time and no space; that an empty space is unthinkable (as elaborated in his attack on the Atomists); that time, like every number, presupposes a soul that counts. He proves that spacial motion and, of spacial motions, circular motion, is the only uniform and perpetual motion which can be without beginning or end. Aristotle is convinced, however, that spacial motion will not alone suffice to explain phenomena. He maintains that matter is qualitatively different. He brings against Plato's mathematical construction of the elements and also against the atomic theory arguments against which the latter in form propounded by Democritus could not be defended in the state of natural knowledge at that time. In his attacks on opposing theories he attempts to show that the "stuffs" and especially the elements change qualitatively one into the other, in that the qualities of the one change under the action of the other. This relation of activity and passivity is, however, as he believes, only possible when two bodies are partly similar and partly dissimilar, that is when they are differentiated within the same genus. In the same spirit Aristotle, in opposition to the mechanical theories, supports the doctrine according to which mixture of stuffs is not merely physical but gives rise to a new substance (chemical mixture). Still more important for him is the principle that the process of nature is not to be regarded as a physical activity, but as tending rather towards a definite end. The end and aim of all becoming is the development of potentiality to actuality, the incorporation of form in matter. Thus in the Aristotelian doctrine of form and matter, just as in the Platonic theory of ideas, the teleological explanation of nature predominates over the physical. "Nature", says Aristotle, "does nothing without a purpose"; "it strives always towards the best"; "it makes everything as beautiful as possible"; nothing in it is superfluous, nothing in vain and nothing incomplete; in all her works, even the least, there is something divine. Even the waste products she puts to some use like a good housekeeper. This is shown by observation of nature, which reveals to us the wonderful purpose in the arrangement of the world and in the creations of nature, whether great or small. We are compelled to refer this purpose or design in the world to an all-pervading purposive activity by the consideration that whatever occurs regularly cannot be ascribed to chance. Even when we can attribute no deliberation to nature, this only proves that she, like a consummate artist, produces what is relevant to her purpose with the unerring certainty which excludes all choice. The real grounds of natural objects lie therefore in the final causes. The material causes, on the other hand, he regards with Plato (p. 199) as their condition and indispensable aids, but not as their positive causes. The resistance which these intermediate causes offer to the purposive action of nature and their limitation of her success, resulting in a gradual ascent in the scale of earthly being from the less perfect to the more perfect (the matter of the heavenly world is of different nature) has been discussed in a previous section (p. 193).

The most important feature of the Aristotelian teleology is the fact that it is neither anthropocentric nor is it due to the actions of a creator existing outside the world or even of a mere arranger of the world, but is always thought of as immanent in nature. What Plato effected in the *Timæus* by the introduction of the world-soul and the Demiurgus is here explained by the assumption of a teleological activity inherent in nature itself, a thought which must have pervaded the work of Protagoras *On the Primary State*.

49. *The structure of the universe*

The eternity of the universe follows as a natural consequence of the eternity of form and matter and from the fact that motion is without beginning and end (p. 194). The assumption, indeed, that the world is originated but will last for ever (cf. Plato's theory, p. 163ff.) overlooks the fact that coming into being and passing away mutually condition each other. Only that can be everlasting which excludes both the one and the other. Even in the earthly world it is only the particular beings that are born and die. The genera on the other hand are unoriginated. It follows that there have always been men, although as Plato assumes, the race has been from time to time annihilated over wide areas or reduced to savagery by great natural catastrophes. This theory of the eternity of the world, which was first formulated by Aristotle and pervades his whole philosophic system, makes the cosmogonic part of physics superfluous for him. He has not to explain the origin of the world but only its composition and structure.

He takes as his basis the distinction of two dissimilar halves which make up the universe. The sublunary and the superlunary worlds, the heavenly and the earthly, the "Beyond" and the "Here". The imperishable nature of the stars and the unchangeable regularity of their motion proves, as Aristotle had attempted to establish from general grounds, that they are different in matter from the perishable things that are subject to constant change. The former consist of æther, the fifth element (quintessence), the body without an opposite which is capable of no change except that of position, and no motion except circular motion. But the things are composed of the four elements which stand to one another in a double opposition—that of the light and the heavy, which arises from their characteristic rectilineal motion towards their natural positions, and the qualitative, which results from the different combinations possible between the basic qualities warm and cold, dry and moist (fire is warm and dry, air warm and moist, water cold and moist, earth cold and dry). On account of this opposition they pass constantly from one into the other; this transition is brought about between those which are further apart (earth and air, water and fire), by transmutation into one of the intermediate elements. Hence follows not only the unity of the world, which is also secured by that of the first mover, but also its spherical shape, which however Aristotle attempted to prove on many other physical and metaphysical grounds. Earth is at rest in the centre of the universe and is also spherical in shape. Around it are amassed in concentric spherical layers water, air and fire (or more precisely the warm, combustible matter, for flame is the extreme of fire). Then come the heavenly spheres, whose material is purer, the further they are from the earth. The outermost of these spheres is the heaven of the fixed stars, the daily revolution of which is produced by the deity, which encompasses it without occupying space (cf. p. 195). The motion of each sphere consists in a completely uniform motion about its axis. This was presupposed by Aristotle in common with Plato and the whole of contemporary astronomy, but he puts forward a detailed proof of it in the case of the first sphere. We must therefore (according to a view of the problem which proceeds from Plato) assume a number of spheres and ascribe to them the motions which must be presupposed in order to explain the actual motion of the seven planets from mere regular circular motions. On this hypothesis Eudoxus (p. 170) had estimated the number of spheres which will account for the motion of planets at twenty-six including the seven in which the planets themselves are fixed, while Calippus had put the number at thirty-three. Aristotle follows them and elaborates his theory of the first mover on a line with the new astronomical theories. Since, according to this theory, the outer spheres stand to the inner in the relation of form to matter, of mover to moved, each sphere must communicate its motion to every sphere which it encompasses. This happens in the case of the outermost sphere which carries all others around with it in its daily revolution. It is therefore obvious that the individual motion of each planet would be disturbed by every sphere which surrounds it, if particular precautions were not adopted against this. Aristotle assumes therefore that between the spheres of each planet and the one next below there are as many "backward moving" spheres as are necessary to counteract the influence of the one on the other. He estimates their number at twenty-two; with the addition of these to the number calculated by Calippus he arrives at the total of fifty-six heavenly spheres, including the sphere of the fixed stars. Each of these, however, must receive its motion from the same source as the "first heaven", that is from an eternal, unmoved and therefore incorporeal substance, from a spirit belonging to it. Hence there must be as many sphere-spirits as there are spheres. The stars are on this account regarded by Aristotle as animate beings endowed with reason and far superior to man. But he does not claim anything more than probability for his account of the number of the spheres and the sphere spirits (*Metaphysics*, Λ8, Simplic. on *de cælo*, 488, 3ff. Heib).

The friction caused by the motion of the heavenly spheres, especially in the places which lie beneath the sun, in the air produce light and heat. This however varies in amount from time to time in every place according to the inclination of the sun's path at the different seasons. The result of this is the circular course of creation and destruction, the copy of the eternal in the perishable, the ebb and flow of matter and the transmutation of the elements into one another, in a word, all that which gives rise to the atmospheric and terrestrial phenomena which form the subject-matter of Aristotle's *Metereology*.

50. *Living beings*

Aristotle devoted a great part of his scientific work to the study of organic nature (cf. p. 182ff). While for this purpose he could doubtless have availed himself of numerous researches by natural scientists and physicians, such as, for instance, those of Democritus, yet his own achievements, from all indications, so far surpass those of his predecessors that we may without hesitation call him not merely the most eminent representative, but even the chief founder of comparative and systematic zoology among the Greeks. Even if he was not the author of the work on plants attributed to him, his activity as a teacher alone is sufficient to justify his claim to the title of founder of scientific botany.

Life consists in the capacity of self-movement. Each motion presupposes two things—a form which moves and matter which is moved. This matter is the body, while the form is the soul of the living being. The soul, therefore, does not exist without body nor is it itself something corporeal. It is at the same time unmoved, not the self-moved, as Plato thought. Its combination with its body is the same as that of form generally with matter. As the form of its body it is also its final end (cf. p. 193). The body is only the instrument of the soul; its nature is determined by this function. This is what Aristotle meant by the term "organic", a conception that he was the first to formulate. If, therefore, the soul is defined as the first entelechy of an organic body, this means that it is the life-principle, the force which moves it and constructs it as its instrument. It is natural on this account that the purposive activity of nature appears most clearly in living beings; for here everything is from the beginning calculated on the soul and the effects which it produces. Since, however, every purposive action can only gradually overcome the resistance of matter (cf. 194), organic life is unequal in quality. The life of plants consists in nourishment and reproduction. In animals we have the additional capacity of sense-perception and in the great majority of locomotion as well. Finally in man both these capacities are found in combination with thought. Aristotle assumes therefore, in partial agreement with Plato (p. 152), three kinds of soul. These, when combined in one individual soul, form three parts of that soul, which are so related to one another that the higher cannot exist without the lower, nor the lower without the higher. The three are the nutritive or plant soul, the sensual or animal soul and the intelligent or human soul. The progressive development in the vital activities corresponds to the scale of living beings, which shows a continuous and gradual ascent from the most imperfect to the highest. The numerous analogies we find between the different parts of this series show that it is governed throughout by the same laws.

The lowest stage is formed by the plants, whose functions are limited to those of nutrition and reproduction. They have no uniform middle point for their life and are consequently incapable of any feeling or perception. In the extant works Aristotle bestows on them no more than a casual attention. His treatment of animals is on that account all the more exhaustive. He is always at pains to combine the most exact knowledge of the particular with that of its significance for and position in the whole. The bodies of animals are composed of matter consisting of equal parts, which in their turn are a mixture of the elements; among them the flesh is of particular importance as the seat of sensation (the nerves were a later discovery). The direct bearer of the soul is the "pneuma" as the basis of vital heat, a stuff related to the æther with which it passes in the seed from the father to the child. The chief seat of the vital heat is the central organ, which in sanguineous animals is the heart; in the heart the blood is prepared from the nutritive substances conveyed to it by the veins (the distinction between veins and arteries was unknown to Aristotle). The blood serves partly for the nutrition of the body and partly for the communication of particular sensations. The genesis of animals takes various forms, which he carefully investigated. Besides sexual reproduction he assumes spontaneous generation even in the case of certain insects and fishes. He regarded however the first species of propagation as the most perfect. Here the male stands to the female as form to matter; he gives the child its soul and she its body. The physiological reason for this lies in the fact that the female sex on account of its colder nature cannot completely boil out the blood which is needed for the formation of the generative substance. The organism in its development passes from the form of a worm into an egg and finally reaches its organic structure. There are, however, fundamental differences in their physical structure, habitats, mode of life and locomotion as in their mode of generation. Aristotle endeavours to demonstrate the gradual ascent from lower to higher which he assumes in all of these respects. It is hardly surprising that he failed to carry through this point of view in all its applications without some deviation, or to establish on this basis a natural classification of the animal world. Among the nine classes of animals which he usually enumerates (viviparous quadrupeds, oviparous quadrupeds, birds, fishes, whales, molluscs, scaly animals, soft-scaled animals, and insects) the most far-reaching distinction is that between bloodless and sanguineous animals, of which he himself remarks (*H. An.* III, 516b, 22ff.) that it coincides with that of vertebrates and invertebrates.

51. *Man*

What distinguishes man from all other living beings is mind, which is combined in him with the animal soul. His physical structure, too, and his lower spiritual activities correspond to the higher destiny which they receive through this combination. In the former it is proclaimed by his upright position and the symmetry of his figure; he has the most and the purest blood, the biggest brain and the highest vital heat; he is endowed in the organs of speech and the hand with the most valuable instruments. Among the activities of the soul, perception is a change produced in the soul through the agency of the body; more precisely it consists in the communication of the form of the perceived object to the perceiving subject. The individual senses as such give us information merely about the quality of things to which they are specially related. What they tell us of these things is always true. Their common qualities, however, about which we obtain information through all our senses, unity and number, size and shape, time, rest and motion—all these we perceive not through an individual sense but only through the "common sensory", in which the images produced in the sense organs are united. Through this common sensory we are enabled to compare and distinguish the perceptions of the various senses, to relate the images which they communicate to objects and to become conscious of our perceptions as our own. This organ of the common sensory is the heart; the medium through which the motions of the sense organs reach the heart seems to be the "pneuma" (see p. 202). When the motion in the sense organ continues beyond the time of actual perception and is communicated to the central organ and produces there a renewal of the sensory image, this is called phantasy (the term also denoting the power of imagining). This, like all the communications of the common sense, can be both true and false. If an image is recognised as a copy of an earlier perception, a matter in which we are not infrequently mistaken, we call it remembrance; the conscious calling up of a remembrance is recollection. Thus memory, too, has its seat in the common sensory. A change in the central organ produced by digestion causes sleep, while the extinction of the vital heat in it causes death. Internal movements in the sense organs or even such as have been evoked by external impressions produce dreams on reaching the central organ; thus dreams can under circumstances be indications of incidents which in waking have passed unnoticed. If the perceived object is regarded as good or evil, pleasure or its opposite arises (these feelings as is indicated in *De an.* III, 7, always contain a judgment of value), which in their turn cause desire or repulsion. These states of mind proceed, too, from the central seat of feeling. Between feeling and desire no further distinction is made; for although Aristotle like Plato contrasts *epithymia* and *thymos* as the purely sensual and the nobler form of irrational desire, he gave no closer definition of *thymos*. He understands by it anger, courage and the whole collection of moods.[13]

All these functions however as such belong to the animal soul; only in men do we find the additional factor of mind or thought. Whereas the animal soul is born and perishes with the body whose form it is, mind is unoriginated and imperishable. It enters from outside into the soul-germ which is transmitted from the father to the child, it has no bodily organ and is not subject to suffering or change and remains unaffected by the death of the body. But as the mind of a human individual, in combination with the soul, it is affected by the change of its states. In the individual the capacity of thinking precedes actual thought; his mind is like a clean unwritten tablet, on which a definite content is written, first by thought itself (that is, however, not by sense perceptions, but by contemplation of the things perceptible [by the mind]); his thought is always accompanied by sensory images. Aristotle, therefore, distinguished a twofold *nous:* that which causes everything and that which becomes everything, the active and the passive. The latter he supposes to arise and pass away with the body, while the active is by its very nature eternal. Our thought, however, as something individual, is due to the co-operation of both factors; we have no recollection of the previous existence of our mind, nor can any of the activities which are characteristic only of beings composed of *nous* and the soul be attributed to the disembodied mind, whether before or after the present life. A more exact account of the nature of passive reason and its relation to the active will be sought in vain in Aristotle. We see, of course, that he hoped to find in it the link connecting *nous* and the animal soul; but he does not show how the different qualities which he attributes to it can be united without contradiction; nor does he raise the questions where the seat of the human personality is, how the disembodied *nous* can lead a personal life without remembrance etc., how, on the other hand, self-consciousness and the personal unity of life of which it is the expression arise from a combination of *nous* with the animal soul, of the eternal with the transient, or how the nature compounded of both can be their subject.

On this combination of the reason with the lower functions of the soul depend the mental activities which raise man above the animals. The activity of the *nous* purely as such is every direct apprehension of the highest truths (see above, p. 189). From this Aristotle, like Plato, distinguishes mediate knowledge and from this opinion, which is related to the not-necessary, without however giving any more detailed psychological explanation of either. If desire is guided by reason, it becomes volition. Aristotle presupposes quite arbitrarily the freedom of the will and attempts to prove it by the fact that virtue is voluntary and that we are universally held accountable for our actions. He asserts further that the constitution of our will decides the aims and ends of our actions (the most general judgments of moral value); it is virtue on which the rightness of our aims depends (*Eth. N.* VI, 1144a, 6, etc.). What means, however, are best for realising those aims has to be decided by reflection. In so far as the reason performs this task it is called the reflective or practical reason, in the development of which prudence consists. We find in Aristotle no closer examinations of the internal processes which result in acts of will nor into the possibility and limits of freedom of the will.

52. *Aristotle's ethics*

It is in the *Nicomachean Ethics* that Aristotle gave his views on morality their final shape. They signify a complete break with the Platonic dualism which had still dominated his *Protrepticus* (p. 177), while the standpoint of the *Eudemean Ethics,* with its concept of thoughtfulness as contemplation of the divine first principle, which also provides the norm for the Ethics, is also given up. Aristotle now takes up his stand in the present life and analyses the moral nature of man with the intention of including the irrational parts of the soul as well in the process of moral perfection. This, however, is not derived from a transcendental principle but from the nature of man itself.

The aim of all human activity is in general (and no Greek writer on ethics ever doubts it) happiness, for it is alone that which is desired for itself alone and not for the sake of something else. But Aristotle finds the criterion by which the conditions of happiness are determined not in subjective feeling but in the objective character of the activities of life. "Eudaimonia" consists in beauty and perfection of existence as such. The pleasure which the individual derives from this perfection is only the result of this perfection; it is neither its final aim nor the measure of its value. The good for every living being consists in the perfection of its activity; thus for man, as Aristotle explains in detail, the good consists only in the perfection of the peculiarly human activity. This is the activity of the reason, and the activity of the reason that is consonant with its function is virtue. Hence the happiness of man as such consists in virtue. Or if two kinds of rational activity and two series of virtues are to be distinguished, the theoretical and the practical, the scientific or pure activity of thought is the more valuable, while practical activity or ethical virtue is the second essential constituent of happiness. To these, however, further additions must be made. To happiness belong maturity and perfection of life. A child cannot be happy because it is still incapable of any perfect activity. Poverty, illness and misfortune disturb happiness and withhold from virtuous activity the means which wealth, power and influence provide; delight in children, intercourse with friends, health, beauty and noble birth are all valuable in themselves. But the positive, constitutive element of happiness is only inward excellence, of which external and material goods are only the negative conditions (like the relation in nature of the material to the final causes); even the most extreme misfortune cannot make a virtuous man miserable, although it may stand in the way of his Eudaimonia. Pleasure is by no means an independent factor of the highest good in the sense that it may be made itself the end of our actions. For even if it is the natural result of every complete activity and consequently inseparable from this, and, although it does not deserve the reproaches which Plato and Speusippus have made against it, nevertheless its value depends absolutely on the activity from which it arises. It is the natural completion of every activity, its immediate consequence (*Eth.* X, 3, 1174, 631). Only he is virtuous who is satisfied by the perfection of the good and beautiful without any addition and who gladly sacrifices everything else to obtain this satisfaction (*Eth.* I, 5-11; X, 1-9; VII, 12-15).

Of the qualities on which happiness is thus seen to depend the advantages of thought and will, the dianoetic and ethical virtues, the latter actually form the subject of the ethics. The concept of ethical virtue is determined by three characteristics, it is a constitution of the will which keeps to the mean that is proper to our nature, fixed by the reason in the way that a wise man would fix it. These determinations are indicated first in a general way (*Eth.* I, 13-II, 9); a more detailed treatment follows, the first in III, 1-8, the second in III, 9-V, 15, and the third in VI. Aristotle took over this concept of the right mean partly from popular ancient Greek ethics of the mean and partly perhaps from the dietetic and therapeutic theories of the Hippocratean physicians.

1. All virtues have their foundation in certain natural ca-

pacities; but they only become virtues in the real sense when they are guided by wisdom. On the other hand ethical virtue has its seat essentially in the will. When Socrates ascribed it to knowledge, he overlooked the fact that it is not a question of knowledge of moral laws but of their application: it is a question of the control of the emotions by the reason, where free decision is left to the will.

Aristotle now proceeds to examine in great detail the concepts which denote the various forms of determination by the will, those of the voluntary, the intended, etc. This determination by the will can, however, only become a virtue when it acquires an enduring quality, when it becomes a firmly established state of mind, such as is only to be found in men of mature age.

2. The quality of will may be called moral when it preserves the correct mean between excess and defect; this mean is determined by the peculiarity of the active agent; for what is right for one can be too much or too little for another. Each virtue is therefore a mean between two errors, between which it oscillates. Aristotle illustrates this by examples of individual virtues such as courage, self-control, generosity, etc., without however attempting, like Plato, to derive his basic virtues from a definite principle. His observation and analysis of the actual behaviour of men led him to make interesting and vivid sketches of character-types such as his pupil Theophrastus elaborated in his *Characters*. He accords the most complete treatment to the main political virtue, justice, devoting to it the whole of the fifth book of his Ethics, which remained until after the Middle Ages the basis of natural law.

Its function, he thought, was the correct apportionment of rewards and punishment; he distinguishes further between private and public law, to which distributive and corrective (better "directive") justice corresponds. The former has to apportion according to merit the honours and rewards which are bestowed upon the individuals by the community; the latter has to see to it, that in voluntary contracts a balance is held between the profits and loss of each contractor and in obligatory contracts, the punishment is proportionate to the crime. For the first—as Aristotle curiously observes—the principle of geometrical proportion holds good and for the second, that of arithmetical proportion. Law in a strict sense, political law, which is to be distinguished from paternal, domestic and slave law, is applicable only among free and equal men. It is to be divided into natural and conventional law. Through the correction of the second by the first we arrive at the proper.

3. Who is to determine in any given case where the correct mean lies? This, says Aristotle, is the business of *Phronēsis*, that is, practical wisdom (cf. § 51 end), which is distinguished from the dianoetic virtues by its relation to the will; for some of these are directed only to the necessary, such as *nous, epistēmē* (*vide*, p. 187, 189, 207ff.) and *sophia*, which is a combination of these two, while others such as *technē* are indeed concerned with the changeable, but make production and not conduct their aim (cf. 169).

Aristotle makes a distinction (VII, 1-11) between virtues and vices in a real sense, that is correct and perverse qualities of will and those conditions which are due not so much to an habitual direction of the will as to the strength or weakness of the will in relation to the emotions—on the one hand moderation and endurance, on the other excess and effeminacy. Finally in the essay on love and friendship (VIII, IX), which is full of the most delicate observations and shrewd remarks, he turns his attention to a moral relation in which it is evident that man is by nature a social being, that each man is a friend and relation of everyone else (VIII, I, 1155a, 16ff., 13, 1161b, 5) and that a common law unites all men (*Rhet.* I, 13 init.). This forms the transition to the treatment of the family and the state.

The Aristotelian ethics shows a twofold character. Since he had rejected the transcendental idealism of Plato, he was faced with the difficult problem of deriving an ethical ideal from experiential reality. He lapses, therefore, for long intervals from an imperative into a descriptive ethics. We find a trace of the Platonic idealism in his recognition of a divine element which is immanent in man, the mind. It is with reference to this divine spark that he makes his appeal that we should immortalise ourselves by our conduct in life. In this sentence he upholds the autonomy of ethics in a true Socratic spirit.

53. *Aristotle's politics*

That Aristotle's *Politics* is not a work written on a preconceived plan but a patchwork of constituents of various chronological origin has been mentioned before (p. 179f.). The first book belongs to the latest parts of the work. It forms the introduction to the whole work which originated in a series of lectures and in many parts remained incomplete. Its main content is the following.

In the nature of man there lies an impulse towards communal life with his kind. He needs this community not only for the self-preservation, security and perfection of his physical existence, but above all because only in it is a good education and control of life by law and justice possible (*Eth.* X, 10). The perfect community that embraces all others is the state. Its aim is not confined to the maintenance of law and order, defence against external enemies and the preservation of life; its function is higher and more comprehensive—the happiness of the citizens in a perfect communal life. Consequently the state must by its very nature come before the individual and the family, just as indeed the parts of any whole are determined by the whole as the aim which they subserve (*Pol.* I, 2, 1252b, 27ff.). Since then virtue forms the most essential constituent of happiness, Aristotle, like Plato, sees the chief function of the state in the education of the young to virtue. He disapproves most expressly of a state's being intent upon war and conquest instead of the peaceful cultivation of moral and scientific education.

Chronologically, however, the family and the village community are prior to the state. Nature first brought man and wife together to set up a household; the families developed into village communities; the combination of several village-communities forms a city community, which Aristotle as yet does not distinguish from the state. The village community forms a mere transition stage to the state in which it is merged. Aristotle points out in a telling criticism (*Pol. II*, 1ff.) that Plato's demand that family and private property should be sacrificed to the ends of the state, is not merely in every respect impracticable, but also that it rests on a false conception of the community; for the state is not merely a unit, but a whole composed of many different parts. He himself treats of marriage and the other relations of family life with a moral understanding which is seldom found in ancient times (*Pol.* I, 2, 13; *Eth.* VIII, 14, etc.). He yields however to the national Greek prejudice and the existing social conditions when he makes an indefensible attempt to justify slavery by the presupposition that there are men who are only capable of manual labour and must on this account be ruled by others; this is in general the relation of the barbarians to the Greeks (*Pol.* I, 4ff.). The same is true of his discussion of acquisition and property (I, 8ff.) in which he asserts that the acquisitions permissible are those which directly serve the satisfaction of our needs. All financial business he treats with distrust and contempt and considers all "banausic" activities unworthy of the free man.

In his theory of State constitutions he does not follow Plato in adjudging one constitution to be the only right one and all others wrong. He sees that the constitutional system must be adapted to the character and needs of the people for which it is intended; that under different circumstances different things are right and that what is in itself imperfect may well be the best that can be attained under the given conditions. For if the correctness of the constitution depends on what we consider the aim of the state, and correct constitutions are those whose aim is the common good and not the advantage of the rulers, and all others are wrong, the form of the constitution is determined by the distribution of political power. This however has to be adapted to the real significance of the different classes for the state; for a constitution can only survive when its supporters are stronger than its opponents and it is only then just when it accords to the citizens equal political rights so far as they are equal, and unequal rights so far as they are unequal (cf. p. 209 on corrective justice). The most important differences among the citizens relate to their virtue (that is their personal capacity in everything on which the welfare of the state depends), their wealth, their noble or ignoble birth and their freedom. Aristotle follows, therefore, the traditional method of classifying constitutions according to the number of the rulers. He enumerates six chief types of constitution (cf. Plato, *Pol.* 300ff. and p. 160): kingdom, aristocracy, polity (*Eth.* VIII, 12, 1160a, 33, also called timocracy) as right, and democracy, oligarchy, and tyranny as wrong. He remarks, however, that this numerical division is only derivative. Monarchy arises naturally when one man surpasses all others in capacity, and aristocracy when a minority is so superior to all others that they are born rulers. A polity is formed when all citizens are roughly of equal merit (which of course would only be roughly the case with regard to warlike qualities). Democracy arises when the mass of the propertyless and free population have the guidance of the state in their hands, oligarchy when a minority of rich and noble-born men rule the state and tyranny when a single man sets himself up as a despot by the force of arms; in the mixed constitutions the share of one or other of these elements in the government is regulated by the same principles (III, 6-13, cf. 17, 1288a, 5ff.; IV, 4, 11F; VI, 2, etc.). It is obvious however, that Aristotle has not succeeded in reconciling these different points of view or in carrying them out with perfect consistency.

His description of the best state (VIIf.) is based, like Plato's, upon the conditions present in a Greek city-republic; Greek, because it is only among the Hellenes that he and Plato could find the qualities which make possible the union of freedom and civic order; republic, because he can find the conditions for a kingdom only in the heroic age. He believed that in his time it was no longer possible for an individual to rise so far above all others that a free people would willingly endure his undivided domination. His model state is an "aristocracy" which is closely allied to that of Plato in its basic ideas, however far removed from it in its conception. All citizens of the state are to have the right of participating in the administration and are to be called upon to exercise this right when they have reached mature years. But in the best state only those are to be citizens who are capable by their position and education of taking a responsible part in government. Aristotle demands therefore—like Plato in the *Laws*—that all manual labour, agriculture and industry, should be performed by slaves or metœcs. He prescribes an education which is to be under the complete control of the state and bears a close resemblance to that of Plato. But neither the section on education nor the description of the best state is brought to a conclusion. Thus, for example, the question how far the state should control scientific education is not even touched.

Together with this model state Aristotle discusses also the imperfect forms of state with minute care. He distinguishes the different kinds of democracy, oligarchy and tyranny which arise partly from the different qualities of the rulers and partly from the fact that the peculiarities of each form of constitution are carried through with varying degrees of thoroughness. He examines the conditions on which the origin, preservation, and decay of each form of State depend and the principles and machinery of administration which are proper to them. He asks finally which constitution is best suited to the majority of states under usual conditions. He answers: it is such a combination of oligarchic and democratic institutions as makes the prosperous middle classes the centre of gravity of civic life. This would be the best way of securing the progress of the state that stability and following of the correct mean which are the best guarantee for the endurance of a constitution and best correspond to the ethical principles of the philosopher. Aristotle calls this form of state a "polity"; he gives however no explanation of its relation to the constitution of the same name which he had mentioned among the correct forms but not further described (*vide* p. 212, 1). It approximates to the form which is called aristocracy (IV, 7). But this part of the Aristotelian *Politics* is also left unfinished.

A comparison of Aristotle's theory of the state with that of Plato shows, despite the agreement between the two philosophers that the aim of the state is to educate the citizens into a community based on moral principles, a striking difference. Plato's state is in accordance with his dualistic philosophy of life. It is ultimately directed towards the other world and, in its modified form, is a concession to the supposed reality of earthly existence. Aristotle, however, stands with both feet firmly on the ground of earthly life and confines his endeavours to moulding it according to moral ideals within the given possibilities. Thus Plato claims absolute validity for his ideal state while Aristotle varies his constitutional forms according the different nature and needs of the people. It is probable that many ideas are present in Aristotle's philosophy that had been anticipated in the lost Sophistic literature. Even his main idea that man is by nature a community-forming being, inspires the myth of Protagoras in Plato, while the advantages and disadvantages of the different constitutions had also been discussed by the Sophists. The occurrence in Euripides of the theory that the middle classes form a stabilising element in the state shows that it must have found champions among the Sophists. It forms in the *Politics* the parallel to the value attached to the mean between the extremes in the *Ethics*.

54. *Aristotle's attitude to art, history and religion*

Another inheritance of the Sophists is Aristotle's inclusion of rhetoric in the circle of the sciences taught by him. Plato had never recognised it as such but had always assigned it to the arts. In Aristotle it appears as a theory of art which borders on dialectic and is subsidiary to ethics and politics. The first two books deal with the proof by probability and give an introduction to the art of conviction in the various spheres of forensic, "symbouleutic" and epideictic oratory. The third book, which was originally a separate treatise, deals with form, expression, style and arrangement of the speech and thus leads to a consideration of its æsthetic qualities.

Art, according to Aristotle, has a double function, to transcend nature and to imitate it. Hence imitation consists not in a simple reproduction of the sensible appearance of things by art; it has rather to represent their inner reality; their forms are types of general laws. In this sense poetry, for the theory of which we have only the incomplete *Poetics,* has the right and the duty to idealise. Thus poetry is more philosophic and serious than history. Of music Aristotle remarks that it serves a fourfold end (*Pol.* VIII, 5-7); amusement, moral education, recreation and purification. Every art can be used in any one of these directions, but mere amusement cannot be their ultimate end. The other three effects, however, are only produced when the work of art embodies and illustrates by the particular laws of general validity. Even purgation, that is the relief of the emotions of pity and fear, which in the famous definition of tragedy is said to be its effect, is to be understood in an ethical and æsthetic sense: that these emotions are satisfied and appeased when the relief is accompanied by a feeling of pleasure. It is obvious that Aristotle derived the idea of Catharsis which he applied in his theory of art from contemporary medicine. It is also unquestionable that his conception of poetry owes much to Sophism, especially Gorgias with his theory of rhetorical suggestion. Aristotle's contribution to the theory of art was incomparably more positive than Plato's. The same is true of the science which had until then stood completely outside the scope of philosophy. This was history together with ethnology. Plato occasionally expressed the thought that we must find out whether foreign peoples have not produced wise men. His reason for this is not any historical interest; he will only leave no means of reaching the truth uninvestigated. Aristotle however in proposing a collection of barbarian customs is inspired only by ethnological interests. As a basis for his theory of the state he collected 158 constitutions which he even traced in their historical development, such as in the *Constitution of the Athenians;* he writes on the territorial rights of states, endeavoured to compile the list of Pythian visitors and laid the foundations of a history of the sciences. In all these works he did not merely follow in the footsteps of the Sophists, but went far beyond them; for the Sophists, in their observation of the customs of foreign peoples, were concerned only with shaking the belief in the absolute validity of native customs. For Aristotle, however, these historical and anthropological facts are valuable as items of knowledge. He was the first philosopher to recognise that there is not merely one science of the general, a science of concept and law, but that investigation of particular historical events and processes may lay claim to the name of science.

We have finally to discuss Aristotle's attitude to religion. He rejects personally the popular religion on account of its anthropomorphic ideas of the nature of the gods. He recognises however that it has a practical value for popular education, a view that is reminiscent of certain theories of the Sophists.

To Aristotle himself God is the mind that thinks of itself, is the origin of all things and moves the world just as the beloved object does the lover.

When however he endeavours to give a philosophical proof of the necessity of the existence of God as the first mover, he turns his attention to religious experience. Not only does the Cosmos demand a final cause, but the soul, too, is aware intuitively of the existence of God. For the absolute mind and the highest in the human mind are similar in nature. He stands before the deity in reverence and wonderment, without however expecting any intervention or interest in the details of the world or the individuals of mankind. He gives all the greater emphasis to the unity and intellectuality of God and opposes the Platonic dualism with the monarchy of the self-thinking mind.

55. *Character and influence of the Aristotelian philosophy*

The philosophy of Aristotle developed slowly from and progressed beyond Platonism. A critical estimate of his philosophy as a whole can only deal with it in the finished form in which Aristotle found himself and formed his own system. A comparison with Plato's system reveals, despite many connecting links, to which belongs the retention of an idealism in the sense of referring the universe to a mental principle and referring the spiritual to the material, a far-reaching fundamental difference between the two philosophers. Plato with his definite dualism belongs to the series of philosophers who extend from the Orphics to Pythagoras and Empedocles and thence to neo-Pythagoreanism and neo-Platonism. Aristotle continues the tradition of the Ionian physicists and partly that of the Sophists. He is a contemplative character, an observer and a discoverer. He regards the world, which he is convinced is eternal, as a given magnitude which he analyses with his thought. At the same time he is a powerful organiser of science. But although endowed with a great gift for speculation, he lacked completely the ardent spirit of a Plato fired with a passion for reform that in the final instance was inspired by mysticism. His attitude to the world is therefore quite different; his reason is cooler, his sense of reality stronger, his criticism less severe and inclined more to observe than to guide. In his system the Platonic dualism is, except in a few small unessential details, completely abandoned. Nothing remains of Plato's conviction of the worthlessness of the material world and the everlastingness of the human soul. His deity, however reverent his attitude towards it, this first mover, is scarcely more than the Nous of Anaxagoras. That it is in reality nothing more than a necessary assumption for his physics is shown by its later transformation into a large number of sphere-movers. And although he criticises Anaxagoras for not having made better use of his Nous for a teleological explanation of nature, he himself becomes liable to the same reproach, in as much as his deity, apart from its significance as the origin of motion, seems in connection with the teleological purpose immanent in nature to be superfluous. While this faded dualism can by no means be compared with Plato's theory of two worlds, it is nevertheless a meagre remnant of the Platonic doctrine of the immortality of the soul, when Aristotle derives the active part of the mind from an external source which he declares to be imperishable. This, however, is not to be interpreted as signifying a belief in personal survival after death. Aristotle's break with dualism finds its final expression in his practical and theoretical attitude to the world.

Both his ethics and politics are concerned exclusively with this world. It lacks the transcendental standard which Plato found in constant contemplation of the supersensual world of the ideas. This explains Aristotle's far more favourable attitude to the arts, especially poetry, the different genres of which he endeavoured to understand and appreciate in the light of their own peculiar nature and problems. His attitude to science, too, is quite different. Plato placed a value only on mathematics and astronomy, owing to their relations with the supersensual and superterrestrial world, while all other natural sciences are merely a probable judgment, since they are concerned with objects which have no real being. Aristotle agrees with Plato in placing a high value on astronomy. His assumption of star-gods is indeed the only bequest of Plato that he preserved. On the other hand mathematics in his philosophy is passed over in favour of the natural sciences which provided his gift of observation with a wide field of joyful activity. The forms that he seeks are not beyond the earthly, but immanent in nature that develop and evolve in it. Apart from nature he recognises in human history, which he imagines as progressing in a periodical circle, an important field of research and turns his attention to the establishment of particular historical events and facts. This combination of a healthy empiricism with philosophical speculation is especially characteristic of the Aristotelian philosophy as distinct from the Platonic.

Aristotle's influence denotes a beginning and an end. His philosophy may be regarded as the conclusion of the whole of the previous development of Greek philosophy and science, which he embraced with the universality of his mind. The Peripatetic school in its later development made no essential alteration in the fundamentals of his metaphysics. Later philosophers, especially the neo-Platonists, made mistaken attempts to harmonise the two systems and to reconcile their fundamental differences. What was far more important was that the schools of science organised by Aristotle flourished after his death not only in the sphere of natural science but also in history and literature. The Alexandrian scholarship is indirectly a creation of the Aristotelian spirit.

But whereas he had embraced all sciences and included them in philosophy, in Hellenistic times they began to break loose from it and to make themselves independent, so that the field of philosophy grew narrower and narrower. For the Christian scholastics and the Arabic philosophy of the middle ages Aristotle signified the whole sum of human knowledge. It was a consequence of this petrification of the Aristotelian philosophy in scholasticism that modern philosophy had first to shake off the burden of his authority, before it could understand and appreciate him anew. It was Leibnitz, the only philosopher of modern times who can be compared with Aristotle in the universality of his mind, who called his own philosophy a "reformation" of Aristotle's. But it was not only in the form of Leibnitz' monads that Aristotle's entelechy concept lived again. It found a place in Goethe's philosophy of nature, and in the neo-vitalism of today it has experienced a surprising and splendid revival.

56. The Peripatetic school

After the death of its founder, the Peripatetic school received in his loyal friend, the learned and eloquent Theophrastus of Eresus in Lesbos (who died according to Diog. V, 36, 40, 58, c. 288-86 at the age of eighty-five) a head, who by his long and successful career as a teacher and his writings, that covered the whole field of philosophy, contributed greatly to the growth and consolidation of the school, to which he bequeathed an estate. As a philosopher he made no departure from the Aristotelian system, but contented himself with supplementing and rectifying it in detail by independent research. The Aristotelian logic underwent at his and Eudemus' hands various extensions and modifications. The most important consist in the separate treatment of the theory of propositions, the limitations of their differences of modality to the degree of subjective certainty and the enrichment of the syllogism by the theory of hypothetical inferences among which, however, the disjunctive were reckoned. Furthermore, as is shown by the fragment of his metaphysical work (Fr. 12), Theophrastus found difficulties in the treatment of certain essential problems of the Aristotelian metaphysics, such as the teleological purpose in nature and the relation of the first mover to the world. We do not know if he offered any solutions to these problems and we must suppose that he himself remained faithful to Aristotle's views. He modified the theory of motion and raised important objections to his definition of space. In the vast majority of points, however, he followed the Aristotelian physics and defended specially its doctrine of the eternity of the world (perhaps against the Stoic Zeno *vide* Philo, *de aetern. mundi, c.* 23ff.; *Doxogr.* 486ff.). Both of his extant works on plants, of which the first contains a systematics of botany, including plant geography and the second a sort of plant physiology, follow Aristotle in their leading ideas. But through his treatment of an extraor dinarily rich material, to which the discoveries of Alexander's expeditions made important contributions, and the fineness of his observation Theophrastus began a new era in this department of science and became the authority on botany until the close of the middle ages. Of his zoological studies his work on colour-change in animals is important and shows that he had grasped the law of adaptation to environment. His conception of thought shows a departure from Aristotle. He regards it as a motion of the soul and made penetrating criticism of the theory of the active and passive reasons, without however definitely rejecting this distinction. He expounded his ethical system in numerous writings which exhibit a shrewd and penetrating knowledge of human character, as we can judge from his most famous work the *Characters*. He was charged by the Stoics with over-estimating the value of external goods but in this respect the degree of difference between him and his master is very slight. He shows a greater departure from his teacher in his prejudice against marriage, which he thought would disturb the tenor of scientific activity and his disapproval of blood-offerings and flesh-foods, an opinion that was based on his belief in the kinship of all living beings. On the other hand he was only following his master's precedent (see p. 210) when he declared that all men and not merely those of one nation are connected and related with one another. Finally, we owe much to Theophrastus' historical researches. His *History of Physics,* of which the treatise *On Sense-Perception* has been preserved, form the source from which the whole of later doxography derived its information on earlier Greek philosophy. His *Inquiries into the Deity* must have been a religious history of the Greek and barbarian peoples. From this religious foundation grew the works on the philosophy of religion *On the Gods* and *On Piety,* remains of the later of which are preserved in Porphyrius.

Beside Theophrastus stands Eudemus of Rhodes, who was a teacher of philosophy, probably in his native city. He was the most respected of the personal pupils of the Stagirite. Through his learned historical works he performed a great service for the history of science. In his opinions he adheres to his master even more closely than Theophrastus. Simplicius calls him (*Phys.* 411, 14) the most faithful of his pupils, In his logic he adopted Theophrastus' improvements, but in his physics as the fragments show, he kept closely to Aristotle, often repeating him word for word. His ethics which are included under his name in the Aristotelian Corpus follow Plato in combining ethics with theology. He derived the disposition to virtue partly from the deity and sets up knowledge of God as the standard of value for all things and actions. It was regarded as a work of Aristotle himself of an earlier period than any of the other pedagogical works.

A third Aristotelian, Aristoxenus of Tarentum, is famous for his harmonics and other works on music. He came into the Peripatetic school from the Pythagoreans, and combined Pythagorean and Aristotelian elements both in his ethical precepts and his theory of music. He agreed with certain of the later Pythagoreans in declaring the soul to be a harmony of the body and on that account denied its immortality. With his lives of the Greek philosophers he founded Peripatetic biography. His fellow pupil Dicæarchus of Messene differed from Aristotle in giving practical life the preference over contemplative. His *Tripoliticus* however rests on the basis of the Aristotelian theory of the state. It recommends as the best constitution a combination of the three main types. With his history of civilisation in Greece, which later served as a model to Varro's *De vita populi Romani,* he continued with the happiest results a tradition started by the Sophists. He asserted that mankind existed first in a state of primitive savagery. In the second stage of development they became nomads living by hunting while the third stage was marked by the cultivation of the land. Theophrastus' pupil, Demetrius of Phaleron, was a popular philosopher and an extraordinarily copious writer. From 317 until 307 he was head of the Athenian government and it was he who advocated the founding of a library and the organisation of science in Alexandria.

Of far greater significance was Strato of Lampsacus, the "Physicist", the successor of Theophrastus, who for eighteen years was the head of the Peripatetic school in Athens (*c.* 287-269). This shrewd investigator not only found it necessary to correct Aristotle's assumptions in many details, but was opposed to his whole dualistic and spiritualistic conception of the world. He identified God with the unconscious force of nature and endeavoured to replace the Aristotelian teleology by a purely physical explanation of phenomena, the underlying elements of which he found in the Warm and the Cold, especially the first as the active principle. In connection with this he rejected the idea that mind in man is of a different nature from the animal soul and regarded all activities of the soul, thought and feeling, as motion of the same rational principle which has its seat in the head between the eyebrows, and is poured from there (apparently with the pneuma, that is moving air, as its substrate) into the different parts of the body. He denied, therefore, the immortality of the soul and showed the inadequacy of the proofs put forward in Plato's *Phædo.* He laid great stress on the necessity for exact research. In his transformation of the Aristotelian system into a pure monism by placing the principle of motion within Nature itself, the influence of Democritus is unmistakeable.

Strato was followed by Lyco, who presided over the school for forty-four years until 228/25 B.C. He was followed by Aristo of Ceos, who in his turn was succeeded by Critolaus of Phaselis in Lycia. The last-mentioned together with the

Stoic Diogenes and the Academician Carneades was a member of an embassy which was sent to Rome on a political
mission in the year 155 B.C. During their stay in the city they
held public lectures and thus brought the Romans for the
first time into real contact with Greek philosophy. The philosophic achievements of the later Peripatetics, of whom Hermippus and Sotion deserve mention, seem to have been confined almost entirely to the transmission of the Peripatetic
doctrines. They seem to have been mainly interested in practical philosophy, although the lectures of Lyco, Aristo and
Critolaus were famous for their form. Critolaus defended
the eternity of the world against the Stoics. His theories approximated, however, more closely to theirs in that like
Strato, he regarded æther as the substrate of the divine and
human *nous*. No further development of the Peripatetic philosophy took place. It was replaced more and more by
learned research until Andronicus' edition of Aristotle gave
a new impulse to the study of the works of its founder.

HELLENISTIC PHILOSOPHY. STOA. THE LATER CYNICISM. EPICUREANISM. SCEPTICISM. ECLECTICISM

57. *Character of Hellenistic philosophy*

The revolution which the rise of the Macedonian power and the conquests of Alexander had caused in the life of the Greek people was bound to have a profound influence on science. Whereas in the countries of the south and east an immeasurable field of work was opened up, minds were quickened by an abundance of new ideas, new international, social and educational centres were created and the Greek schools received an influx of Hellenised oriental pupils and teachers, the Greek motherland, robbed of its independence and political activity, became an object of contention for foreigners and the scene of their strife. The prosperity and population of the country declined steadily. The old beliefs had long ceased to have any moral influence, and now that the disappearance of a vigorous political activity which had been directed to high and liberal ends removed a strong controlling influence, morality threatened to become swamped in the petty interests of private life, in the pursuit of enjoyment and gain and in the struggle for daily subsistence. Under these circumstances it was natural that the desire and power of a free and purely scientific view of the world should disappear; that practical problems should come to the fore and philosophy should find its chief value in providing a refuge from the miseries of life; yet for this, too, the speculative tastes of the Greek people and the conviction which since Socrates had become firmly rooted found a definite scientific theory indispensable. It is however easy to understand that this mission of philosophy could only be fulfilled if the individual made himself independent of all external circumstances and withdrew completely into his inner life, and that human communities, in accordance with the conditions in the Alexandrian and Roman world, were commended by those who ascribed any value to them more in a cosmopolitan than a political sense. Hence in the systems of Hellenistic philosophy ethics and social theory occupy the most prominent positions, while they go back to the speculations of the pre-Socratic thinkers, especially Heraclitus and Democritus, for their metaphysical basis. Until Aristotle there had been no definite division between philosophy and science. In Hellenistic times the separate sciences began to break loose from philosophy and found in Alexandria, Antioch, Pergamon and later in Rhodes, richly equipped centres for their activities. Eratosthenes was the first to call himself a scholar, is definite distinction from the philosophers. The last who attempted to combine philosophy and science in a comprehensive system was Posidonius. In general however philosophy and the separate sciences tended to drift further and further apart. In this period, too, Athens remained the centre of philosophy and continued to be so until the end of the ancient world. But whereas philosophy and science now went different ways, religion and philosophy now tended to become united. Philosophy began gradually to emerge from the narrow circles of the schools within which it had been the property of a powerful, if only intellectual, aristocracy. It became popular and tried to provide a substitute for the discredited ideas of popular religion. It made use of the methods of proselytism which were especially characteristic of the oriental religions and found in the Cynic and Stoic diatribes, the popular philosophic sermon and the literary tract powerful instruments for the dissemination of their ideas. The proud

reserve which philosophy had exhibited in its older aristocratic representatives, especially in the Pre-Socratic period,
was now broken down. It won however an influence on the
life of the public to an extent which it possessed neither in
the middle ages nor in modern times. Its influence was
strengthened, too, by the fact that, apart from many garrulous and ostentatious hangers-on, not a few of these Hellenistic philosophers not only taught but lived their philosophy
either at the courts of princes, where they filled the office of
spiritual advisors, or in the bustle of the great cities, where
they gathered the multitude around them.

The two chief systems of this period, the Stoa and Epicureanism, returned to the principles of the old Ionic monism. Even in the Academy the Pythagorean-Platonic dualism
made way for a sceptical mode of thought. It was only at the
end of our period that it emerged from its obscurity to
achieve in the last period of ancient philosophy a new popularity.

I. THE STOIC PHILOSOPHY

58. *The earlier Stoa*

The founder of the Stoic school was Zeno of Citium in
Cyprus, a Greek city with a Phœnician element. His death
seems to have taken place 262/261 B.C., his birth, since he
was then about seventy-two years old (according to Persæus
in VII, 28, against which nothing is proved by the inter-
polated letter *ibid.,* 9) in 334/33. Of Semitic extraction, he
came to Athens in his twenty-second year and attached himself to the Cynic Crates and later to Stilpo, while he availed
himself also of the instruction of the Megarean Diodorus
and the Academician Polemo. About 300 B.C. he came forward as a teacher and philosophic author. His pupils were
called at first Zenonians, but afterwards Stoics from the Stoa
Poikile, their meeting place. Honoured for the loftiness of
his character both by the Athenians and the Macedonian
king, Antigonus Gonatas, he died a voluntary death. He was
succeeded by Cleanthes of Assus in the Troad, a man of

singular strength of will, self-sufficiency and moral strictness, but distinguished more by the warmth of his religious feelings, which he expressed in his famous hymn to Zeus, than by the versatility of his thought. He was born *c.* 304/03 and died *c.* 233/32 at the same age as Zeno by voluntary starvation. Besides Cleanthes the following are the most important among Zeno's personal pupils: his countryman Persæus, with whom he lived, Aristo of Chius and Herillus of Carthage, Sphærus of Bosporus, the tutor of the Spartan king, Cleomenes, the poet Aratus of Soli in Cilicia, famous for his didactic poem on astronomy, which begins also with a hymn to Zeus. Cleanthes' successor was Chrysippus of Solsus (ol., 143, 208/04 B.C., died at the age of seventy-three, consequently born in 281/77), the shrewd dialectician and industrious scholar was honoured as its second founder; for he not only contributed greatly to the spread of the Stoic doctrines by his numerous writings, which are however too diffuse and careless in style and exposition, but made the system into a complete whole and reconciled the factions which threatened to split the school. Chrysippus was succeeded by two of his pupils, first Zeno of Tarsus and then Diogenes of Seleucia (Diogenes the Babylonian), who also took part in the embassy of philosophers to Rome in 155 B.C. (v.p. 205) but probably did not long survive it. Of the numerous pupils of Diogenes, Antipater of Tarsus (died 129 B.C.) was his successor in the chair at Athens, while Archedemus, also of Tarsus founded a school in Babylon.

59. *Character and divisions of the Stoic system*

Of the numerous writings of the Stoic philosophers in the first three centuries of the school only fragments remain. The later accounts usually treat the Stoic doctrine as a whole without expressly saying what belongs to Zeno and what belongs only to his successors, especially Chrysippus. We can therefore only set forth the system in the form which it had after Chrysippus and at the same time note the differences of doctrine within the school so far as they are known to us or can with probability be conjectured.

What led the founder of the Stoic system to philosophy was in the first instance the necessity of finding a firm support for his moral life. At first he sought to satisfy this need with the Cynic Crates. His followers also regarded themselves as the descendants of the Cynic branch of the Socratic school. When asked who came nearest their ideal of a sage they always bracketed Diogenes and Antisthenes with Socrates. Like these philosophers their object was to make men happy and independent by virtue. They followed them in defining philosophy as the practice of virtue (studium virtutis, sed per ipsam virtutem, Sen., *ep.* 89, 8) and made the values of theoretical enquiry dependent on its significance for the moral life. Their conception of moral duties, too, resembles that of the Stoics. But what fundamentally divided the Stoa from Cynicism and carried even its founder beyond them, was the importance which the Stoics attached to scientific research. The final end of philosophy lies for them in its influence on man's moral state. But true morality is impossible without knowledge; virtuous and wise are regarded as synonymous, while philosophy, although identified with the practice of virtue, is nevertheless defined as "knowledge of the human and the divine". When Herillus declared knowledge to be the highest good and the final object of life, that signified a return from Zeno to Aristotle. It was, however, an attempt to keep Stoicism within the bounds of Cynicism when Aristo despised not only culture and learning but repudiated all knowledge of dialectics and physics on the grounds that the former was useless and the latter passed beyond the possibility of human knowledge. In the same spirit he attached a value only to the discussion of ethical principles while declaring the special rules of life to be unnecessary. Zeno himself saw in scientific knowledge the indispensable condition of moral conduct, and borrowed from the Academics the division of philosophy into logic, physics and ethics (v.p. 152). For the systematic basis of ethics he went back primarily to Heraclitus, whose physics most appealed to him through its uncompromising working out of the idea that all individual things in the world are only manifestations of one and the same primary substance

and that there is a law which governs the course of nature
and which should govern human action. He was repelled on
the other hand by the dualism of the Platonic and the Aristotelian metaphysics, which placed the action of necessity by
the side of that of reason in the world and thereby seemed
to endanger the absolute rule of reason in human life. Moreover the idealism and spiritualism of Plato and Aristotle,
apart from the difficulties in which it had involved its authors, could not be reconciled with the nominalism which
Zeno had derived from Antisthenes, and the theory seemed
to him too little suited to secure a firm basis for conduct that
he could contribute to it. The more decidedly did he and his
school adopt the Socratic-Platonic teleology and the belief in
providence involved in it. In his physics he supplemented the
theories of Heraclitus by those of Aristotle. Still greater was
the influence of the Peripatetic logic on the Stoic, especially
after Chrysippus. In ethics, too, Zeno endeavoured to temper
the harshness and severity of Cynicism. Thus the Stoic philosophy is by no means a mere continuation of the Cynic. It
altered and supplemented it on all sides making use of everything that the earlier systems had to offer.

The three divisions of philosophy, which the Stoics enumerated (although Cleanthes added rhetoric to logic, politics
to ethics and theology to physics) were not always taught in
the same order and opinion varied as to the relative value,
the highest place being assigned sometimes to physics as the
knowledge of "divine things", and sometimes to ethics as
the science which is most important for men. Zeno and
Chrysippus belonged to those who began with logic; they
followed this by physics and ended with ethics.

60. *The Stoic logic*

Under the name Logic, which Zeno was perhaps the first
to use, the Stoics after Chrysippus comprehended all inquiries which dealt with inward or outward speech. They divided it therefore into rhetoric and dialectic. The latter is
sometimes made to include the theory of criteria and defini-

tions which, however, is sometimes treated as an independent science.

In dialectic they distinguished the theory of the sign from the thing signified. Under the former they included poetics, musical theory and grammar, to the development of which in Alexandrian and Roman times Stoicism largely contributed. The theory of the thing signified corresponds in all essentials to our formal logic, while that of the criteria contains the theory of knowledge which was held by the school.

In contrast to Plato and Aristotle the Stoics were pronounced empiricists. Antisthenes had ascribed reality only to the particular things. Zeno concluded from this that all knowledge must proceed from perception of the particular. According to the Stoic doctrine the soul at birth is like a clean tablet (cf. p. 164, 1; hence the expression "tabula rasa" in the Scholastic Philosophy and Locke). It must receive its contents from the objects; representation is according to Zeno and Cleanthes an impression of the things in the soul, and according to Chrysippus a change produced by them in the soul. We derive our knowledge of inner states and activities also from perception (according to Chrysippus). But since these, too, consist of material processes, the Stoics did not need to assume any distinction between internal and external perception.

From the perceptions arise recollections and from these experience. By inferences from the data of perception we arrive at general concepts. So far as these are derived from nature and simply from generally known experiences[1] they form the "common concepts", which are presupposed by all scientific inquiries and were called Prolepses, a term borrowed from Epicurus and apparently used for the first time by Chrysippus. Science proceeds by fixed methods of proof and building of concepts. Its peculiar advantage is that, in contrast to opinion, it consists of a conviction which can be shaken by no objections or of a system of such convictions. As all our representations have their origin in perception, their epistemological value depends on the question whether there are perceptions of which it is certain that they agree with the perceived objects. This was maintained by the

Stoics. They held that a part of our representations are so constituted that they compel us to give assent to them in that they are connected with consciousness; that they can only originate in something real in that they are directly evident. Hence, if we assent to them, we apprehend the object itself. According to Zeno, it is in this assent to a representation that the concept consists. The concept has therefore the same content as the mere representation, but is distinguished from it through its consciousness of its agreement with the object and through the unchangeability which results from this. A representation which carries this consciousness with it is called by Zeno a "conceptual representation" (i.e., one that is fitted to apprehend its object). He asserts accordingly that the conceptual representation is the criterion of truth. Since however the "common concepts" are a consequence of perceptions, they too can be regarded as natural norms of the truth, and *Æthesis* and *Prolepsis* could both be termed criteria by Chrysippus. The possibility of knowledge in general was proved by the Stoics in the last resort by the assertion that otherwise no conduct based in reasonable conviction would be possible. That, however, involved them in the contradiction that on the one hand they made perception the standard of truth and, on the other expected perfectly certain knowledge only from science. This, of course, answered not only the demands of science, but also the practical requirements of a system which made the virtue and happiness of man dependent on their subordination to a general "law".

The part of dialectic which corresponds to our formal logic deals with what is signified or expressed and this is either incomplete or complete, in the form of concepts and propositions respectively. The most important part of their treatment of concepts is the theory of categories. The Stoics enumerated only four instead of the ten Aristotelian categories. These are so related that each gives a closer definition of the one which precedes and contains this in it. They are the substrate, the essential constitution, which is further subdivided into the accidental constitution and the relative accidental constitution. The generic concept under which all categories fall was called by some (probably Zeno) Being and by others (Chrysippus) the Something, which was further subdivided into Being and Not-being. Of the complete statements or propositions, judgments or assertions are those which are either true or false.

The Stoics divided these into simple (categoric) and compound, and of the latter they devoted particular attention to hypothetical judgments. In their treatment of syllogisms too they gave such prominence to the hypothetical and the disjunctive that they held that only these were to be regarded as inferences in the proper sense. The scientific value of this logic is very slight. Although in a few details the Stoics made a more precise examination, the pedantic external formalism which Chrysippus especially introduced into logic could not promote the progress of the science as a whole.

61. *The Stoic physics: first principles and the universe*

The metaphysical system of the Stoics is governed by a threefold tendency. In contrast to the Platonic-Aristotelian metaphysics it concentrates on the unity of final cause and the world-order which arises from it: it is monistic. In contrast to their idealism it is realistic and even materialistic. Nevertheless when their ethical principles demanded it, they regarded everything in the world as the work of reason and the absolute reason as the ultimate basis of the world. Their point of view was essentially teleological and even their monism developed into pantheism.

According to the Stoic doctrines corporeal objects constitute the only reality. For only what acts or endures is real and this quality belongs only to corporeal nature. They declared, therefore, not only all substances, not excepting the human soul and the deity, to be corporeal but also that all qualities of things consist of something corporeal, of air-currents which are diffused throughout them and impart to them the tension which holds them together. And since this is naturally true also of the soul-bodies, virtues, emotions, wisdom, walking, etc., as states of the soul, are also called bodies and living beings. It was, of course, an unavoidable inconsistency that empty space, place, time and thought were not to be regarded as bodies. In order to explain from their standpoint how the soul is spread throughout the body and the qualities of things throughout the things to their whole extent, the Stoics denied in their theory of the universal intermingling the impermeability of bodies. They asserted that one body could permeate another in all its parts, without, however, becoming one substance with it. Nevertheless, in spite of their materialism, they distinguished between matter and the forces which work in it. Matter taken by itself is without qualities. All qualities or things are derived from the rational force which permeates it. Even the filling up of space is produced by two motions, a condensing motion which proceeds inwards and a rarefying motion which proceeds outwards. All forces at work in the world can however arise only from one original force, as is shown by the unity of the world and the connection and agreement of all its parts. Like all that is real, this one force must also be corporeal. It is warm breath or, what is the same, fire; for it is warmth that begets, animates and moves all things. On the other hand the perfection and finality of the world-structure and especially the rationality of human nature shows that this final world-cause must at the same time be the most perfect reason, the most beneficent and philanthropic of all beings, in a word God. It is this because it consists of the most perfect substance. Since everything in the world owes its qualities, its motion and its life to it, it must bear the same relation to the universe as soul to our body. It permeates all things as the pneuma or the artificial fire which animates them and contains the seeds of the forms within itself. It is the soul, mind and the reason of the world, providence, fate, nature, universal law, etc.; for all these ideas denote the same object from different aspects. Just as, however, with the human soul, although it is present in the whole body, the dominant part is distinguished from the rest and is assigned a special seat, this happens in a similar way with the soul of the universe. God or Zeus has his seat in the outermost circle of the world (according to

Archedemus in the centre of the world, according to Cleanthes in the sun) and is from here diffused throughout the world. But its distinction from the world is only relative, the distinction between what is directly and what is indirectly divine. In themselves both are the same; it is the same being of which a part assumes the form of the world, while another retains its original form and in that shape appears as the moving cause or the Deity.

In order to form the world, God first transformed a part of the fiery vapour of which he consists into air and then into water, in which he was immanent as the formative force. He then caused a part of the water to be precipitated as earth; another part remained water and a third was turned into air, and after rarefaction this became the elementary fire. Thus the body of the world was formed as distinguished from its soul, the Deity. But this opposition which has arisen in time will likewise pass away in the course of time. After the present world-period has run its course, a conflagration will transform all things into a huge mass of fiery vapour: Zeus takes back the world into himself, to emit it again at a preordained time. Thus the history of the world is an endless succession of creation and destruction. Since however this motion always obeys the same laws, all the innumerable successions of worlds are so exactly similar that the same persons, things and events occur in them all down to the minutest detail. For an inviolable necessity, an unbreakable chain of cause and effect determines all events. This is perfectly consistent in so strict a pantheistic system and it is expressed in the Stoic definitions of fate or destiny, nature and providence. The human will, too, is no exception in this connection. A man acts voluntarily so far as it is his own impulse that determines him; and he is also free to do what fate ordains, that is with his own assent; but he must do it under all circumstances: volentem fata ducunt, nolentem trahunt. On this connection of all things rests the unity of the world; on the rationality of the cause from which it proceeds depend its beauty and perfection; and the more eagerly the Stoics strove to establish their belief in providence by proofs of every kind, the less could they escape the problem of proving the complete perfection of the world and defending it against the obvious objections which the existence of numerous evils would suggest. Chrysippus seems to have been the chief author of this physico-theology and theodicy. We know, however, that it was he who worked out the proposition that the world was made for gods and men with the most petty and superficial teleology. Although the basic idea of the Stoic theodicy, that the imperfection of the individual subserves the perfection of the whole, became the model for all later attempts, nevertheless, the problem of reconciling moral wickedness with their theological determinism became the more difficult the more lurid the colours in which they painted the extent and power of this evil (v.p. 239ff.).

62. *Nature and man*

In their theories on nature the Stoics, as was to be expected in the existing state of natural science, adhered less to Heraclitus than Aristotle. Apart from a minor deviation they followed Aristotle in their theory of the four elements and whereas they found it unnecessary to postulate æther as a fifth, they made a distinction between the æthereal and the terrestrial fire, the former moving in a circle and the latter in a straight line. The Stoics insisted again and again that all elementary substances pass continually into one another and that all things are in a state of perpetual change; and it is on this that the cohesion of the world depends. They did not thereby intend to deny any fixed state of things nor like Aristotle to limit this change to the sublunary world.

In their views on the structure of the universe they adhered to the prevailing theories. They imagined the stars as fixed in their spheres; their fire was renewed by exhalations from the earth and water; their divinity and rationality were deduced from the purity of this fire. The whole realm of nature was divided into four parts, which were distinguished by the fact that in inorganic things the creative pneuma is operative as a mere *hexis,* i.e., through the cohesion of their parts; in plants as the formative force of nature, in animals as the desiring soul and in men as the rational soul. Every living being has from its birth onwards a consciousness of itself, which is explained by the close connection of body and soul. From this grows self-love and the instinct of self-preservation, which is the indispensable condition for the survival of all beings.

Of these beings man has the greatest interest for our philosopher, and in man the soul. It is, like every real thing, of corporeal nature and it arises together with the body in the physical way of begetting; but its matter is the purest and the noblest, a part of the divine fire which descended from the æther into bodies of men when they were first created and passes from the parents to the children as an offshoot of their souls. This soul-fire is nourished by the blood. It is in the centre of the circulation of the blood, in the heart, that (according to Zeno, Cleanthes and Chrysippus, etc., from whom only a few authors deviate) the dominant part of the soul has its seat. From here it puts out its seven offshoots, namely the five senses and the powers of speech and reproduction, to their repective organs. But the seat of the personality lies only in the dominant part as the reason, to which both the lower and higher activities of the soul belong, and in the power of which the decisions of the will and assent to the representations rest, both, however, only in the sense which the Stoic determinism permits. After death the souls were supposed to endure until the end of the world, when they returned with everything else to God. Whereas, however, Cleanthes supported that this happened in the case of all, Chrysippus held that only those souls which had gained sufficient strength for this, namely those of the wise, could so return. In the Stoic system, therefore, there was nothing that resembled a belief in personal immortality.

63. *The Stoic ethics: its general principles*

Although everything obeys world-wide laws, man is enabled by his reason to know these laws and to follow them consciously. This is the leading idea of the Stoic moral the-

ory. Their fundamental principle is in general the life according to nature. That this was first formulated by Zeno's
successors, while he himself demanded only a life at harmony with itself (Arius Did. in Stob. II, 7, 6a, p. 75, 11W.),
is all the more improbable in that Diog. VII, 87 says precisely
the opposite and that Zeno's teacher Polemo had laid stress
on the natural life. If Cleanthes denoted the nature according to which life must be lived as the common nature and
Chrysippus the general and in particular human nature, the
correction is really nothing more than verbal.

The most general natural instinct is that of self-preservation. For each being only that can have a value which con-
tributes to his self-preservation and his happiness. Hence for
rational beings only what is reasonable can have any value;
only virtue is a good for them, it is only in virtue that their
happiness can consist, which is therefore affected by no further conditions (virtue is self-sufficiency for happiness). Con-
versely the only evil is wickedness (*kakia*). Everything else
is indifferent; life, health, honour, possessions, etc., are not
goods; death, disease, insult, poverty, etc., are not evils. Least
of all may pleasure be held for a good at all, to say nothing
of the highest good, or sought for its own sake. It is a result of our activity if this is of the right kind (for correct conduct ensures the only true satisfaction); but it may not be
the aim of our actions (cf. Arist., p. 207). While not all the
Stoics went so far as Cleanthes, who did not reckon pleasure
among the things according to nature, nevertheless they all
denied that it has any value in itself. They sought therefore
the real happiness of the virtuous man predominantly in
freedom from disturbance, tranquillity and inward independence. As virtue alone is a good for man, the effort to
attain it is the general law of his nature. This concept of law
and duty is given far more prominence by the Stoics than
the earlier moralists. Since however we have in us besides
rational also irrational and uncontrolled impulses or affects
(which Zeno reduced to four chief affects—pleasure, lust,
anxiety and fear), the Stoic virtue is essentially a struggle
with the affects. They are something opposed to reason and
morbid, they should not be merely moderated (as the Acad-

emicians and the Peripatetics thought) but eradicated. We have to attain freedom from affects, "apathia". In contrast to the affects, virtue consists in the rational constitution of the soul. Its first condition is right opinions on what we have to do and what not to do; for we always strive (as Zeno following Socrates says) after what we hold to be good, even if it lies in our power to give or refuse our assent to an opinion on this. Virtue is therefore defined as knowledge and vice as ignorance, while the affects are attributed to false judgments of value. But the Stoics imagined moral knowledge as so closely bound up with strength of mind and will, which Cleanthes especially stressed, that the nature of virtue is to be found equally well in them. Zeno held that meditation was the common source of all virtues, Cleanthes strength of soul and Aristo the health of the soul. After Chrysippus it became usual to find it in wisdom as the science of human and divine things. From this four basic virtues were derived, of which the most important, meditation, was subdivided into bravery, self-control and justice. Cleanthes, however, replaced meditation by endurance. According to Aristo (and at bottom also Cleanthes), the different virtues were distinguished from one another only by the objects in which they express themselves; Chrysippus and later writers held that there were qualitative differences between them. They adhered however to the principle that they were all indissolubly connected as expressions of one and the same character, so that where one virtue is all must be and similarly where one vice is all must be. Therefore all virtues are equal in value and all vices equally to be condemned. Only the character comes into consideration. It alone makes fulfilment of duty virtuous conduct; it is immaterial in what form it expresses itself. This character the Stoics believed could either be wholly present or wholly absent. Virtue and vice are essential qualities which admit of no difference of degree. Hence there is no mean between them, we cannot possess them partially, but either have or not have them. We can only be virtuous or depraved, only a wise man or a fool; the transition from foolishness to wisdom is instantaneous; those who are still progressing still belong to the fools. The wise man is the ideal of all perfection and, since this is the sole condition of happiness, it is the ideal of all happiness; the fool is the ideal of all depravity and misery. The former is alone free (as the Stoics expounded with declamatory pathos), alone beautiful, rich, happy, etc. He possesses all virtues and all knowledge; in all things he alone acts rightly; he is the only true king, statesman, poet, prophet, pilot, etc. He is completely free from needs and sorrow and is the only friend of the gods. His virtue is something which he can never lose (Chrysippus makes an exception for the case disease of mind); his happiness is equal to that of Zeus and cannot be increased by the time which it lasts. The fool for his part is completely bad and miserable, a slave, a beggar, an ignoramus; he can do no good or anything that is not wrong; all fools are mad. The Stoics believed that all men are fools with but few rapidly disappearing exceptions. Even to the most celebrated statesmen and heroes they made at most the inconsistent concession that they are afflicted with the common failings, only to a less degree than the others. The extent and depth of human depravity was described by later adherents of the school like Seneca, in colours as lurid as those of the contemporary and later Christian theologians.

In all this the Stoics followed essentially the principles of Cynicism, with the differences, however, which resulted from their scientific basis and method of exposition. Yet Zeno could not hide from himself the fact that these principles required considerable moderation and limitation. These moderations were not only the conditions on which alone they could pass beyond the narrow limits of a sect and become an historical power, but they were the result of the general hypotheses of the Stoic ethics. For a system which recognised in practice accordance with nature, and in theory universal conviction as standards, could not place itself in so glaring a contradiction to either as Antisthenes and Diogenes had not hesitated to do. Hence in the theory of goods three classes of morally indifferent things are distinguished; those which are in accordance with nature and therefore have a value, are desirable and are to be preferred for themselves alone; those which are contrary to nature and consequently

have no value and are to be avoided; and finally those
which have neither value nor its opposite, the "adiaphora"
in a narrow sense. Aristo, who contested this distinction and
regarded complete indifference to it as man's highest aim,
exposed himself by this return from Zeno to Antisthenes to
the objection that he made all action on principle impossible.
Herillus deviated from Zeno in asserting that a moral of
the morally indifferent things could, without being referred
to the final aim of life, nevertheless form an independent
and separate aim. It was only by this modification of their
theory of values that the Stoics made it possible to gain a
positive relation to the problems of practical life; but not
seldom they made use of it in a way which was not consistent with the strictness of the Stoic principles. The conditioned or "middle" duties, which are distinguished from the
perfect duties, are referred to the relation to the desirable
and the worthless; for in all these we have to do with precepts which under circumstances can lose their force. Furthermore, just as a conditioned valuation of certain "adiaphora" is permitted and indeed demanded, the apathy of
the wise man is so far moderated that it is said that incipient
affects occur in him, too, without however gaining his assent, and that certain rational emotions are found in him
alone. Finally the less the Stoics dared to indicate anyone of
their number as a wise man and the more doubtful they became in their assertions about a Socrates or a Diogenes, the
more unavoidable was it that the abrupt contrast of the wise
and foolish should lose more and more of its practical value
and should finally come to contain no more than an ideal
and regulative significance, so that the "proficients" received
an intermediary position between the wise and the foolish
and finally attained such importance in the Stoic accounts
that they became almost indistinguishable from the wise.

64. *Continuation. Applied morals. Theory of society. Relation to religion*

The detailed discussion of particular moral relations and
problems was a common feature of the post-Aristotelian phi-

losophy. The Stoics (with the exception of Aristo, cf. p. 209) were particularly prone to them. They seemed to have had a particular predilection for the casuistic questions raised by the collision of duties, the more so that such discussion provided them with an opportunity for the display of their dialectic art. But however important these detailed treatments may have been for the practical influence of the Stoic ethics and for the spread of purer moral ideas, their scientific value seems to have been very slight and their treatment not seldom characterised by a regrettable triviality. As far as they are known to us they exhibit a double tendency; to make the individual independent in his moral self-assurance of all externals and to do justice to the problems which arise from his relation to the greater whole of which he is a part. On the one side lie the features which characterise Stoicism as the descendant of Cynicism and on the other those whereby it supplements and passes beyond Cynicism. The complete independence of all that does not influence our moral constitution, the exaltation above all external circumstances and bodily states, the self-sufficiency of the wise man, the needlessness of a Diogenes are all Stoic ideals. The Cynic mode of life was by no means essential, nevertheless it was considered worthy of a philosopher, should circumstances permit. The principle that the morality of conduct depends only on the inner character and not on the external act, led the Stoics, like their predecessors, into many strange and one-sided assertions; nevertheless what was most repellant and objectionable in their doctrines seems to have been partly a mere hypothesis and partly a conclusion from the opinions which they opposed. Finally in order to secure for man independence in every circumstance, they permitted voluntary withdrawal from life not merely as a refuge in extreme distress, but because they saw in it the final assertion of moral freedom. It is a step by which a man proves that he counts even life along with the indifferent things and which a man is justified in taking as soon as external circumstances make it appear that it would be more in accordance with nature to leave this earthly life than to remain longer in it. We know that Zeno, Cleanthes, Eratosthenes, Antipater and many other Stoics ended their lives in this way.

But however independent the attitude of the Stoic to everything which he himself was not, he nevertheless felt himself closely connected with his kind. In virtue of his rationality, man recognises himself as part of the universe and thereby pledged to work for this whole. He knows that he is related to all rational beings in nature; he sees that they are similar in kind and of equal rights and that they stand under the same law of nature and reason as himself; he regards it as their natural destination to live for one another. The communal instinct is therefore implanted in human nature, which demands the two qualities, justice and love of one's fellow-men which are the fundamental conditions of a community. In the first place the Stoics held that all wise men are naturally friends. They placed indeed so high a value on friendship in general, that they did not quite succeed in reconciling the self-sufficiency of the wise man with the need for friendship. They recognised, too, the moral significance of all other human relations. They recommended marriage but required that it should be carried out in a pure and moral spirit. For politics they had no particular interest; nevertheless of the philosophical schools of later antiquity they made the deepest study of political problems and produced the most independent political characters. For them, however, the connection of a man with the whole of humanity is far more important than his connection with his nation. Cosmopolitanism took the place of politics, a creed of which the Stoics were the most zealous and successful prophets. In this respect Zeno had followed the Cynics so closely that it was said of his work *On the State* that it was "written on the dog's tail" (Diog. L., VII, 4). Nevertheless the idea of social and communal life formed a sharp contrast to the Cynic idealism. For since it is on the equality of reason in the individual that every human community is based, this must be co-extensive with humanity. All men are interrelated, all have the same origin and destiny, all stand under the same law and are citizens of one state, members of one body. All men have as men a claim to our good-will. Even slaves can claim their rights from us and are shown to be worthy of our esteem. As men we owe even to our enemies mercy and forgiveness and ready support, a view that was expressed repeatedly and emphatically by the Stoics of the Roman empire. This cosmopolitanism was one of the most impressive of the characteristics which made the Stoicism the real representative of the Hellenistic and Roman periods and gave it its significance for the rise and spread of Christianity.

If the community of all rational beings is extended still further we arrive at the conception of the world as a community consisting of gods and men and the necessity of unconditional submission to the laws and requirements of this community. It is in this obedience to the laws of the universe and the submission to destiny, on which the Stoics incessantly insist, that religion from their point of view essentially consists. Piety is knowledge of worship of the gods. But in its essence religion consists in correct notions about the gods, in obedience to their wills, in imitation of their perfection (Sen., *ep.* 95, 47; Epict. *Ench.* 31, 1), in purity of heart and will (Cic. *De nat. deo.*, II, 71; Sen. *Fr.*, 123), in a word in wisdom and virtue. True religion is not different from philosophy. The Stoics found much to criticise in what popular belief contained over and above this.

The impurity of "anthropomorphic beliefs", the unworthiness of the mythical tales of gods and heroes, the inanity of the traditional ceremonies were after the time of Zeno objects of condemnation by members of the school. In spite of this the Stoics as a whole were not opponents but defenders of popular religion, partly because they saw in its general acceptance a proof of its wisdom and partly because they could not decide to withdraw from the masses a support that was indispensable to morality. The real content of mythology (p. 161) was to be determined by philosophical theology: the one God of the Stoics was to be worshipped partly directly and partly indirectly in the form of the gods of mythology; directly under the form of Zeus, whom Cleanthes and Aratus celebrated as the universal God, the origin and the

supporting force of the universe, as a cosmic and moral law
of the universe (p. 209); indirectly in the forms of the
other gods, so far as these are no more than representations
of divine forces, which are revealed to us in the stars, the elements, the fruits of the earth and in the great men and bene-
factors of humanity. The means, however, whereby the
Stoics demonstrated the philosophic truth in the myths was
allegorical interpretation. This procedure which was used
before them only in isolated instances,[2] was first made into a
system by Zeno.

It was then applied by Cleanthes and Chrysippus to such
an extent and with such incredible arbitrariness and want of
taste that could not be surpassed even by their successors on
heathen, Jewish and Christian ground. Prophecy, on which
they laid the greatest value, was treated in the same spirit by
Zeno, Cleanthes and Sphærus but especially by Chrysippus
and his followers. The irrational received here, too, an elaborate rationalisation; in virtue of the connection of all things
future events are predicted by certain natural signs, which
we may come to know and interpret partly by a natural gift
arising from the relationship of God and man and partly by
technical observation. No story of fulfilled prophecy was so
far-fetched or poorly substantiated that it could not be justified by this expedient. Hence although the Stoics may even
before the time of Panætius have distinguished three kinds
of theology—that of philosophers, that of statesmen and that
of poets—and although they may have made trenchant criticism of the last, which is nothing more than the mythology of
popular belief, yet this did not deter them from deprecating
any serious attack on existing religion. We see this in Cleanthes' attitude to Aristarchus of Samos, whom he accused of
atheism in a work directed against him (Diog. L., VII, 174),
on the grounds of his assertion that the earth, "the hearth of
the world", moved of itself (Plut. *De fac.*, 923A) and in
the severity of Marcus Aurelius towards the Christians.

With regard to the historical position of the Stoa, a recent
comparison of the outline of Peripatetic ethics by the Stoic
Arius Didymus preserved in Stobæus (*Ecl.*, II, p. 116-
152W.) with the ethical works of Aristotle and the frag-

ments of Theophrastus has shown that Zeno derived the basic ideas of his ethics through his teacher Polemo (p. 227) from the common ground of the old Academy and the Peripatetics. Thus apart from the idea of life according to nature he owed to the same source that of self-preservation, duty, virtuous conduct and especially the idea of humanity, which can by no means be traced back to the Cynics.

Original, however, was the fusion of all these elements with the Heraclitan physics into a strictly monistic system of pantheism, exhibiting the remarkable combination of an optimistic view of nature with a pessimistic conception of the moral capacity of humanity, the prominence given to the emotions with the Socratic-Platonic intellectualism and finally an imperatival ethics with a clearly defined fatalism, contradictions which were later bound to demand modifications of doctrine.

II. THE LATER CYNICISM

65. *The Cynics of the Hellenistic age*

Cynicism lived on in Hellenistic times side by side with the Stoa; but it is as if it had lost its logical and ethical strength to the latter. The earlier Cynics had laid particular stress on suppression of desire, freedom from needs and physical inurance. This heroic ethics now underwent an obvious moderation in that the essential quality of the Cynic philosopher was replaced by an elasticity and an easy adaptbility to all situations of life. They made a grateful use of the simile of a play written by God or destiny the different rôles of which are allotted to individual men; those of the poor man or the rich, the ruler or the slave, the healthy man or the sick. The wise man must be able to play them all equally well. Other characteristics of Cynicism were of course retained, such as its cosmopolitanism, its criticism of belief in gods, its individualism, its contempt for science and its denial of traditional culture. These were combined with a low estimation of life, which seemed too fleeting and transient to be worth taking seriously. In this lies the reason for the change in the external form of philosophic exposition, which was prepared by Diogenes and Crates (p. 128) and made its appearance among the Cynics of this period—they turned to the satire, the serio-comic, the "ridendo dicere verum". Thus on the one hand the popular philosophic diatribe took the place of a strictly logical exposition, at first with logical constituents through the introduction of fictitious opponents, the prose being broken up by the insertion of numerous passages from the poets and the citation of witty and often coarse anecdotes, with vivid sketches, personifications and antitheses; on the other hand, a sort of parodic poetry which chose the most varied aspects of life as the objects of its ridicule.

The first representative of this new, so-called hedonistic Cynicism was Bion of Borysthenes on the Black Sea. He was the son of a freedman and himself the slave of a rhetor who made him his heir so that he could become familiar with the various tendencies in philosophy in Athens, the Academy, the Peripatetics, Cynicism and the Cyrenaic school. Of these the last two made the greatest impression on him. He succeeded in reconciling the differences between the two systems, so that he did not scorn a lengthy attendance at the court of Antigonus Gonatas (243-240). He wrote diatribes on anger, serfdom, burial, etc., in a style scintillating with brilliant wit and sarcasm, which brought upon him the reproach that he had adorned philosophy in the cloak of an hetæra. We can best obtain an idea of his philosophy and manner of writing from the diatribes of Teles preserved in Stobæus. Teles was engaged in teaching in Megara, *c.* 240 and made use of Bion, besides Aristippus and Stilpo, Diogenes and Crates. They deal with appearance and reality, independence, poverty and wealth, exile, the relations of life, pleasure and the control of the emotions. Menippus of Gadara (*c.* 250 B.C.) went a step further than Bion in the mixture of the serious and the ridiculous. He was also a liberated slave and the pupil of Metrocles. He neglected the systematic side of philosophy and was a satirist through and through: "the secret dog who bites as he laughs". Inspired by the comedy, the satyr-play and the mime, he became the creator of the satire which is called after him, which was imitated by Varro in his *Saturæ Menippeæ,* by Seneca in his *Apocolocyntosis* and especially by Lucian in many of his works. Under various forms (Journeys to Hades, exorcism of the dead, wills, letters to the gods, etc.) he criticised in the sharpest vein human life, belief in gods and the attempts to defend it and also the doctrines of the philosophic schools. The positive content of philosophy dwindled more and more until it finally had nothing more to advise than adaptability and surrender. The Cynic Menedemus seems to have been of more serious character. He was a former pupil of the Epicurean Colotes with whom he engaged in a violent literary controversy.

This later form of Cynicism stimulated a new activity in gnomological poetry. In imitation of the old beggar-poet Hipponax of Ephesus, Phœnix of Colophon (3rd cent.) revived the form of the Choliambus and made it the vehicle of Cynic doctrines. Here may be mentioned further the meliambs of the statesman and general Cercidas of Megalopolis mentioned by Polybius (II, 48ff.), the epigrammatist Poseidippus of Pella, Leonidas of Tarentum (3rd cent.) and Meleager of Gadara (1st cent. B.C.), who imitated his countryman Menippus.

III. THE EPICUREAN PHILOSOPHY

66. *Epicurus and his school*

The rival brother of the Stoa was Epicureanism, which was engaged in constant controversy with the other school and yet had many points in common with it. Its founder was Epicurus (341-270). The son of an Attic "clerouch" and born in Samos, he heard in his early years the Democritean Nausiphanes in Teos, spent his "ephebus" year in Athens in 323 and then devoted himself to study in Colophon for twelve years, a fact which explains his claim to be self-taught. In the year 310 he founded a school in Mitylene, which he later transferred to Lampsacus and in 306 to Athens. Here the permanent headquarters of the school were his house and garden, which he bequeathed to it in his will. This gave rise to the name by which his adherents, who included women and slaves, were called—"the philosophers of the garden". He carried on an extensive correspondence with his friends abroad, both with individuals and whole philosophical schools. As head of the school he was worshipped during his life and after his death with almost divine reverence. This is the reason why his basic doctrines, despite vigorous controversy on isolated points, retained dogmatic authority in the following centuries. This was further supported by the fact that his main theories were collected together at an early date in concise collections of dicta, which were intended to be learned off by heart. Epicurus regarded philosophy as a medicine for the soul. The aim of the acquisition of knowledge is not mere knowing as such, but the practical regulation of life; hence his contempt for the special sciences. Epicurus' name has without justification become proverbial for a life of pleasure. Those who knew him praised his contentedness, his tenderness and goodness, qualities to which his last note, written shortly before his death to his pupil Idomeneus (Diog. L., X, 22), bears witness. Of Epicurus' writings, which comprised some 300 volumes, only a little has been preserved. Most important are the three didactic letters to Herodotus, Pythocles and Menœcus in the tenth book of Diogenes Lærtius. Of these the first and the third contain a short outline of the physics and the ethics and were certainly written by Epicurus himself, while the second, which is perhaps the work of a pupil, is nevertheless a trustworthy extract from the works of Epicurus and deals with meteorology. Of Epicurus' chief work *On Nature* (thirty-seven books) fragments have been preserved in the so-called Herculanean rolls, which formed a part of the library of the Epicurean Piso (probably the consul, L. Piso, 58 B.C.). He expounded his theory of knowledge in a book which bore the title the *Canon*. Of his other numerous works the three most important on ethical subjects may be mentioned: *On the Highest Good*, *What Is to Be Sought and Avoided* and *On Lives*.

Together with Epicurus his pupils Metrodorus, Hermarchus and Polyænus were regarded as spiritual fathers of the school. Of these Metrodorus of Lampsacus, who was a man of no great originality, but on that account the more faithful an adherent of his master, died seven years before him. Polyænus, too, who was also of Lampsacus, met an earlier death than his master. Hermarchus of Mitylene, who succeeded him in the headship of the school, wrote among other things a work comprising two volumes on Empedocles, whose philosophy and especially its mystical tendency, he subjected to a searching criticism. Apart from these men Colopes was a prominent member of the school. Fragments of his literary polemic against Plato are preserved in the Herculanean rolls, while his pupil Menedemus went over to the Cynics and was attacked by Plutarch in a special work.

The successor of Hermarchus, Polystratus, wrote *c.* 230 B.C. a remarkable work *On the Unfounded Contempt of Popular Opinion* in which he contested the Sophistic view of the conventional origin of moral ideas and their invalidity which resulted from this opinion. Considerable remains of this work have been preserved to us through the Herculanean rolls. Philonides of Laodicæa, who occupied a prominent position at the court of Antiochus Epiphanes (175-164 B.C.), departed, both in his political activity and his interest in mathematical problems from the principles of the school. He collected, however, and made extracts of the works of Epicurus and his friends probably for the library in Antioch. To the second half of the 2nd cent. B.C. belong Apollodorus, the so-called "lord of the garden", who wrote over 400 works, and Zeno of Sidon, whom Cicero held in high esteem. Dependent on these were Phædrus, who was scholarch in Athens between 78 and 70. Cicero heard him in Rome about 90 B.C. and used his work *On the Gods* in his own work of similar title between 78-80. Apart from him may be mentioned Siro, the teacher of the poet Virgil and his friend Alfenus Varus, and Philodemus of Gadara, the contemporary of Cicero and protégé of his opponent L. Calpurnius Piso Cæsonius (p. 249). Of the numerous works which this questionable Epicurean threw off in rapid succession the Herculanean rolls contain considerable remains; thus for example of his works *On Defects of Character* which is manifestly indebted to the works of the Peripatetic Aristo of Ceos, *On Vain-Glory, On Anger, On Death* (B4), *On Piety, On the Gods, On Music,* etc. Long before this Epicureanism had spread to Rome; about 150 B.C. there were Latin prose writings of Epicurean content by C. Amafinius (Cic., *Tusc.,* IV, 3, 6ff.). The Epicurean doctrines however were proclaimed with the greatest enthusiasm to the Roman people by T. Lucretius Carus (91-51 B.C.) in his poem *De Rerum Natura* (6B.) as a gospel of liberation from all superstitious madness. Lucretius seems to have been closely connected with the physician Asclepiades of Prusa or Cios in Bithynia, who lived in Rome at that time and was also a devotee of the Epicurean philosophy. After the early death of the poet his work was edited by Cicero. It formed for the whole of after times the only complete exposition and the chief source of information of the Epicurean system.

67. *The Epicurean system: general. The Canonic*

With Epicurus far more exclusively than with Zeno his philosophic system was simply meant to be a guide for practical problems. He had little use for learned research or the mathematical sciences, to which he objected that they were useless and did not correspond to reality. His own education was in both connections very perfunctory. Among the branches of philosophy he valued only that part of dialectics concerned with the criterion. This part of his system he called the Canonic. Of physics he said that we only need it because the knowledge of natural causes frees us from fear of the gods and death, while knowledge of human nature shows us what we have to desire and avoid. Hence this part of philosophy, too, has no independent significance.

If the empiricism and the materialism of Stoicism are connected with its one-sided interest in practical life, the same connection is to be observed still more strongly in Epicurus. It is fully in accordance with an ethical system which asserts the full independence of the individual that only the particular, material object is considered to be real and original, and sense-perception to be the source of our ideas. If man finds his greatest problem in keeping his individual life free from disturbances, he will not try to find signs of a reason in the universe on which he has to support himself and to whose laws he must submit, nor will he make any attempt to provide a theoretical basis for his conduct through knowledge of these laws. The world appears to him as a mechanism within which he arranges his life to the best of his ability. He has no need to know more of it than concerns his own woe or weal. For this purpose experience and the natural understanding seem to suffice without much logical apparatus.

From this point of view Epicurus in the Canonic regards perception as the criterion of truth in theory, while in practice (§ 69) it is the feeling of pleasure or pain. Perception is the obvious, which is always true; we cannot doubt it without making both knowledge and action impossible (cf. p. 232). Deceptions of the senses prove nothing against it, for the error lies here not in perception but in judgment. The image which we believed we saw (cf. p. 255) did really touch our soul, but we have no right to suppose that it corresponds to an object or that it is a perfect representation of an object. (We do not hear what will enable us to distinguish the images to which an object corresponds from those to which none corresponds.) From perceptions, which penetrate[3] us in the form of images or influences, ideas or generic concepts[4] are formed by memory, in that what has been repeatedly perceived stamps itself on the memory. Since these concepts are always related to previous perceptions, they are always true. Hence besides perception and feelings, concepts can be reckoned among the criteria. Since imaginative ideas are according to Epicurus also produced by the actual objective images present to the soul (cf. p. 255), these are also included in the criteria. It is only when we pass beyond perception as such, when we form from the known an opinion on the unknown, that the question arises whether this opinion is true or false. In order to be true, an opinion, if it refers to future events, must be confirmed by experience; if it refers to the hidden causes of phenomena it must not be contradicted by experience. Epicurus mentions in Diog. X, 22 four ways in which we may proceed from perception to conjecture; but no scientific theory of induction is found in his own works or in his school, however notable the attempt which Zeno of Sidon (p. 250) made (as appears from Philodemus II. *On Signs and Interpretations*) to justify inductive-analogical methods of inference against the attacks of the Stoa.

Remarkable is the Epicurean philosophy of language, which departed from Democritus in regarding language not as a product of convention, but as something natural and necessary, and in explaining its origin by comparison with expressions of feeling in animals.

68. *The physics of Epicurus: the gods*

Epicurus' view of nature was in the first instance determined by the wish to exclude all interference of supernatural influence in the course of the world, since this deprives man of his peace of mind and keeps him in constant fear of incalculable powers. He hoped to attain this most surely by a purely mechanical explanation of nature. In his search for such an explanation among the older systems (for he was neither inclined nor qualified to form a theory of his own on natural science) he found none which suited his purpose more completely than that which also seemed to offer the best basis for his ethical individualism. This system which was the first to attract him and was perhaps the only one of which he had any detailed knowledge was the atomism of Democritus. Epicurus followed Democritus in asserting that atoms and empty space are the basic constituents of all things. Things consist partly of aggregates, that is mere collections and partly of entanglements of atoms with greater or smaller spaces between them. He takes the same view of the atoms as Democritus, except that he ascribes to them not an infinite but merely a limited variety of shapes, the number of which however cannot be determined. The particular atoms he regarded as of material composition but physically and mathematically indivisible. In contrast to Democritus' theory of a rotary motion Epicurus conceived the atoms as falling in empty space. Since however they fall with the same velocity and thus would not impinge on one another and since without a certain spontaneous motion immanent in the primary bodies necessity and fate could not be broken and the freedom of the human will would remain unexplained, Epicurus assumed that the atoms spontaneously, without any external cause, deviate to an infinitesimal degree from the perpendicular. Thus they collide, become entangled with one another, rebound and are partly forced upwards and thus produce the rotary motions which create innumerable worlds in the different parts of endless space. These worlds, which are separated by portions of empty space present the most varied conditions; but they have all arisen in time and in the course of time they will pass away.

Worlds are thus seen to owe their origin to the action of mechanical causes. Epicurus accordingly attaches the greatest value to the explanation of all particulars in the world from a purely mechanical point of view to the exclusion of the teleological. How it is to be explained is a matter of little concern to him. If we can only be certain that something has natural causes it does not matter much what these causes are. For the explanation of particular natural phenomena Epicurus leaves us the choice between all possible hypotheses, although one may be more probable than the others. He does not even reject such obvious absurdities such as the assumption that the moon really increases and diminishes, or that the sun is actually not bigger or only a little bigger than it appears to us.

Living beings he supposed to have originally come forth from the earth. In the beginning there may have been some monstrous forms among them, but only those fitted for life survived. We find in Lucretius many attractive and intelligent conjectures on the original state and the gradual development of man (V, 925ff). The souls of animals and men consist, besides fiery, airy and pneumatic constituents, of a still finer and more mobile substance which cannot be named. This is the cause of sensation and is derived from the souls of the parents. In man a rational part (in Lucretius mens or animus) is added to the irrational soul (anima).

This Epicurus needed for his ethics (cf. p. 256). It had, like the Stoic dominant part (p. 236f.) its seat in the breast, while the anima was spread throughout the whole body. We are given however no information on its material composition. Epicurus regarded the soul as a mixture of four constituents: fire, air, pneuma and an unnameable. At death the soul-atoms are scattered, since they are no longer held together by the body. This was a great consolation to Epicurus, for only the conviction that after death we cease to exist can free us from the fear of the horrors of Hades. He follows Democritus in deriving our idea of hell from the guilty conscience. Hence death is of no concern. Of the activities of the soul not only are perceptions explained (following Democritus, from whom Epicurus deviates only in a few unimportant points) from a contact of the soul with the images which are given off from the surface of bodies and reach the soul through the senses, but the same explanation is given of the imaginative ideas. In the latter case however the soul comes into contact with images the objects of which no longer exist or which have been formed only in the air from the mixture of different "idola" or from new combinations of atoms. Through the movements which the images produce in the soul by their penetration, previous movements of the soul are revived, or, as the process is described we are caused to direct our attention to those of the innumerable idola that continually surround us which are similar to those images and this constitutes remembrance. From the combination of a memory-image with a perception opinion arises, and with it the possibility of error (cf. p. 252). By inferences from the perceived (that is by an independent action of thought, the possibility of which remains unexplained) we come to know what is hidden. Will consists in movements which are produced by representations in the soul and are transmitted by it to the body. The freedom of the will, in the sense of a moderate indeterminism, was strongly maintained by Epicurus and as vigorously contested by the Stoic fatalism and of course by the professors of divination.

By this physics Epicurus hoped he had dispelled for ever fear of death and the gods. He did not, however, make any attack on belief in the gods, partly because the universality of this belief seemed to prove that it rested on real experience, and that the images from the appearance of which alone he can explain it arise at least partly from real beings and are therefore perceptions and not merely imagined images; partly because he himself felt the need of beholding his idea of happiness realised in the gods. He could however only partly accept the prevailing notions about gods, for he was definitely opposed to the popular ideas on their relation to the world. He assumed, indeed, a plurality of gods, in fact according to him they are innumerable; that they have the most beautiful form that can be imagined, the human form, he regards as self-evident. He attributed to them sex-distinctions, need of food and language, even the Greek language. But the happiness and immortality of the gods, the two main factors of his conception of the gods, required in his opinion that their bodies should be composed of fine light instead of the coarse material of our bodies, that they should live in the intermundia, for otherwise they would be affected by the decay of the worlds in which they dwelt and their happiness disturbed by the prospect of this fate. Their happiness also demands that they should not be burdened by cares about the world and men which the belief in providence lays upon them. Still more indispensable is this supposition for the tranquillity of men, who has no more dangerous enemy than the belief that higher powers interfere with the course of the world. Epicurus is thus the most pronounced opponent of this belief in every form. He can only derive popular religion from uncertainty and above all fear. He believed that the Stoic doctrine of providence and fate was not only contradicted by the actual constitution of the world but that it was even more comfortless than the absurdities of mythology. It was extolled by his admirers, like Lucr. I, 62, as Epicurus' undying service to humanity that he freed mankind from this delusion, from the oppressive fear of the gods (religio), while at the same time they praised his piety and his participation in the traditional worship of the gods.

69. *The ethics and social theory of Epicurus*

Just as Epicurus in his physics had declared atoms to be the basis of all being, in his ethics he declared the individual to be the aim of all action. The standard for the estimation of good and evil is our feelings (cf. p. 227). The only unconditional good is that after which all living beings strive—pleasure; the only absolute evil is that which they all shun—pain. Hence Epicurus, like Aristippus, considers pleasure to be the final aim of all our actions. Yet by pleasure he did not mean the individual sensations of pleasure as such, but the happiness of an entire life. It is according to their relation to this that we must judge the particular enjoyments and pains. He believes further that the real significance of pleasure consists only in the satisfaction of a need and thus in the removal of a pain. Our final aim is not positive pleasure but freedom from pain, not the motion but the repose of the spirit; since the most essential condition of this repose lies in the state of our feelings. Epicurus, like Democritus (p. 85), regards the pleasures and pains of the intellect as far more important than those of the body. For however openly and coarsely he declares (despite an occasional expression of the contrary) that all pleasure and pain are occasioned in the last resort by bodily states, yet he observes that only present pleasure and pains affect the body, while the soul is moved by those of the past and future. These feelings, which rest on recollection, hope or fear, are in his opinion so much stronger that he believes himself justified in speaking of the power of the mind over bodily suffering with the same exaggeration as the Cynics and the Stoics. For the most severe pains are of short duration and quickly put an end to our lives, while the less severe can be endured and are overcome by greater intellectual pleasures. Thus the art of life consists in a sort of art of mensuration, which can weigh correctly pleasure and pain and their consequences one against the other. Virtue is only one condition of tranquillity, but so indispensable a condition that Epicurus believes that happiness is indissolubly connected with it,

however small the independent value which his system allows him to attach to it. Understanding frees us from preju-
dices, which disturb us, from empty fancies and wishes. It
teaches us the true art of life. Self-control preserves us from
suffering by its right attitude to pleasure and pain, and bravery does the same by the contempt for death and pain; to justice we owe it that no fear of punishment disturbs our peace
of mind. Epicurus himself led a model life and his sayings
frequently reveal a purity of sentiment and a correctness of
moral judgement which far transcends their inadequate scientific foundation. His ideal of the wise man approaches
very closely to the Stoic. He requires from the wise man neither the Stoic "apathy" nor his renunciation of sensual enjoyment; nevertheless he represents him as so completely
master of his desires that they never lead him astray. He
pictures him as so independent of externals, his happiness so
perfect and his wisdom so inalienable that he can say of
him, no less than the Stoics of their ideal, that he walks as a
god among men and that even on bread and water he need
not envy Zeus (*Fr.*, 602). This complete contentment was
often compared with the calmness of the sea or the clear and
sunny heavens.

In accordance with his ideal Epicurus formulates precepts
for life with the aim of procuring for the individual as such
an existence of self-contained contentment and independence of the external world by freeing him from prejudice
and limiting his desires. He himself lived an unusually mod-
derate and contented life and preached the gospel of contentment. Even of the natural desires only a part are directed to
what is necessary, while by far the most desires are unnatural and vain. Among the latter Epicurus counts especially
the thirst for honour and glory. He did not however demand the suppression of sensual impulses, nor did he forbid
a rich enjoyment of life. He did however insist that we
should not become dependent on these things. The point is
not to use little but to need little. A man should not bind
himself unconditionally even to life. Epicurus permitted him
to withdraw from intolerable suffering by a voluntary death,

though he believes that such a case will rarely arise. Thus he adhered to the independence and self-sufficiency of the wise man which Socrates had taught.

It was more difficult for Epicurus with these hypotheses to establish the necessity and significance of social life for man. His system left only one way open—the consideration of the advantages which accrue to men from union with one another. Even these advantages the philosopher who looked upon freedom from disturbance as the highest good sought more in protection from injury than in any positive benefit which the moral community confers on the individual. This holds good especially of the state. The purpose of all laws is to secure society against injustice. Only the wise in their knowledge of its harmfulness abstain from unjust actions, whereas the masses of men must be deterred by punishment. Thus, as in Sophism, the origin of law and the state is traced back to a social contract (Diog. L., X, 150). To enjoy this security without being disturbed by the effort and danger to which the statesman is inevitably exposed seems to our philosopher to be the most desirable thing. Hence he recommends obedience to the laws, since if we transgressed them we should never be free from fear of punishment; but he considers it best to hold aloof from public life unless special circumstances require a different course. His favourite maxim was "Live hidden", i.e., withdrawn from the world (*Fr.*, 551). He expresses doubts, too, about marriage and the family. On the other hand his school had a keener sense of friendship. It seems indeed rather paltry when he attributes the value of this relationship to the mutual support and feeling of security which arises from it, but in reality he went far beyond the bounds of this supposition. The Epicurean friendships are as renowned as those of the Pythagoreans and the supposed communism of goods among the Pythagoreans was condemned by Epicurus on the grounds that such an institution was unnecessary among friends. It would however have contradicted his principles if he had limited his benevolence to the circle of his personal friends. In actual fact both he and many men of his school were renowned for

their kindliness and philanthropy. In his own case this is expressed by the saying that it is pleasanter to do a kindness
than to receive one.

The most pronounced characteristics of the Epicurean philosophy and ethics are its strong sense of reality which finds
expression in the physics as materialism and in the ethics
centres the interest on the present life with special insistence
on its corporeal side. It always has the happiness of the individual in mind and is thus, as it were, a system of the art
of living, a dietetics of the soul. It is individualist and quiet-
ist in principle. Like the Stoa, Epicureanism is a consistent
monism which goes back for the physical basis of its ethics
to the pre-Socratic philosophy, while its theory of civilisation
is based partly on those of the Sophists whose rationalism it
continued in its war against all religious madness.

IV. THE SCEPTICS

70. Pyrrho and the Pyrrhonians

The Pyrrhonian school was founded rather earlier than the
Stoic and Epicurean. In its practical aim it resembles closely
these schools; but it sought to attain this end not by definite
scientific conviction, but on the contrary by disclaiming science. Pyrrho of Elis had probably become acquainted with
the doctrines of the Elean-Megarean school when he accompanied Anaxarchus (p. 85) on Alexander's expedition to the
east. He may too have learned of Democritus' theory of
sense qualities (p. 84) and the Scepticism of Metrodorus
(p. 86) from the same source. He probably became familiar
too with the subjectivism of Protagoras and Aristippus
(pp. 98, 130), which may be regarded as the precursors of
Scepticism. Later he founded a school of his own in his native city, where he lived in poor circumstances but was universally honoured. This school did not however spread to
any great extent. He lived to be nearly ninety years of age
and seems to have died about 275 B.C. Even in antiquity
his doctrines were known only through those of his pupil
Timon of Phlius, who later lived in Athens and died there

about 230 B.C. also at the age of ninety. He renewed in a clever and witty form the genre of "sillography" founded by Xenophanes, in that under the guise of a visit to Hades he subjected the dogmatic philosophers to a merciless criticism. Besides this he composed a didactic poem in elegiac metre which has the title of *Sketches*. In order to live happily a man must, according to Timon, be clear on three things—what is the nature of things, what should be our attitude towards them and what benefit this attitude will bring us.

To the first two questions we can only answer that the nature of things is completely unknown to us; for perception reveals them to us not as they are but only as they appear to us, and thus our opinions are completely subjective. We may never make any assertion; we may never say "that is so", but always "that seems to me so", so that reservation of judgment is the only correct attitude to things. If we preserve this attitude, then, as Timon believes, we achieve by this alone *ataraxia* or *apathia*. For whoever has renounced the possibility of any knowledge of things cannot attach a higher value to one thing than to another. He will not believe that anything is good or bad in itself, but will rather refer these ideas to law and tradition. He will be indifferent to all else and his only aim will be to achieve the correct temperament or virtue and will thus find happiness in tranquillity. So far, however, as he is compelled to act, he will follow probability, nature and tradition. Pyrrho made no more profound attempt to establish a scientific basis for these doctrines. The ten sceptical tropes which were later attributed to him certainly belong to Ænesidemus (vid. infra.). After the middle of the 3rd. cent. the Pyrrhonian scepticism was replaced by the Academic.

71. *The new Academy*

The man who led the Academy in its new path was Arcesilaus of Pitane in Æolia (315/14—241/40 B.C.), the successor of Crates (p. 173). We are only imperfectly acquainted with his doctrines and, as he wrote nothing, they were known even to the ancients only at third hand. The Socratic negation of knowledge, the shaken belief in the reality of the material world which was the consequence of the Platonic idealism and the epistemology of the Megarian school may have caused him to open the doors to the Pyrrhonian Scepticism. This is indicated at any rate by the character-sketch made of him by a Stoic opponent.

According to Cicero (De Or., III, 67), he contested the possibility of obtaining knowledge of anything through the senses or the understanding (sensibus aut animo). The main object of his attacks however was Zeno's theory of conceptual re-presentation (p. 231f.). Apart from some more formal criticisms his main objection was that there are no ideas which bear a certain hall-mark of truth. This he attempted to prove in various applications. He seems also to have contested the Stoic physics and theology. Hence, in agreement with Pyrrho, he held that nothing remains for us but to withhold judgment. He himself adhered so strictly to this point of view that he would not even assert this principle as a piece of knowledge. This makes all the more incredible the testimony of some of our authorities that this scepticism was intended to serve only as a preparation for the Platonic dogmatism. He seems rather to have been convinced that by this scepticism he was remaining faithful to the spirit of the Socratic dialectic as reflected in the early dialogues of Plato. He did not, however, assert that with knowledge the possibility of reasonable action must be abandoned; for the representation sets the will in motion even when we do not consider it knowledge and in order to act rationally it is sufficient to follow probability which forms the highest criterion for practical life.

The successors of Arcesilaus remained faithful to his doctrines. Scepticism entered upon a new stage with Carneades of Cyrene (214-129 B.C.). This shrewd and learned man, remarkable for the persuasive force of his eloquence, probably took over the headship for the school before 156/155, when he came with the embassy of philosophers to Athens (p. 259). He fulfilled the office with the greatest renown and success until the year 137. He left no works behind him, his doctrines being expounded in the work of his pupils, especially Clitomachus (187-109 B.C.). The teaching of Carneades marks the culmination of the Academic scepticism. Arcesilaus had made the Stoic doctrine of the criterion the chief object of his attacks and Carneades, too, regarded the Stoics, the most influential dogmatists of the time, as his chief opponents. He investigated, however, the question of the possibility of knowledge on a more general basis and subjected the views of the different philosophers to a more comprehensive and penetrating criticism than his predecessors and at the same time defined more precisely the degree and conditions of probability. He first posed the general question whether knowledge is at all possible and believed that this should be denied, for (as he demonstrated in detail) there is no conviction which does not deceive us, no true representation which is not indistinguishably resembled by false ones. Thus there is no criterion of truth in the sense of the Stoic "conceptual representation". He denied therefore the possibility of any process of proof, partly because this could only be done by proof, that is by a *petitio principii;* partly because the premises of the proof require proof in turn and so on *ad infinitum.* He subjected the contents, too, of the philosophic systems to a detailed examination and contested the Stoic theology in particular from all sides. The Stoics inferred the existence of God from the finality in the structure of the universe. Carneades denied both the validity of this conclusion and the correctness of its presupposition by pointing out the existence of numerous evils in the world. He attacked the idea of God itself in that he pointed out with great shrewdness that we cannot think of God as a living, rational creature without attributing to him qualities and states which contradict his eternality and perfection. We can here only touch upon his criticism of polytheism and his attacks on the Stoic belief in prophecy, with which his polemic against the Stoic determinism is also connected. A still greater impression seems to have been made by the criticism of moral concepts, of which a sample was given by his two lectures for and against justice delivered in Rome. In these lectures he followed the precedent of the Sophists in employing the opposition of natural and positive law. Our information on this criticism is of course very imperfect, and indeed the records give us no very exhaustive account of the scientific activities of Carneades. The final result of his sceptical inquiries was naturally that which had long been declared—the absolute impossibility of knowledge and the demand for an unconditional suspension of judgment. The earlier sceptics had at least recognised probability as the norm for our practical conduct. Carneades carried this idea still further. He distinguished three grades of probability. We should strive the more to reach the highest possible grade in every question, the more important the question is for our happiness. Of the probable representations he said that some were probable in themselves, while the probability of others is strengthened by that of all others which are connected with it; in a third class investigation confirms this impression with regard to the last mentioned themselves (the probable presentation, a convincing and uncontradicted presentation and the presentation probable and uncontradicted, and tested from all sides.) Carneades also seems to have made a detailed study of the characteristics by which probability is to be judged. We cannot establish with certainty how he treated ethics from this point of view. It is most probable, however, that he (with the reservation of course of the Sceptic withholding judgement) adhered to the Academic principle of the life according to nature and found virtue in striving after natural goods.

V. ECLECTICISM

72. Its origin and character

Vigorous as were the disputes between the philosophical schools of the post-Aristotelian period, it was natural that in the course of years their contrasts should be softened and that the relationship which despite these contrasts existed between Academic, Peripatetic and Stoic schools should make itself more distinctly felt. In this process there were two factors of decisive significance present—the success which the

Academic scepticism won through Carneades and the connection into which Greece entered with Rome. The more
deeply the beliefs, which the dogmatic schools had in the
irrefutability of their doctrines, had been shaken by the penetrating criticism of Carneades, the more inclined they must
have become to withdraw from the distinctive doctrines
which were exposed to so many objections to the convictions
on which a compromise could be reached in all essentials,
which the critic himself recognised as standards for practical
conduct and considered adequate for the main purpose.
On the other hand the more strongly that Carneades had felt
in his theory of probability the need to secure such practical
standards, the more easy it was for this school to continue
this tendency and come to lay the chief weight on this part
of his doctrines. Thus they departed more and more from
his scepticism in that what in his doctrines had been a mere
probability in time came to acquire the significance of a
known certainty. The Roman spirit, too, which now began
to win an influence on Greek science, worked in the same
direction. After the conquest of Macedonia by the Romans
(168) Greece was actually—what it became more and more
in form—a part of the Roman Empire. Soon there grew up
an interchange of scientific ideas between Greece and Rome,
promoted by men like Flaminius, Æmilius Paulus, Scipio
Æmilianus and his friends. This brought Greek teachers to
Rome and young Romans in ever growing numbers to the
philosophic schools of Athens and other Greek cities. Still
more lasting than the visit of the embassy of philosophers
(pp. 223, 259, 262) was the influence of Panætius' stay
in Rome (§ 73), together with the simultaneous spread of
Epicureanism among the Romans (v. p. 250), so that
after the beginning of the 1st cent. B.C. Greek philosophy
was regarded in Rome as an indispensable part of higher education. At first the Greeks were the teachers and the Romans the pupils, but it was natural that the former should
adapt themselves to the needs of their distinguished and
influential hearers and that they themselves in intercourse
with the Roman world should become affected by the spirit
which had created that world. It was fully in accordance

with this spirit that every point of view was estimated more by its value for practical life than its scientific tenability. These circumstances must have been favourable to the tendency to an amalgamation of the philosophic schools, to throw their distinctive doctrines into the background and to make prominent all that they had in common, especially in points of practical importance. But in order to select what was true or probable from their different and not directly reconcilable views, some sort of criterion was necessary. They were finally led to certain convictions which, as they supposed, are present in man before every process of proof and the truth of which is guaranteed by general accept-ance—the consensus gentium. The idea of "humanity", too, grew up on the soil of this eclecticism, the roots of which of course reach down to the time of the Sophists and the beginnings of Cynicism. It first received however its full content through the fusing of the Hellenic spirit with the Roman character. It was the Romans who gave it the lin-guistic term which no Greek word can render exactly.

This eclecticism appeared first in the Stoic school; later it came to dominate the Academic school in a still higher de-gree and found an entrance also into the Peripatetic school. In the Epicureans of this time, however, we cannot observe any important departure from the doctrines of their founder.

73. *The Stoics of the middle period*

The polemics which the Stoics conducted with other schools, especially the Academy and the Peripatetics, had an influence on their own system. They destroyed its unity and moderated its rigid dogmatism so as to adapt themselves partly to the doctrines of other schools and partly to meet the demands of practical life. Thus Boëthus of Sidon (d. 119 B.C.), a pupil of Diogenes of Seleucia, approached closely to the Peripatetic theories in that he identified God with æther but separated him substantially from the world. He assigned him an abode in the sphere of the fixed stars.

and replaced its doctrine of a periodic conflagration by the Aristotelian theory of the eternity of the world.

The real founder, however, of the middle Stoa and especially its influence on the Roman world was Panætius of Rhodes (c. 180-110). He was also a pupil of Diogenes and his successor Antipater of Tarsus and stayed for a considerable time in Rome where he was a member of the circle of younger Scipio and his friend Lælius. He exerted a profound influence on numerous distinguished Romans, such as the Q. Mucius Scævola and the Greek historian Polybius, who was then living in Rome as a hostage. His chief works, *On Duty, On Action and Inaction, On Tranquillity* and *On Providence* were used by Cicero in various sections of his philosophic works, especially the *De Officiis (ad Att.,* XVI, 11, 4). He was a pronounced rationalist, as is most clearly shown by his repudiation of divination, including astrology, whereby he made considerable breaches in the foundations of the Stoic doctrine of providence. He distinguished three kinds of theology; that of the poets, the philosophers and the statesmen. The first he rejected as childish and trivial; the second, after the manner of Euhemerus, traced the gods of popular religion back to eminent men and replaced them by the idea of an unlimited Deity; the third he saw in public virtue, which is necessary for the control and education of the people. In physics he abandoned the theory of a conflagration. On the other hand he laid the greatest emphasis on the connection between man's mental life and on its physical and physiological conditions. Here belongs his attempt to explain the habitability of the hot zones and the importance which he ascribes to a temperate climate for the production of men with superior intellectual powers. This is the reason for his rejection of Plato's dualistic psychology by pointing out the fact that mental qualities can be inherited (*Cic. Tusc.,* I, 3, 2, 79ff.), although in other respects he was an admirer of Plato and called him the Homer of philosophers. In ethics he adhered to the identification of the moral and the useful, but abandoned the insistence on apathy and the harsh ideal of the Stoic wise man, in favour of co-operation among men. It is to his influence that the development of the ideal of humanity in the circle of Scipio is due. This explains, too, his interest in political activity. He regarded, like Plato and Dicæarchus before him (pp. 160, 222), the best constitution as a mixture of monarchy, aristocracy and democracy, an ideal which, in the opinion of Polybius (VI, 4, 10, 11), was most closely approached by the constitutions of Lycurgus and the Romans. Thus Panætius was not distinguished by any remarkable philosophical originality. His mind was free from any fantastic mysticism or esoteric doctrinaire and he transformed the Stoic system so that it could serve the practical-minded Romans as a guide in life. Both Scipio and his brother-in-law Tiberius Gracchus, the great social reformer, were obviously influenced by Stoic ideas.

One of the pupils of Panætius was his countryman Hecaton. He too was the author of a book on duties, which he dedicated to the nephew of the younger Scipio, Q. Aelius Iubero (tribune of the people 129 B.C.). In this book he showed himself not entirely free from casuistry but remained loyal to the old Stoic idea, that not success but character is the deciding factor in the judgment of human conduct.

The most important pupil of Panætius was Posidonius of Apamea (135-51 B.C.). After extensive travels which took him to Egypt and Nubia, Massilia and Spain he settled in Rhodes in 97 B.C., where Cicero heard him in 78 B.C. while Pompey twice honoured him with a visit in order to honour Hellenistic science in his person. He himself came as an ambassador to Rome in the year 86 and paid a further visit to that city shortly before his death. He was on terms of personal friendship with many distinguished Romans. He was the most universal mind that Greece had seen since the time of Aristotle. He was as an historian the successor of Polybius, while he was as much at home in geography as the various branches of natural science and familiar with the philosophical problems current at that time. Although in speculative power he is not to be compared with the great pre-Socratics or Plato or Aristotle, the term eclectic does not convey his full significance; for it is the unity of his system that is most imposing in him. He did not form his system of heterogeneous parts from various philosophical schools, but he remained essentially on the basis of the Stoic monism. He not only supported the dogmas of this system by the whole of the empirical knowledge of his time and infused it with new life, but breathed into it with his strong religious feelings a satisfying warmth. He shows an unmistakable tendency towards the mysterious, a feature which was characteristic of that period, disturbed as it was by war and revolution. Of his numerous works only relatively few fragments have been preserved. We have to rely for the most part on the accounts of later authors, in which we often have to extract the real Posidonian philosophy from a mass of irrelevant material.

In his *Protrepticus* Posidonius defined philosophy as knowledge of divine and human things and their causes. This he sought in every sphere of knowledge. It was the discovery made on the shore at Gades that the periodical movements of the sea in ebb and flood are caused by the moon that opened his eyes to the sympathy that prevails in the world in which he found the key to the riddle of the universe. This was an idea which had already been familiar to the early Stoics. What was new in Posidonius' contribution to the Stoic physics was the idea of force, more precisely vital force. He regarded the sun as the source of this force which permeates the whole world with its warming breath. The world appeared to him as a graduated structure which ascends in innumerable transitions from the inorganic forms, to the plants and animals and finally to man. In this structure everything is arranged by the divine wisdom down to the smallest detail. His special merit lies in the fact that he attempted to give an empirical and detailed demonstration of this truth. The structure of the cosmos is divided into the world above and that below the moon; the latter is the earthly, the former the heavenly world; the latter is perishable, the former imperishable; the second is nourished by and lives from the heavenly forces which are poured into it from the first. Man forms the bridge between these two worlds. He is, as Posidonius says, with an idea borrowed from the Platonic *Timæus* (31 B.C.), the chain which holds both worlds together. With his combination of body and spirit, the perishable and the eternal, he stands on the border between the divine and the earthly. Apart from him there exist of course other spiritual beings. In the work *On Heroes and Demons* he developed the theory that the souls come from the sun, from which all life is derived, and travel to the earth by way of the moon. These souls, after their departure from the region of the sun, dwell in the space beneath the moon. As beings of light and fire they become demons and then, as beings of air, heroes. Hence the air is full of them and intercourse with them is possible. The Deity himself he regarded, like all Stoics, as a thinking, fiery breath, which has no shape but can change itself into any form it pleases. Posidonius adhered to a belief in prophecy and endeavoured to explain it by the sympathy that prevails in the universe. He made a special distinction between divination by signs and the capacity which the soul has in sleep, in ecstasy, at the approach of death and in any states in which the bonds of the soul with the body are loosened, of catching a glimpse of the underlying connection of world events and thus looking into the future. Thus every single being is organically connected with the universe. On this sympathy of all that is depends sense-perception, knowledge and finally the communal instinct, especially among human beings. In his psychology, which was contained in his works on the soul and the emotions, he departed from the Stoic dogma that the emotions depend on false judgments and approached the standpoint of Plato in postulating not three parts of the soul like him, but three functions of the soul, instinct, feeling, and reason, the affects being derived from the feeling. The lowest beings lead only an instinctive life, the higher have feeling in addition, while only man is gifted with reason. Its mission (in accordance with the general Stoic ethics) is to discipline the lower impulses of the soul. Posidonius, too, was unable to solve the antinomy between the concept of fate and the theory of free will. In contrast to the Stoa, however, he repudiated suicide. Remarkable is his theory of the origin of civilisation of which Seneca (*Ep.* 90) contains an account. He shares with Theophrastus and Dicæarchus the romantic conception of the innocent, primitive state of the first men and then depicts the rise of civilisation with the use and adaptation of Democritean ideas. It appears that the impulse to progress is to be found not in want but in philosophy. The philosophers instruct primitive man on the nature of God and the community of the human race. After the demand for property has been followed by the growth of vice, legislators and founders of states make their appearance and promote the progress of civilisation by inventions of all kinds from the plough to the building of houses. In a book on the gods Posidonius expounded his ideas of the origin of religion. He assumed that there had once existed a religion common to all men, which grew up partly from the wonder of the stars, partly from thanksgiving for the gifts of the earth and partly from fear of punishment of evil. Just because the first men were nearer the divine they had an in-born idea of him and a strong feeling for his power in the world. Then religious ideas, customs and usages were given shape by poets and legislators and a binding authority was ascribed to them. In history, too, Posidonius perceived an organic connection, while in ethnology and in his description of individual persons he was at pains to bring out the connection between the soul and the external conditions of life. In his work on the ocean he attempted to demonstrate the influence of climate on the nature and life of the different nations. This work contained, besides his theory of ebb and flood (p. 268), his investigations on the size of the earth and its habitable parts, on the connection between the various parts of the world-ocean and on its variations of depth, etc.; also the idea that if we travelled from the furthest west with the east wind, we should be bound to reach India, an idea which 1500 years later Columbus, inspired by Toscanelli, attempted to realise.

Thus the philosophy of Posidonius forms a great pantheistic system, in which the whole of empirical knowledge finds a place; but unfortunately not only knowledge but also the whole superstition of his time. That he did not find the

strength to overcome this by philosophy, but merely endeavoured to justify it before the reason, that is the slavish
imitative, the Hippocratian feature of his system, which already proclaims the decline of philosophic thought. He gave
a powerful impulse to the process of the demonisation of
ancient religion, which culminated in neo-Platonism. His
monism, too, is on closer examination merely a veiled dualism in which the two worlds of the heavenly and the earthly,
the mental and material, interpenetrate without the problem
of their contrast being fully solved, or turned, as in Heraclitus
or the orthodox Stoa, into a unity. With his acceptance of
bodiless souls, heroes and demons, Posidonius stands on the
border-line of the two tendencies which we have followed
throughout the history of Greek philosophy—the monistic
and the dualistic. He smoothed the path for the revival of
the latter tendency and unnoticed changed philosophy into
theosophy.

Posidonius had a profound and far-reaching influence
both on his contemporaries and after-times. Traces of his
doctrines are found in the solar monotheism of the 4th cent.
as represented in Julian's speech on king Helias and in the
work of the Christian bishop, Nemesius of Emesa, on the
nature of man (c. 400). The treatise on the world contained among the works of Aristotle shows an unmistakable
dependence on Posidonius. It was in reality the work of an
Eclectic of the 1st cent. A.D. who took up an intermediate
position between the Peripatetics and the Stoa and looks up
in wonderment to Plato. He lays strong emphasis on the
transcendence of God, but makes him in virtue of his power
the cause of everything in the world, a thesis which he illustrates by a number of remarkable similes. Thus the work
is a characteristic product of popular eclectic philosophy.

74. *The Academicians of the last century* B.C.

It was in the Academic school that eclecticism found most
favour. Even among the personal pupils of Carneades there
were some who abandoned the belief that absolute knowledge of things is possible. This step was taken more defi-

nitely (at least in his later years) by Philo of Larissa, the pupil and successor of Clitomachus (*vide* p. 263). He fled to Rome in 88 B.C., where he became the teacher of Cicero and died probably before 79 B.C. He did not merely set philosophy the problem of showing men the way to happiness but attempted to achieve this end by a detailed ethical theory, by attacking false and imparting correct moral opinions (Stobæus, II, 7, 2, p. 39, 20ff. W.). Furthermore he disregarded the withholding judgement, which Carneades had not abandoned even in his ethics. Thus he could not consistently maintain a point of view which questioned the truth of all convictions. Hence although he contested the Stoic doctrine of the criterion and regarded any absolutely certain knowledge of things in the sense of the Stoic "conceptual representation" as impossible, he did not wish to deny all possibility of knowledge of things. He asserted that even Arcesilaus and Carneades had not intended to deny this possibility, but had only refuted the Stoic doctrines in defence of pure Platonism. There is an obviousness, which creates a completely sure conviction that satisfies the investigator although it does not attain the unconditioned certainty of the concept. He sought therefore something intermediate between mere probability and knowledge.

The untenability of this intermediate position was recognised by Philo's successor Antiochus of Ascalon (d. 68 B.C.), who had heard both Philo and the Stoic Mnesarchus. It was his objection to the neo-Academic theories that brought him finally into conflict with Philo. He was the friend of Lucullus and the teacher of Cicero in Athens. Through his influence the Academy made finally and definitely the transition from Scepticism to Eclecticism. Whereas Philo had still adhered to the doctrine that there is nothing absolutely certain, Antiochus made this assertion anew and returned to a pronounced dogmatism. Among other objections to Scepticism, which carried particular weight for him as for the Stoics, was the consideration that without firm convictions no rational content of life is possible. He conducted his attack on logical lines and pointed out that without truth there can be no probability and no obvious ness; that it is a contradiction to assert that nothing can be asserted or to prove that nothing can be proved; that we cannot speak of false ideas and at the same time deny the distinction between false and true. To the question where truth is to be sought Antiochus answered: in that on which all reputable philosophers are agreed. In order to prove that there actually exists such an agreement on all more important points, he expounded the Academic, Peripatetic and Stoic systems in such a way as to show that these three schools deviate from one another only in minor points, and then more verbally than essentially. This, of course, was impossible without considerable inaccuracies. He himself was chiefly interested in ethics, in which he tried to find a middle way between Zeno, Aristotle and Plato. For instance he said that virtue suffices for happiness, but for the highest grade of happiness bodily and external goods are necessary as well. The reproach was made against him that he called himself an Academician but was more a Stoic. Actually he was neither but merely an Eclectic.

After the death of Antiochus, as is shown by Cicero (*Acad.*, II, 11) and Ænesidemus (in Phot. Cod., 212, pp. 170, 14), this mode of thought continued to be the prevailing one in the Academy. Suidas calls the Alexandrian Potamo a contemporary of Augustus. This philosopher himself gave his school the name of "Eclectic". What we know of his doctrines is a superficial combination of unoriginal ideas that are chiefly reminiscent of Antiochus.

75. *The Peripatetic school*

This eclecticism was less prevalent among the contemporary Peripatetics. Andronicus of Rhodes, who was head of the Peripatetic school at Athens from 70-50 B.C., published with the help of the grammarian Tyrannio an edition of Aristotle's pedagogical works (pp. 175, 180, 223). His investigation into their authenticity and his commentaries to many of these works gave an impulse to the diligent study of Aristotle to which the Peripatetic school from now on devoted itself. It was a necessary result of this study of their founder's works that it now became difficult to attribute views to him which did not belong to him. Nevertheless neither Andronicus nor his pupil Boëthus of Sidon, who in his denial of immortality and in other points represented a naturalistic conception of the Peripatetic doctrines, surrendered their independence of judgment in favour of Aristotle.

That individuals were not lacking who were ready to introduce foreign elements into the Aristotelian theory is shown by two treatises from the Aristotelian Corpus: the book *On the World* and the short essay *On Virtues and Vices*. The latter resembles the Platonic theory of virtue more than the Aristotelian, but seems to be the work of a Peripatetic.

76. *The Roman eclectics*

The Eclecticism of the 1st cent. B.C. appears in a peculiar form in the Roman philosophers. The man whose historical influence far exceeds that of any other was M. Tullius Cicero (106-43). He owes his success not to the acuteness or independence of his thought but to the skill with which he could expound the doctrines of the Greeks—superficial as his acquaintance with them was—in a clear and appropriate manner for the contemporary and succeeding generations of Latin readers.

Cicero was familiar with the main tendencies in philosophy: he had studied Epicureanism with Phædrus and Zeno of Sidon, Stoicism with Diadobus and Posidonius, and the doctrines of the Academy with Philo and Antiochus. He considered himself one of the neo-Academic school and gladly followed the school in their method of discussing the *pros* and the *cons* without any final decision. The chief motive for his scepticism lay not so much in scientific reasons which he borrowed from the Academicians as in the conflict of philosophic authorities. Thus he is ready to abandon his scepticism to the degree that these contradictions can be reconciled. Hence although he believed that we must despair of knowledge in the full sense, yet he attributes to probability a far greater significance than Carneades. In the things which most concerned him, moral principles and the theological and anthropological questions connected with them, he speaks with great decision; for he was convinced that right concepts are implanted in us by nature, that they can be drawn directly from our own consciousness and upheld by universal agreement. The theories which he erected on this basis were neither original nor free from vacillation. In his ethics he is definitely opposed to Epicureanism although he failed to find any firm footing between the Stoic and the Academic-Peripatetic doctrines. While he found the sublimity of the Stoic principles pleasing, he could not approve of the one-sidedness inseparable from them. In theology the belief in the existence of God and Providence, and in psychology that in the immortality of the soul and the freedom of the will, harmonised with his own deep-seated convictions. But he could not reach any definite decision on the nature of God or our mind. In general he ranged himself on the side of the Platonic spiritualism, without however being able to withdraw himself completely from the influence of the Stoic materialism. He stood in no intimate relation to the popular religion as such, but in the interest of the community he wished to preserve it, while freeing it as far as possible from superstition. The ideal of humanity first formulated by the Stoics of the Scipionic circle was elaborated by him into an ethical principle and an educational principle. Close to Cicero stands his friend M. Terentius Varro (116-27 B.C.), who was, however, more scholar than philosopher. A pupil of Antiochus, whom he is made by Cicero to represent (*Acad. post.*), he followed his master in his ethics (in Augustine *De civ. dei*, XIX, 1-3), which was for him by far the most important part of philosophy; but like his teacher he approached in many respects the standpoint of the Stoics, especially the Stoic materialism. In theology he allied himself still more closely with the Stoics, especially Panætius and Posidonius. He followed them in describing God as the soul of the world and believed that in the form of the Gods of polytheism the forces of this soul were honoured as they operate in the various parts of the world. On the other hand he adopted their distinction of a threefold theology and their sharp criticism of the mythology of the poets and went so far as to express his open disapproval of important parts of the public religion.

An offshoot of Stoicism was the school which was founded *c.* 40 B.C. by Q. Laertius, a Roman of good family who abandoned a political career for philosophy. It was presided over after his death by his son but soon died out. To this school belonged Sotion of Alexandria, who *c.* 18-20 A.D. was the teacher of Seneca, the learned encyclopædist Cornelius Celsus, Fabianus Papirius and L. Crassicius. What we know of these men shows that they were moral philosophers who were earnest advocates of the Cynic-Stoic principles. The impression which they made was due more to their own personality than to any peculiar philosophic merit. They combined Pythagorean elements with Stoic; for example, in Sextius the self-examination to which he submitted himself every evening, his abstinence from animal food, which however he recommended only on general moral grounds, whereas his pupil Sotion adduced the transmigration theory as a reason for this abstention. Finally Platonic influence seems to have been at work in the Sextian view of the incorporeality of the soul.

77. *The Jewish-Greek philosophy*

The Jewish-Greek philosophy as represented by Philo and his predecessors exhibits a thorough-going eclecticism combined with a religious syncretism and a transition to mysticism. The Jews, despite their peculiar exclusiveness, did not remain unaffected by the fusion of the Greek and oriental worlds which took place in the Hellenistic period. We find many traces of mutual influence. On the Greek side religious monstrosities such as the cult of "the Highest" or "the Lord" in Asia Minor, in which the Phrygian Sabazius and the Jewish "Lord Zebaoth" conflicted, while to many Greeks the Jewish religion with its image-free worship of God appeared as a religion of philosophic enlightenment. The Jewish "diaspora" extended to most of the great cities and this enabled Greeks and Romans to make their acquaintance with Jewish belief and customs. On the other hand the Jews who had settled in the middle of the Hellenistic world could not escape its influence. Thus the book Koheleth of the so-called *Preacher Solomon,* written about 200 B.C., clearly betrays the influence of Stoic philosophy, while the *Book of Wisdom* also attributed to Solomon and written about 30 B.C. contains unmistakable Pythagorean and Platonic elements in its idea of the pre-existence of the soul and its imprisonment in the body, its assumption of a primary matter and its hypostatising of divine wisdom. But the strongest proof of the Hellenisation of the Jews in the "diaspora" is afforded by the fact that in their greatest community, that in Alexandria, they had so completely forgotten the native Hebrew language that they needed a Greek translation of their Sacred writings, the so-called Septuagint, which was probably begun under Ptolemæus II, Philadelphus (285-247 B.C.). The mythical creation of this book through the agency of 70 (or 72) interpreters is depicted in the *Epistle of Aristeas,* written about 100 B.C. This is the work of a Jewish writer who puts on the mask of a pagan and delights in the tropes of the Stoic philosophy. Its allegorical methods, in which it anticipates Philo, are applied to the interpretation of the law-code of the Old Testament. Rather earlier is the Jewish so-called Peripatetic Philobulus who dedicated to the king Ptolemæus Philometor his commentary on the Pentateuch. In the fragments preserved in Eusebius he attempted to trace the doctrines of Greek philosophers such as Pythagoras, Socrates and Plato to the Mosaic writings, partly by allegorical interpretation of these writings and partly by falsifying the Greek texts, as can be seen in a large Orphic fragment the text of which has been preserved elsewhere. Another Jewish forgery of the 1st cent. A.D. is the poem of the Pseudo-Phocylides, a collection of moral aphorisms which were attributed to the old gnomic poet of the 6th cent. B.C. There remains to mention two religious sects which in their views and customs present a remarkable mixture of Jewish belief and Jewish piety with Greek, and in particular Orphic-Pythagorean, speculations and precepts. The one is the sect of the Therapeutes which had its origin in Egypt. It was a society of ascetics who lived a life of extreme piety, and engaged in allegorical interpretation and theological speculation. Their principles were described by Philo in his works on *The Contemplative Life*. The other is the far more important religious society of the Essees (or Essenes) which grew up on the soil of Palestine and is mentioned by Josephus together with the Pharisees and the Sadducees as having flourished about 160 B.C. They lived as a sort of religious order with strict discipline and hierarchical division of authority. They had secret doctrines which were based on the interpretation of sacred writings. They practised communism of goods and in the higher grades celibacy, while marriage for the lower grades was subject to severe restrictions. They disapproved of blood-offerings, consumption of flesh and wine and maintained a sharply defined dualism which formed the basis of their asceticism. They believed in the pre-existence of the soul and its survival after death and assumed that the opposition of good and evil pervades the whole world. They worshipped the light of the sun and the elements as manifestations of God and attributed great importance to the belief in angels. The power of prophecy was regarded as the highest reward of piety and asceticism and many of them were supposed to have possessed this gift. It was inevitable that this close contact of Jews and Greeks should provoke reactions. Antiochus Epiphanes in his attempt to Hellenise the Jews in Palestine by force could rely on a numerous party which favoured the Greeks, while the growing number and importance of the Jews in Greek cities provoked strong anti-Semitic movements. This whole development reached its culmination in the life and works of Philo of Alexandria.

Philo's birth falls between 20-30 B.C., his death not long after A.D. 40. He was a true son of his people, filled with the deepest reverence for their sacred writings and especially for Moses. He held that these writings were literally inspired not only in the original text but also in the Greek translation. But he was at the same time the pupil and admirer of the Greek philosophers Plato, Pythagoras, Parmenides, Empedocles, Zeno and Cleanthes. He was convinced that one and the same truth is to be found in both; this is, of course, pure and perfect only in the Jewish revelations. He justified this belief by the traditional methods; on the one hand he assumed that the Hellenic sages used the Old Testament writings and on the other he pushed to its furthest limits the allegorical interpretation of these writings so that he could discover any meaning he chose in any passage whatsoever. Hence although he desired to be nothing more than an interpreter of the Holy Scripture and expounded his view almost solely in this form—for the knowledge of God in his revelation is the "Royal road" as distinguished from all merely human thought—his system is in reality a combination of Greek philosophy with Jewish theology, the scientific parts of which are derived predominantly from the former. The philosophy which he followed belonged completely to the form of Platonism which had been developing for more than a century, especially at Alexandria, and was named sometimes after Plato and sometimes after Pythagoras, although Stoicism, especially in Philo, contributed largely to it.

The idea of God forms the starting point of Philo's system. It is here, however, that the various tendencies from which Philo's speculation emerged cross. He had so lofty a conception of the elevation of God above all that is finite that he thought that no idea and no word could correspond to his greatness. God appears as more perfect than all perfection, better than the good, without name or quality, inconceivable; we can, as Plato says, only know that he is, not what he is; only the name of the Being (Jehovah) can be applied to him. Furthermore God must include all being and all perfection in himself; for the finite can derive these qualities only from him and it is only to avoid approaching too closely to his perfection that no finite predicate is to be attributed to him. Above all he must be thought of as the final cause of everything; we must ascribe to him an unceasing activity, and all perfection in created things must be derived from him. It was self-evident for the Platonists and the Jewish monotheists that this activity can only be directed to the best ends, and that of the two basic qualities of God—

power and goodness—the second expresses his nature more directly than the first.

In order to unite this absolute activity of God in the world with his absolute transcendence Philo had recourse to the assumption which was familiar to other thinkers of that time (cf. pp. 200, 269, 307), but which no one before Plotinus worked out so systematically as he. This was the assumption of intermediate beings. In defining the nature of these beings, besides the belief in angels and demons and Plato's statements on the world-soul and the ideas, it was above all the Stoic doctrine of the effluences of God that permeate the world that served him as a model. He called these intermediate beings forces and described them on the one hand as qualities of the Deity, as ideas or thoughts of God, as parts of the general force and reason that prevails in the world; on the other hand as servants, ambassadors and satellites of God, or the executors of his will, souls, angels and demons. He found it impossible to harmonise these two modes of exposition and to give a clear answer to the question of the personality of these forces. All these forces are comprehended in one, the Logos. The Logos is the most universal intermediary between God and the world, the wisdom and reason of God, the idea which comprises all ideas, the power that comprises all powers, the representative and ambassador of God, the instrument of the creation and government of the world, the highest of the angels, the first-born son of God, the second God. He is the original pattern of the world and the force which creates everything in it, the soul which is clothed with the body of the world as with a garment. In a word he has all the qualities of the Stoic Logos (p. 234), in so far as this is thought of as distinguished from God as such and free from the characteristics which were the result of the Stoic materialism. His personality is, however, as uncertain as that of the "powers" generally. This must be the case; for only so long as the concept of the Logos hovers between that of a personal being distinct from God and that of an impersonal divine force or quality can it provide even an apparent solution of the insoluble problem for which it is required—to make it comprehensible how God can be present in the world and all its parts with his force and activity, when he is by his very nature completely external to it and would be defiled by any contact with it. The constitution of the world can be however only partly understood from the divine force operating in it. In order to explain the evil and defects of finite existence, but especially the evil which adheres to the soul on account of its connection with the body, we must postulate a second principle which Philo, like Plato, can only find in matter. In his detailed description of matter, too, he follows Plato except that he regards it, in the usual way as occupying space and thus calls it variously not-being (like Plato) and real being (like the Stoics). God formed the world out of the chaotic mixture of matter through the agency of the Logos; hence the world has a beginning but no end. Like the Stoics Philo considered the world as entirely supported by the force of God operating in it; this is manifested in its most glorious form in the stars, which are visible gods. He defended their perfection on the lines of the Stoic theodicy, but he does not omit to give expression to the thought that everything is arranged according to numbers by the frequent application of the Pythagorean numerical symbolism. In his anthropology, the part of physics to which he attached most importance, he adhered to the Platonic and Pythagorean fall of the soul, the corporeal survival of the purified souls after death, the migration of those in need of purification, the relationship of the human mind with God, the divisions of the soul and the freedom of the will. But what was most important for him was the sharp contrast between reason and the sensual. The body is the tomb of soul, the source of all the evils under which it sighs. Through the combination of the soul with the body every man has innate in him the inclination to sin, from which no one can free himself from birth until death. Hence the greatest possible emancipation from the sensual is one of the basic requirements of the Philonian ethics; like the Stoics he demanded apathy, a complete eradication of all passions, looked up to virtue as the only good, rejected sensual pleasure and professed Cynic simplicity; he adapted the Cynic and Stoic doctrine of the virtues and the emotions, their description of the wise man, their distinction of the wise and the proficient and their cosmopolitanism. But in his philosophy trust in oneself was replaced by trust in God. All good in us is the work of God alone. He alone can implant virtue in us; only he who does good for his sake is truly good; from faith alone is that wisdom derived on which all virtue rests. But even in this virtue Philo places less value on conduct than on knowledge or more correctly on the inner life of the pious soul. For not only does active ("political") life repel him, because it involves us in external things and distracts us from ourselves, but even science is in his eyes only valuable as an aid to piety. Even religious perfection, however, has grades. Thus "ascetic" virtue, that is virtue based on practice (that of Jacob), is lower than that which is founded on instruction (that of Abraham); both are lower than that which proceeds directly from a divinely-favoured nature (that of Isaac). The last and highest aim of virtue is God, to which we approximate more and more as we come more immediately into contact with it. Hence however indispensable science may be, we can only attain the highest when we pass beyond all mediacy, even the Logos, and in the state of unconsciousness, in ecstasy, receive the higher illumination into ourselves and thus behold God in his pure unity and allow it to work upon us.

This illumination is effected by the influx of the invisible divine spirit into man, of the cosmic force that proceeds from God. The "unmixed wisdom" thus revealed in ecstasy has nothing to do with human knowledge that can be learned. It is heavenly wisdom, in short that which is elsewhere called "Gnosis", an expression which Philo himself avoided.

With such views Philo, despite his dependence on Plato, Xenocrates, the Stoa and especially Posidonius, passes beyond the bounds of philosophy into mysticism. His ideas are completely different from those of Greek philosophy. In the latter we have the principle of the autonomy of reason and the bold search after human knowledge; in the former, the contempt of reason and science and faith in the revelation of

sacred books; in the latter, the close connection of God
and the world, generally in the form of immanence; in
the former, the complete transcendence of God, the most
pronounced dualism between God and the world which
makes necessary the introduction of intermediate beings to
connect the two; in the latter, the recognition of the sensual
and at the same time the moral power of man for its control; in the former the oriental and ascetic conception of the
corporeal as the source of evil and a belief in the innate corruption of human nature; in the latter, the goal of mental
endeavour is insight into the nature of the world and moral
perfection, both attained by our own efforts, in the former
the contemplation of God in ecstasy, which as an act of divine mercy signifies liberation from the bonds of the flesh;
finally in the latter, the wise man as the highest type of man,
in the former, the priest and the prophet. Thus Philo's system appears more as Jewish theology mixed with Greek
mysticism than as real philosophy. Nevertheless he was soon
forgotten by his Jewish compatriots and fellow-worshipers,
while on the other hand he became the precursor of neo-
Platonism and exerted considerable influence in the elaboration of the dogmas of the Christian church.

THE PHILOSOPHY OF THE ROMAN EMPIRE

78. *Introductory*

Philo's life and activity falls chronologically in the Period of the Roman Empire; intrinsically, however, he belongs to the Hellenistic age, which provided the fundaments of his thought. It was mentioned above (p. 37) that the beginning of the Roman Empire does not denote any important period in the development of philosophy. The transition from the republican to the monarchist constitution and administration of the Empire did not directly affect philosophy. The world-empire on whose soil the cosmopolitan ideas of philosophy had been strengthened if not originated, remained the same, and the Greeks, who still remained the main purveyors and creators of philosophic ideas, had long ceased to play any active part in politics when the same fate overtook the Hellenised upper-classes of Rome. Even the very different attitudes of the Roman emperors to philosophy did not have any decisive significance. Alone of importance was the fact that Marcus Aurelius, who himself became an adherent of the Stoic school, endowed chairs in Athens for the four great philosophic schools of the Academy, the Peripatetics, the Stoa and the Garden. Furthermore it is hardly disputable that the endeavour to realise the idea of the

"Optimus princeps", of the sovereign who rules according to the principle of justice and who regards the "salus publica" as his highest criterion, which we observe in emperors like Augustus, in the first five years of Nero under Seneca's regency, Trajan and especially Hadrian, Antoninus Pius, and M. Aurelius, was a result of the spread of political ideas which philosophy and especially the middle Stoa had carried into the Roman world. For the old philosophical schools lived on, and many which seemed almost to have disappeared, such as Pythagoreanism, Cynicism, and Scepticism experienced a revival. Nevertheless we may recognise in the philosophy of the Empire certain distinctive features which give it its own peculiar stamp; not merely that the process of mutual rapprochement of the schools which had begun in the Hellenistic period continued, but above all that a note of weariness, even exhaustion, made itself felt which heralded its extinction. In the Stoic ethics particularly, the heroism which had lent a Cato and many Stoics of the early empire the strength to turn their back on a life that was no longer worth living was replaced by an honourable, yet rather weak resignation and surrender to fate. Furthermore the renewal of scepticism reveals an enfeeblement of philosophical speculation and the corresponding growth of mysticism that is especially characteristic of the last phase and of Greek philosophy and its approaching end. In the lower classes of the people it gained ground through the spread of oriental mystery-religions and in the upper classes through neo-Platonism and neo-Pythagoreanism, systems in which, too, mysticism predominated over philosophy and thus prepared its end.

The whole attitude of mind on which neo-Platonism rests is at bottom the same as that of its youthful and vigorous opponent, the Christian religion, which explains why it could offer no successful resistance to the latter. Nevertheless the victory of the new religion was by no means complete; many ideas of the ancient wisdom of Greek philosophy passed into the speculative theology of the Christian faith and lived on in the dogmatism of the church.

I. CONTINUANCE AND REVIVAL OF THE OLD SCHOOLS

79. *The later Stoics*

In the later Stoa, the development of which belongs to the first two centuries of the empire, two tendencies may be distinguished; the one was occupied with the scientific exposition of the Stoic doctrines, while the other laid main emphasis on the dissemination and practical application of the moral principles of the school. In this it recognises the ancient principles of the system but approaches Cynicism to some extent. They stressed the religious ideas of the Stoics—the kinship of man with God and of men with one another and the consequent duty of love of those who are nearest to us, mercy and forgiveness—and occasionally borrowed ideas from Platonism.

To the first of these two tendencies belongs Arius Didymus of Alexandria, the friend and teacher of Augustus. He wrote, perhaps for the use of the emperor, an exposition of the doctrines of the most prominent philosophers which answered the need of rapid orientation in these studies. A few fragments of this work have been preserved. That he actively practiced his Stoic principles is shown by the remains of his consolation addressed to the empress Livia after the death of Drusus (9 B.C.).

Probably the Heraclitus is also to be ascribed to the time of Augustus of whom we know nothing except that he was the author of a work *Homeric Allegories,* which is still extant. In this book he attempted, partly by physical and partly by ethical interpretation of the passages which offended his taste to elicit from Homer a deeper hidden sense. The same spirit inspires the handbook of Greek theology by L. Annæus Cornutus, the teacher and friend of the poets Persius and Lucan, who were banished from Rome by Nero after the Pisonian conspiracy (A.D. 65). He drew on older sources, probably Cleanthes and Apollodorus of Athens (*c.* 180-109 B.C.).

These men are far exceeded in importance by L. Annæus Seneca, a son of the rhetorician Seneca. He was born soon after the beginning of our era in Corduba and was for long the tutor and, with Burrus, the adviser of Nero, at whose command he died in A.D. 65. He was opposed to the doctrines of his school in no important point; nevertheless his philosophy breathes a somewhat different spirit from that of the ancient Stoics. He made use of other authorities than the Stoics, especially the works of Epicurus. In the first place he confined himself almost entirely to morals. He was acquainted with the Stoic logic but had no inclination to make any detailed study of it. He praised the sublimity of physics and in his *Naturales Quæstiones* adopted the meteorology of Posidonius; but of this part of philosophy only such theological and anthropological details as admitted of a practical application had any deeper interest for him. Without contradicting the Stoic materialism and pantheism he laid special emphasis on the ethical features of the Stoic idea of God on which the belief in providence was based; and in anthropology on the doctrine of the kinship of the human mind with God and its survival after death. His moral teaching, however, does not completely coincide with the older Stoicism the principles and precepts of which it repeats. Seneca is too completely obsessed with the weakness and sinfulness of men, in his lively descriptions of which he strikingly resembles his contemporary the Apostle Paul, to be able to face moral problems with the self-trust of the original Stoicism. In his despair of finding a wise man in this world or of becoming one himself he was inclined to mitigate the requirements which he demanded of men. However serious his appeal that we should by moral work on ourselves make ourselves independent of externals and however glowing his praise of this independence might be, he nevertheless frequently ascribed a greater importance to external good and evils than was actually permissible among the Stoics. Furthermore, although he emphatically stressed the natural connection of men in the manner of his school, yet each individual state, as compared with the great world-state of humanity, seemed to him even less worthy of the attention of the wise man than was the case with the older Stoics. In his cosmopolitanism, too, the softer traits such as love of man and compassion are more strongly marked than with them. Finally the effect of his morals on his anthropology and theology is remarkable. The more painfully he felt the power of the senses and the emotions, the more strongly did he, despite his materialism, draw the contrast between the body and the soul. In many cases he expresses a longing for the liberation from the bonds of the body and praises death as the beginning of true life in a tone that sounds more Platonic than Stoic. For the same reason he distinguishes, like Plato and Posidonius, a rational and two irrational parts in the soul itself. The greater the value he ascribes in the battle of reason with the senses to the thought that this reason is the divine part of man and its laws the will of God, the more definitely he had to distinguish the Deity as the moving force from inert matter. Seneca stated expressly that the Deity receives the right worship only through purity of life and knowledge of God and not by sacrifice; only in the shrine of one's own breast and not in temples; and, as a worthy representative of Roman Stoicism, he attacked the absurdities of mythology and the superstition of the existing worship (cf. p. 243).

Musonius Rufus of Volsinii occupied himself still more exclusively with morals. He was a Stoic who under Nero and the Flavians enjoyed a high reputation as a teacher of philosophy in Rome and was twice banished by Nero and Vespasian. Numerous fragments of his lectures, which were taken down by his pupil Lucius, have been preserved in Stobæus. Virtue, according to Musonius, is the only aim of philosophy. Men are morally ill, the philosopher is the physician who must heal them. Virtue, however, is far more a matter of practice and education than of teaching. The disposition to it is born in us and can easily be developed into a conviction. What is most important is the application of this conviction. Hence the philosopher needs only a few scientific propositions. He should show us what is in our power and what not. The application of our ideas lies in our power and nothing else. Thus our virtue and happiness rest on this alone; everything else is indifferent and we must surrender ourselves unconditionally to it. In the application of these principles to human life we find a true moral teaching that in some points inclines to Stoic simplicity, and remains philanthropic and merciful even in the face of insult. Musonius, too, without being blind to the differences of the sexes, was a powerful advocate of the equality of women. His strength lay less in the originality of his thought than the characterful way in which he accommodated his life to his theories.

Epictetus of Hierapolis (c. A.D. 50-138) was Musonius' pupil. He lived at first under Nero as a slave and then as a free man in Rome, and in A.D. 89 or 93, when Domitian banished all philosophers from Rome, he went to Nicopolis in Epirus. Here the historian Flavius Arrianus attended his lectures and embodied their contents in eight books, of which four have been preserved. Furthermore he made an extract of his master's doctrines which he issued as a small handbook in the form of a catechism. Like his master he regarded philosophy as merely a training in virtue, the curing of moral defects. Nevertheless he made a thorough study of the logic and physics of the old Stoa, especially the works of Chrysippus. It was in them that he found the necessary basis for his moral precepts—the belief in God and his care for man; in the rational structure and course of the universe; in the kinship of the human mind with God. Between the mind and the body, despite his materialism, he, like Seneca, drew a contrast that is almost dualistic in character, while he gave up the belief in personal survival after death. His moral theory, too, could dispense the more easily with a complicated systematic apparatus in that like Musonius he believed that general moral principles are implanted in us by nature. Like him he held that only one thing lies in our power—our will, the use of our ideas. Epictetus believed that our happiness depends on this alone; everything else he regarded as so indifferent that the distinction between the desirable and the condemnable had scarcely any significance for him. In this he approached closely to Cynicism, with which he further agreed in his views on marriage and civic life, while it was the Cynic whom he described as the true philosopher. On the other hand he preached not only unconditional surrender to the course of the world, but also the most unbounded and comprehensive philanthropy. This demand he supported above all by pointing to the similar relation of all men to God. His philosophy has in general a religious character. The philosopher appears as the servant and emissary of God and although his attitude towards popular religion was free enough, he was more a moral preacher filled with earnest and enthusiastic piety than a systematic philosopher. This however increased his influence rather than otherwise and an inscription found on the cliffs in Pisidia praises the one-time slave as "the source of blessing and joy".

In the first half of the 2nd cent. lived the Stoic Hierocles described by Gellius (IX, 5, 8) as "vir sanctus et gravis". Sections of a popular book on morals arranged according to provinces of duty have been preserved in Stobæus. Of a more scientific nature are the fragments of this *Elementary Ethics* found in a papyrus. This work, which gives a detailed account of the origin and development of consciousness in living beings according to their peculiarity on the lines of the ancient Stoic conception, seems to have formed the basis for his theory of virtue and duties.

Roughly contemporary was Cleomedes, whose introduction to astronomy is important because he used Posidonius as one of his sources.

The noble Marcus Aurelius Antoninus (b. A.D. 121, co-regent 138, emperor 161, died 180), who was the author of twelve books of *Meditations,* which are partly leaves from his diary written in the field in an aphoristic form, agreed with Epictetus, of whom he was greatly admired, in his distaste for all merely theoretical inquiries, in his religious view of things and his withdrawal into his own consciousness. His belief in divine providence, whose concern for man is shown not only in the whole organisation of the world but also in extraordinary revelations, led him to acquiesce in everything that the order of nature brings with it and that the gods may ordain. His insight into the change of all things and the transience of all particular things taught him that nothing external is to be desired as a good or to be feared as an evil. His conviction of the divine origin and nature of the human mind brought with it the urge to worship only the dæmon in his own breast and to expect happiness from this alone. In the recognition that all others have the same nature he found the impulse towards the most boundless and unselfish philanthropy. What distinguishes Marcus Aurelius from Epictetus apart from their different judgement on political activities, which was a natural consequence of their different stations in life, is the fact that the influence of ethical dualism on anthropology and metaphysics which had already appeared in Posidonius and Seneca is still more strongly marked in Aurelius than Epictetus. He held that the soul returns for some time after death into the Deity, but it is more suggestive of Platonism than Stoicism when he distinguishes the mind or the dominant part as the active and divine principle not only from the body but also from the soul or *pneuma* and he remarks of God that he beholds the minds free from their bodily frames in that his reason comes into direct contact with their effluences. The Stoic materialism is here revealed in the act of passing into a Platonic dualism. A striking contrast to the emperor's general mildness and lenience is formed by his harsh treatment of the Christians, whose influence he was convinced, perhaps by personal experience (I, 17; XI, 3), was corruptive.

The swan-song of Stoic philosophy is heard in the *Painting* of Cebes, an allegorical account of the Stoic theory of goods, which contains a considerable admixture of Cynic and Pythagorean elements. The latter influence is indicated by the pseudonym of the author taken from Plato's *Phædo* and the old simile of the two ways. This work, which was known to Lucian (*De merc. cond.*, 42), is imitated in the Christian *The Herdsman of Hermas*.

Nearly half a millennium intervenes between the founder and the last important representative of the Stoic school. Its consistent pantheism exerted a powerful attraction on many distinguished men, while its ethics which embraced the whole of mankind, afforded the best characters a firm support in the middle of the moral degeneracy which marked the decline of the ancient world. With its doctrine of the kinship of men with God and its universal humanity it prepared the way for Christianity, while its metaphysics and ethics have left ineffaceable traces in modern times in the philosophy of Spinoza, Leibniz, Kant, and Fichte.

80. *The Cynics of the empire*

The Cynicism which made its reappearance soon after the beginning of our era is to be regarded as a more one-sided form of this Stoic moral philosophy. The more that the scientific elements of the Stoic philosophy were thrown into the background by its insistence on the practical, the nearer it approximated to the Cynicism from which it had arisen. The more melancholy the political and moral conditions became after the last century of the Roman Republic, the more necessary did it appear to counteract the corruption and distress of the times in the striking but effective way of the ancient Cynics. Varro in his *Menippean Satires* had already conjured up their shades in order to convey the truth in the bluntest possible way to his contemporaries. The Letters of the Cynics seem intended to support a real revival of the Cynic school. This revived Cynicism, however, was not the same as the hedonistic school of the Hellenistic period (p. 245ff.), but the old strict Cynicism, with its aggressiveness especially towards the religious cults and the wealth of the possessing classes. It is in Seneca, who gives special praise and prominence to Demetrius among the Cynics of his time, that we have the first indication of its revival. Among those who came after, the following are the most worthy of mention: Œnomaus of Gadara under Hadrian; Demonax, who died nearly one hundred years old in Athens; Peregrinus, later called Proteus, who publicly burnt himself to death in 165 in Olympia, and his disciple Theagenes. But this school, remarkable as it is in the history of civilisation, had only an indirect significance for the history of science as an expression of a widespread state of mind. Even in the best of its representatives Cynicism was not free from many excesses and it served not a few as a mere pretext for a life of idleness and parasitism, immorality and the gratification of van-

ity by an attitude of boastful ostentation. These later Cynics
were the creators of no original ideas. Demetrius and even
Peregrinus (praised by Gellius, *Noct. Att.,* XII, 11, 1, as
"vir gravis et constans"), despite their eccentricity, repeat the
moral principles which the Stoa had long made commonplace. Demonax, who philosophically was an eclectic Socratic, was the object of general veneration on account of his
mild, kindly and benevolent character. Œnomaus in the
fragment of his *Conjurers Unmasked* makes a sharp attack on oracles and in this connection defends the freedom
of the will against the Stoics. These men had as moral
preachers a considerable and doubtless beneficial influence
on the thought and feelings of their time. But none of them
made any notable contributions to science. Through the very
fact that they were more concerned with a way of life than
scientific views this later Cynicism was little affected by the
change of philosophic systems. It outlived all schools except
the neo-Platonist and survived until the 5th cent., while
even at the beginning of the 6th cent. it could still count adherents.

Dio and Lucian bear a curious relation to Cynicism. Dio
of Prusa in Bithynia (*c.* 40-120) was first a Sophist and
after his banishment by Domitian turned to the Cynic philosophy (or. 13). During his fourteen years' exile he led the
life of an itinerant preacher, but after his recall under Nerva
and Trajan approached more closely to the Stoa. In the
Speeches of Diogenes (6, 8, 9, 10) he had cherished the ancient Cynic ideal; now he subscribed to the Stoic idea of the
universe arranged and guided by Zeus on a uniform principle (or. 36). In his formulation of a social and political pro-
gramme (or. 7) he regarded monarchy as the best constitution (or. 1-4). Much of his work indicates Posidonius as its
source, especially the remarkable passage on the origin of
religion, which is today still well worth reading. His brilliant style earned him the name of "Chrysostomus." Lucian
of Samosata (*c.* 120-180) is of quite a different character.
He used the form of the Mennipean satire (p. 247) in his
attacks on the Stoic belief in providence, while in *Peregrinus
Proteus* and in the *Auction of Philosophers* he poured ridi-

cule on Cynicism and the whole of philosophy. Lucian cannot indeed be called a philosopher; he is more a sceptical layman and a witty journalist. In his works he proclaims with
biting scorn the bankruptcy of religion and philosophy.

81. *The last of the Epicureans*

Epicureanism, the most dogmatic and conservative of all ancient philosophic schools, clung stubbornly to its old doctrines even under the Roman Empire. This theory of an
intellectual and refined art of life was indeed never lacking
in adherents and its metaphysical basis, directed against all
superstitious delusion, never ceased to be attractive. We have
only to mention poets like Virgil and Horace. This philosophy no less than Stoicism found its way into the upper circles. The empress Plotina, the wife of Trajan, corresponded
with Epicureans and it is due to her influence that Trajan
re-organised the school. What however gave it a new impetus in the 2nd cent. A.D. was the advance of mystical tendencies and the consequent beliefs in far-fetched miracles and
superstitions which had sprung up since the time of Posidonius, Philo and the revival of Pythagoreanism (p. 299). This
philosophy provided an unshakable defence against these
delusions, so that it was with good reason that Lucian dedicated to the Epicurean Celsus his satire *Alexandros* (cf.
chaps. 17, 25, 41), which was directed against this movement. We have a warm-hearted testimony of this re-
blossoming of Epicureanism in the inscription of Diogenes
of Œnoanda excavated in the years 1884-1889. It was put
up in a colonnade of his native city in Lycia by this enthusiastic teacher of Epicurean philosophy for the use and profit
of his fellow-citizens, future generations and the strangers
who came to the city. In a polemic with other philosophic
doctrines, especially those of the Stoa and of Empedocles, he
attempted by an exposition of the main ideas of the founder
of his school to point out to his own contemporaries and the
whole of after times the way to freedom of mind and liberation from all fear. A few extracts from the *Main Doctrines*
and two letters, one by the author to his friend Antipater

and another which was perhaps written by Epicurus himself, were appended to the work. The fragments of the Epicurean *Diogenian* preserved in Eusebius belong probably to the 2nd cent. They are directed against the doctrines of Chrysippus. This was the last flickering of Epicureanism. The tendency of religious mysticism won the day and in the time of the Emperor Julian and the Christian Father Augustine, Epicureanism, on the testimony of both these witnesses, had disappeared.

Epicureanism was in no way scientific but merely drew a sharp distinction between knowledge which determines one's view of the world and life and the peripheral results of scientific research. It owed its lasting importance to its purely causal explanation of the world, which excluded all supernatural interference or deliberate directive influence; and to its ethics, that was completely independent of religion and intent on finding a place for men in the order and course of nature and subduing the passions. It is a proof of the soundness of its scientific basis that modern scientific research with Gassendi could resume its traditions.

82. *The Peripatetics of the empire*

The Peripatetic school continued to move along the lines which had been laid down by Andronicus (p. 273) until its fusion with the neo-Platonic school. Its activity seems to have consisted predominantly in the explanation of the Aristotelian writings and the defence of his theories. That however the Peripatetics in this later period did not entirely exclude views which were originally foreign to this school is shown by the example of Aristocles of Messana (*c.* 180). This distinguished Peripatetic assumed that the divine mind dwells within the whole corporeal world and operates in it; that it becomes the individual human mind when it finds an organism that is fitted to receive it. Thus he treats the deity in the manner of the Stoics as the soul of the world, which according to his contemporary the Aristotelian apologist Athenagoras (*Supplic., c.* 5, p. 22P) was also the view taken by the Peripatetics. This approximation to the Stoic pantheism was not shared by Aristocles' pupil Alexander of Aphrodisias in Caria (*c.* 200), the famous "Commentator." Nevertheless, however well versed he was in the Aristotelian doctrines and however successfully he defended them against the Stoics, he too departed in important points from them because of a too naturalistic conception of its formulæ. He does not merely follow Aristotle in holding the particulars to be something substantial; he departs from him by adding (p. 192) that the particular in itself is more primary than the universal; the universal concepts exist as such only in our minds, their real objects being only the particulars. In man, too, he brought the higher parts of the soul closer to the lower in that he separated the "active *nous*" from the human soul and explained it as the divine spirit working upon the soul, so that man brings with him into life merely the disposition to thought (the "potential *nous*"), which only later develops into the "acquired *nous*" under the influence of the divine mind. In connection with this he denied more uncompromisingly than Aristotle the immortality of the soul. Finally he referred providence entirely to nature or the force which spreads from the upper spheres to the lower. From the nature of its action he was led to exclude the possibility of any teleological provision for the good of man. After Alexander we know of no important teacher of Peripatetic philosophy. The neo-Platonic school became the chief seat of Aristotelian studies even before the end of the 3rd cent. Although individuals like Themestius preferred to be called Peripatetics rather than Platonists, they are nevertheless either mere commentators on Aristotle or Eclectics. The following may be mentioned as eclectic Peripatetics: the astronomer Claudius Ptolemæus of Ptolemais and the philosophically cultured physician Claudius Galenus of Pergamum (2nd cent.).

83. *The later Sceptics*

Although the Eclecticism of Antiochus succeeded in driving Scepticism from its chief abode in the Academy, the victory was not by any means final. It was the loss of confidence in philosophic systems brought about by the criticism of the Sceptics that had given rise to eclecticism. Hence this mistrust of all dogmatism remained its presupposition, so that it was inevitable that it should reassume the form of a sceptical theory. Yet this later Scepticism never attained the influence or the extension which the earlier Academic Scepticism had possessed. This last school of Greek Sceptics, which called its philosophy neither a theory nor a school but a tendency, claimed to be the descendant of the Pyrrhonians rather than the Academics. After the latter had become extinct in the 3rd cent. the school was revived (according to Aristocles in Euseb., *Præp. ev.*, XIV, 18, 22) by Ænesidemus, who was born in Cnossus and taught in Alexandria.

Ænesidemus' transition from the Academy to the neo-Pyrrhonians cannot be placed before Cicero's death (43 B.C.), even if Tubero, to whom he dedicated his chief work *Pyrrhonian Principles,* was the man known to us as the friend of Cicero's youth; for not only is the latter nowhere mentioned in Ænesidemus' work, but the Pyrrhonian school is repeatedly declared to be extinct.

Ænesidemus agrees in all essentials with Pyrrho. Since we can know nothing of the real constitution of things and each assumption may be met with equally strong objections, we may assert nothing, not even our own ignorance. In this way we attain true pleasure, that is tranquillity. So far however as we are compelled to act we should follow partly tradition and partly our own feelings and needs. Ænesidemus attempted to establish this principle in his *Pyrrhonian Principles* by a systematic criticism of prevailing ideas and assumptions; among other things he contested the conclusion that things must have causes. The main grounds of his proo. are collected in the ten (or perhaps with him only nine) *Pyrrhonian Tropes* which are all intended to demonstrate the relativity of all our ideas of things; but these thoughts are worked out almost exclusively for the case of sense-perceptions. Sextus Empiricus (*Hyp.* I, 210) asserts that Ænesidemus intended his scepticism only as a preparation for the Heraclitan philosophy. This however does not imply that Ænesidemus later went over from Scepticism to Heraclitanism. We must rather assume that Ænesidemus merely gave an account of the theories of Heraclitus without actually adopting them.

Of the eight successors of Ænesidemus in the leadership of the school (in Diog. L., IX, 116) none of them except Sextus is known to us as a philosopher in any great detail. On the other hand we hear that Agrippa (we do not know when) reduced the ten tropes of Ænesidemus to five, which could be still further reduced to three main points—the conflict of opinions, the relativity of perception, the impossibility of a proof which does not move in a circle or proceed from unproved premises. Others went still further in simplification and contented themselves with two tropes—nothing can be known from itself, as is shown by the conflict of opinions, nor can anything be known from another thing, since this must be known from itself. How the Sceptics concentrated at the same time on the complete refutation of dogmatism in all its aspects is shown by the works of Sextus, who as one of the empirical physicians bore the nick-name of Empiricus. He seems to have been a contemporary of Galen, so that his *floruit* falls in the period about A.D. 180.

We possess three works of Sextus, of which the second and third are in the tradition combined under the inappropriate title *Against the Mathematicians*. These are the "Pyrrhonian Hypotyposes", that is an outline of the Sceptical philosophy (three books), the tract against the dogmatic philosophers (*adv. Math.*, VII-XI) and that against the *mathē-mata,* that is the sciences belonging to the rounded education, the artes liberales—grammar, rhetoric, geometry, arithmetic, astrology and music (*adv. Math.*, I-VI); by far the greatest part of these works, however, was doubtless borrowed by Sextus from the older members of his school and partly from the Academicians, especially Carneades (Clitomachus); the latest name that is mentioned in the chief work (*adv. Math.*, VII-XI) is that of Ænesidemus. His work may be therefore regarded as comprehending everything that was brought forward in his school in defence of their point of view. He disputed, not infrequently with wearisome prolixity and with reasons of varying validity, the formal possibility of knowledge in his discussions of the Criterium, truth, proof and the symbols of proof, etc. He attacked the concept of causality from every possible side. It was precisely the question of the origin of this concept that he like his predecessors disregarded. He repeated Carneades' criticism of the Stoic theology in attacking the idea of a moving cause. He found the material cause of bodies inconceivable in every respect. He criticised the ethical assumptions especially those on the good and happiness in order to show that in this field, too, no knowledge is attainable. Finally, from these and many other considerations he drew the conclusions that had long been known—that in the balance of the *pros* and *cons* we should forego all decision and despair of all knowledge. Thus alone can we attain tranquillity and happiness and so realise the aim of all philosophy. This however should not deter us from being guided in our conduct not only by perception, natural impulses, law and traditions, but also by experience, which instructs us on the usual course of things and puts us in a position to frame rules for the art of living.

The Scepticism of Ænesidemus did not spread far beyond the narrow circle of his school, the last representative of which known to us, Saturninus (Diog. L., IX, 16), must have belonged to the first quarter of the 3rd cent. The only other member of the school to whom we can point is the rhetorician and historian Favorinus of Arelate, whose life is put approximately between 80 and 150. But as an indication of a scientific spirit this mode of thought has a more general significance, and the extent of its contribution to the development of the Eclecticism of the time into neo-Pythagorean and neo-Platonic speculation is unmistakable.

84. *The Neo-Pythagoreans*

In a period in which much greater importance was attached to the practical effects of a philosophy than to scientific knowledge as such, in which a deep distrust of man's ability to attain knowledge possessed the minds of the majority of thinkers, and a wide-spread tendency prevailed to accept the truth where it was found on the grounds of practical needs and direct intuition of truth even at the cost of scientific consistency—in such a time it required only a slight impulse to lead the mind in its need for truth beyond the bounds of natural knowledge to a supposed higher source. Greek thought seems to have received this impulse from the end of the 4th cent. onwards, partly through the spread of the mysteries and partly from the contact with oriental ideas and culture of which Alexandria was the centre. Here, where the Jewish-Greek philosophy had originated (p. 277), the speculation first made its appearance which after centuries of development culminated in neo-Platonism. The final motive of this speculation was formed by the longing for a higher revelation of the truth; its metaphysical presupposition was an opposition of God and the world, of mind and matter, such as we have observed in the doctrines of the Orphics, Pythagoreans, and Plato. As intermediates between these opposites recourse was had to dæmons and divine powers. The practical consequence of this speculation was the combination of ethics with religion, which led on the one hand to asceticism and on the other to the demand for a direct intuition of God.

Although the Pythagorean philosophy as such became extinct in the course of the fourth century or was fused with the Platonic, Pythagoreanism survived as a form of religious life. Fragments of poets of the middle comedy show that the Pythagorean mysteries actually became more widely spread in connection with the growth of the Orphic-Dionysiac secret worship and speculations during the Alexandrian period in the East and West. That, however, theoretical Pythagoreanism, too, and the interest in it was not quite extinct in the time when the tradition is broken is shown by the work of Lucanus Ocellus, written in the 2nd cent. B.C., *On the Nature of the Universe,* which owes its origin to the endeavour to demonstrate anticipations of the Aristotelian doctrines among the Pythagoreans: namely for doctrines of the eternity of the world and the human race. It is evidence for at least a Pythagorising tendency among the Peripatetics. But it was first at the end of the 2nd or the beginning of

the 1st cent. B.C. and probably in Alexandria that any attempt was made to revive Pythagorean science and to extend
and enrich it by later theories. We have already mentioned
the account of the Pythagorean doctrines by Alexander Polyhistorius (c. 70 B.C.) contained in Diog. L., VIII, 24ff. (p.
72), the exposition of which clearly shows an acquaintance
with Hellenistic and especially Stoic philosophy, and the
remarkable *Anonymus* in Photius (cod. 249), which attempted to combine in an eclectic way the two tendencies
which are to be distinguished in neo-Pythagoreanism, the
Platonic dualism and Stoic monism. A favourite means of
popularising Pythagoreanism in a modernised form were literary forgeries under the names of ancient members of the
school, such as the *Preambles* to the laws of Zaleucus and
Charandas quoted by Cicero (*De leg.*, II, 14f.). In later
times a mass of such alleged ancient Pythagorean, but in
reality neo-Pythagorean, writings (about ninety by more
than fifty authors) is known to us by name and many fragments of these works have come down to us, among which
those of Archytas predominate in number and importance.
the first adherent of the neo-Pythagorean school whose name
we know is Cicero's friend, the learned Publius Nigidius
Figulus (d. 45 B.C.), who was the author of a learned work
On the Gods, and was followed by P. Vatinius. The school
of the Sextians, too, was connected with the neo-Pythagoreans (see p. 277). Definite traces of their existence and doctrines are found in the Augustine period in Arius Didymus
and in King Juba II's predilection for Pythagorean books.
The so-called *Golden Poem* was written about this time,
for it was known to the Pseudo-Phocylides. In the second
half of the 1st cent. A.D., lived Moderatus of Gades and
Apollonius of Tyana. Apollonius traversed the Roman Empire perhaps in the rôle and certainly with the reputation of
a magician. About A.D. 150 Nicomachus of Gerasa seems to
have written the voluminous work of which we possess the
Introduction to Arithmetic and the *Manual of Music.* Numenius (§ 85) seems to have lived somewhat later under
the Antonines, and Philostratus belonged to the first-third
of the 3rd cent. (p. 305).

In the doctrines by which these new Pythagoreans sought to establish the moral and religious principles of their sect the ancient Pythagorean theories and the still more authoritative doctrines derived from Plato, the old Academy and especially Xenocrates were combined with elements borrowed from the Peripatetic and Stoic schools; for this philosophy, like that of the contemporary Academicians, bears an Eclectic stamp. Yet within this common agreement we find many differences of detail. The unit and the dyad were declared to be the ultimate bases; of these the unit is identified with form and the dyad with matter; but whereas a part of the Pythagoreans held that the unit is also the moving cause or God, others distinguished the two and represented God partly as the moving cause (as in the *Timæus,* cf. p. 147) which brings matter and form together, and partly as the One from which the derived unit and dyad proceed. The latter was a theory which combined Stoic monism with Platonic-Aristotelian dualism and thus prepared the way for neo-Platonism. The same opposition is repeated in the statements on the relation of God to the world. Some regarded the deity as higher than reason and placed it so far above all that is finite that it could never enter into direct contact with anything corporeal; others represented God as the soul which is diffused throughout the whole body of the world and followed the Stoics in describing the soul as warmth or *pneuma*. The formal principle was thought to comprehend all numbers while the ideas were completely identified with numbers. There was much fantastic speculation in the school on the significance of the individual numbers; but scientific mathematics, too, were the object of serious and intensive cultivation. The neo-Pythagoreans subjected the Platonic doctrines to a considerable alteration in that they made the numbers or ideas into thoughts of God and thus regarded them not as the substance of things, but merely as the original patterns of which things are copies; for only in this way was it possible to unite the plurality of the ideas with the unity of the world cause. The Platonic accounts of matter were taken literally; the world-soul was placed in the position it occupied in Plato, that is between matter and the ideas (p. 165) and the supposed Locrian Timæus adopted the Platonic construction of the soul. Apart from metaphysics, however, all other branches of philosophy were treated in the neo-Pythagorean writings. An indication of the logical activities of the school is provided by the pseudo-Archytean treatise *On the Universe,* which treats the theory of categories, mainly in dependence on Aristotle, although it deviates from him in many details. In their physics the neo-Pythagoreans chiefly followed Plato and the Stoics in that they praised the beauty and perfection of the world which is not impaired even by the evil in it and above all regarded the stars as visible gods. They borrowed from Aristotle the theory of the eternity of the world and the human race which was maintained by the school after Ocellus. They followed Aristotle, too, in their statements on the contrast of the heavenly and earthly worlds, the permanence of the one and the changeability of the other. Like Plato and the ancient Pythagoreans they deduced magnitudes of space from numbers and the elements from the regular solids; on the other hand we find in Ocellus the Aristotelian theory of the elements. The anthropology of the school is Platonic; only the Pythagorean Alexander (see pp. 88, 302) ranges himself on the side of the Stoic materialism. The soul is regarded with Xenocrates as a number that moves itself and is also denoted by other mathematical symbols, while the Platonic theory of the parts of the soul, its pre-existence and immortality is repeated. Transmigration however, strangely enough, recedes into the background with the neo-Pythagoreans as far as we know, while they attributed considerable importance to the belief in dæmons. As early as Nicomachus the dæmons were connected with the Jewish angels. The extant fragments of the numerous ethical and political writings of the "Pythagoreans" present merely colourless repetition of Platonic and still more Peripatetic doctrines, with comparatively few additions of Stoic elements. The peculiarity of the neo-Pythagorean school is more strongly marked in their religious doctrines. We find on the one hand a more refined idea of God and with reference to the highest God a demand for a purely spiritual worship; on the other hand popular worship is presupposed and a high value is set on prophecy. They insisted on purity of life, to which belong the abstinences common in the Pythagorean mysteries. This element is still more strongly developed in the accounts which represent the ideal of the neo-Pythagorean philosophy in Pythagoras and Apollonius of Tyana and which are to be found in the notices of the biographies of Pythagoras written by Apollonius, Moderatus, and Nicomachus and in *The Life of Apollonius* written (*c.* 220) by Philostratus. Philosophy appears here as the true religion, the philosopher as the prophet and servant of God. The greatest problem of man and the only means of freeing his soul from the bonds of the body and sensuality is purity of life and true worship of God. This consists partly, of course, in possessing noble ideas about God and in a virtuous life devoted to the good of our fellow men; but asceticism, too, is none the less an essential part of it. This in its full extent comprised abstinence from flesh and wine, celibacy, linen garments for priests, forbiddance of all oaths and animal offerings and, in the ascetic and philosophic societies, communism of goods and the other institutions attributed by the legends to the ancient Pythagoreans. The most obvious reward of this piety consists in the power of working miracles and in the prophetic knowledge bordering on omniscience, proofs of which abound in the biographies of Pythagoras and Apollonius. An inscription of the 1st cent. A.D. found in Asia Minor applies the simile of the two ways known from the myth of Prodicus (p. 101) to the neo-Pythagorean asceticism in its contrast with the pleasure-seeking life led by the average man.

85. *The middle Platonism*

After Antiochus of Ascalon (p. 272) had asserted the agreement of the fundamental doctrines of the Academy, the Peripatetics, and the Stoa, the Academy became the chief seat of Eclecticism, which however always excluded Epicureanism. This eclectic tendency was favoured by the lack of dogmatic works by the founder of the school, for which the dialogues of Plato offered no adequate substitute; internally, too, this movement was promoted by the necessity of considering the main theories of the post-Platonic schools of philosophy, such as the Aristotelian logic and the Stoic psychology and ethics (theory of goods and emotions) if they were to remain up-to-date. In this, however, they showed themselves too ready to adapt themselves to other philosophic views and an orthodox reaction then set in which maintained the older Platonism. This middle Platonism bears a double aspect; on the one hand it was engaged like the later Peripatetics in scholarly activities in that it occupied itself with the exposition of Platonic doctrines and the explanation of his dialogues, among which the *Timæus* enjoyed particular popularity; on the other hand they attempted to develop the Platonic theories systematically. In so far as it was subject in this to the influence of neo-Pythagoreanism, it was of considerable importance in preparing the way for neo-Platonism, which cannot be fully understood apart from it. Its most important representatives in the first two centuries A.D. are the following:

Eudorus of Alexandria (*c.* 25 B.C.) combined Platonic, Pythagorean and Stoic ideas. Inspired by the Stoa he formulated a teleological principle for Platonism which from now on became dominant. He derived this principle from the *Theætetus* (176B): As much as we can, becoming like God. In this he believed that he had found an apt definition of the common goal of Pythagoras, Socrates, and Plato. Thrasyllus held the position of court-astrologer to the emperor Tiberius. He was responsible for a new edition of the Platonic dialogues which he arranged in tetralogies and a collected edition of the works of Democritus.

Incomparably more important is Plutarch of Chæronia, who won fame as an historian by his biographies (45-125). He was appointed consul and govenor of Greece by Trajan and was also elected to the archonship of his native city. Plutarch was definitely a Platonist, but was open to the influence of the Peripatetics and in some details even to the Stoic philosophy. Despite his polemics against their principles, he rejected absolutely only the Epicurean system. His conception of Plato's doctrines was almost completely identical with that of the neo-Pythagoreans who had preceded him. He attached little importance to theoretical questions as such and doubted the possibility of ever solving them. He was thus all the more interested in what was of significance for moral and religious life. In opposition to the Stoic materialism and the Epicurean "atheism" and popular superstition he cherished a pure idea of God that was more in accordance with Plato. Nevertheless he had to avail himself of a second principle in order to explain the constitution of the phenomenal world. This principle he sought, however, not in any indeterminate matter but in the evil world-soul which has from the beginning been bound up with matter, but in the creation was filled with reason and arranged by it. Thus it was transformed into the divine soul of the world, but continued to operate as the source of all evil. In divergence from the majority of the neo-Pythagoreans he regarded the creation of the world as an event in time. He represented the divine activity in the world less under the form of the Platonic theory of ideas or the Pythagorean speculations on number than under that of the ordinary belief in providence. In opposition to the fatalism of Epicurus and the Stoics he attached the highest importance to this belief. But the further he elevated the deity above the finite world, the more necessary dæmons became for him as agents of his influence on the world. In this he followed the precedent of Xenocrates and Posidonius, whom he held in great veneration. He has much that is superstitious to say about these dæmons and transfers to them what he hesitated to ascribe directly to God himself. A peculiar feature is his assumption not merely of five elements, but also five worlds. Plato's mythical accounts of the changes in the condition of the world was accepted by him so dogmatically that he in this respect approached the Stoic doctrines which he elsewhere disputed. His anthropology is Platonic but contains Aristotelian elements. The freedom of the will and immortality (with the exclusion of transmigration) were retained and strongly defended. The Platonic-Peripatetic ethics were upheld by Plutarch against the opposing theories of the Stoics and Epicureans and applied in a pure, noble and moderate sense to different circumstances of life. In this it was natural that he should be influenced to some extent by the Stoic cosmopolitanism and that the nature of the times should limit his interest in politics. The most characteristic feature of Plutarch's ethics is, however, its close connection with religion. However pure Plutarch's idea of God is and however vivid his description of the vice and corruption which superstition causes, yet in the warmth of his religious feelings and his distrust of human powers of knowledge he cannot dispense with the belief that God comes to our aid by direct revelations, which we perceive the more clearly the more completely that we refrain in "enthusiasm" from all action; and in his consideration of the natural conditions and aids for these revelations his theory made it possible for him to justify popular belief in prophecy in the way which had long been usual among the Stoics and the neo-Pythagoreans. His attitude to popular religion was similar. The gods of different peoples are merely different names for one and the same divine Being and the powers that serve them. The myths contain philosophic truths which Plutarch extracted from them by allegorical interpretation, in which he showed the traditional arbitrariness. Thus however repulsive and absurd many ritual observances may be, nevertheless, when all else failed, his dæmonic theory provided him with the means of finding an apparent justification for them. He did not demand however any Pythagorean asceticism. Thus Plutarch appears as a typical compromising theologian who could not find the courage to take up a firm stand on the ground of a rational explanation of the world but sought to combine the philosophic and religious conception of things and to remain as close as possible to tradition.

The following philosophers adhered more strictly to the doctrines of the schools. Theon of Smyrna (under Hadrian) wrote a mathematical introduction to Plato and followed him in ascribing a cathartic influence to this science (cf. *Rep.*, VII, 527D). Gaius belonged to the first half of the second century; he was a teacher of Platonic philosophy and was the author of an exposition of Plato's doctrines. The author of the above-mentioned commentary to the *Theætetus* and his pupil Albinus, of whom we possess an introduction to Plato's works (*Prologue*) and a treatise on his doctrines (*Didascalus*), were both dependent on Gaius. In his metaphysics he postulated three principles—the first God, the ideas, which are regarded as thoughts of this "first God", and matter. His physics are based on the *Timæus;* his ethical "telos" is that of Eudorus (p. 306f.). Apuleius of Madaura (*c.* 125), a popular philosopher with a rhetorical education, expounded an eclectic Platonism in his books *De Deo Socratis* and *De Platone et Eius Dogmate* which are written in Latin. Maximus of Tyre (*c.* 180), like Plutarch, endeavoured to bridge the gulf between a transcendent God and matter by the assumption of numerous dæmons as intermediaries. Nicostratus had already raised objections against the Aristotelian "aporiæ" and the importance of the somewhat later philosopher Atticus (*c.* 176) lies in the fact that he opposed the eclecticism which had invaded the school and contested the theories of Aristotle as an aberration from Plato. He was an uncompromising supporter of Plato and regarded the theory of immortality as the basis of his whole system. Nevertheless in this theology he approached more closely to the Stoic idea of immanence. It was a Platonist, Celsus, who in his work *The True Account,* written about 179, made the first literary attack on Christianity. His main ideas can still be reconstructed from the work of his opponent Origines. The roughly contemporary Severus wrote *On the Soul* in connection with the *Timæus* of Plato; in this work he replaced the Platonic divisions of the soul by the Aristotelian functions. Numenius of Apanea (*c.* 160) stands on the border-line between neo-Pythagoreanism and Platonism, but is usually reckoned among the former. Nevertheless Platonism forms the foundation of his views, but he exhibits a far-going syncretism in borrowing from the magicians, Egyptians, Brahmans, and Moses, whom he held in great reverence. He seems also to have used Philo of Alexandria and the Christian Gnostics. Beginning with the distinction of God and matter, the unit and the indeterminate dyad (cf. p. 303), he widened the gap between the two to such an extent that he regarded any direct influence of

God on matter as impossible and was consequently led (like the Gnostic Valentine) to insert the world-creator or Demiurgus as a second God. The world itself he called the third God. Like Plutarch he supposed that an evil soul was combined with matter. From this the mortal part of the human soul is derived, which he described as the second irrational soul. Because of its guilt the soul had to descend from its bodiless life into the body, and after its departure from the body, if it does not need to undergo further incarnation, such as the Stoics assumed after the general conflagration, it becomes indistinguishably united with God. A gift of God is the wisdom which is the highest good for man. And this gift is only granted to those who devote themselves to the ultimate good to the exclusion of all other thoughts. Harpocration of Argos, the pupil of Atticus, was influenced by Numenius. He wrote commentaries to Plato's *Timæus* and other dialogues (*Phædo, Alcibiades I*). Numenius also exerted an influence on Cronius, who anticipated Porphyry with an allegorical interpretation of the Homeric "Grotto of the Nymphs" (see p. 103ff.), and was the author of a work on transmigration.

The majority of the writings which have come down to us under the name of Hermes Trismegistus seem to have their source in an Egyptian branch of the neo-Pythagorean and Platonic school. It is called Poimandres ("the good shepherd") after the title of the first of the eighteen tracts. Here too we find an expression of one of the main features of the school, the endeavour to bridge the gulf between the world and God by means of intermediary beings. God is the creator of being and reason and as such is exalted above them. He is the good but is thought of as a personal willing and thinking being. The *nous* is related to it as light to the sun, different but inseparable from it. The soul (in irrational beings the *physics*) depends on *nous;* between the soul and matter stands air. God arranged and animated matter and thus the world was created. It is sustained by the divine force and filled with visible and invisible Gods and dæmons; it is called the second god and men the third. The inviolable order of the course of the world, providence and fate were taught in a Stoic spirit and the Platonic anthropology was repeated with many, not altogether consistent additions. The only means of securing to the soul its ultimate return to its higher home is piety, which is here identified with philosophy, for it consists essentially of knowledge of God and integrity. It is of course obvious that renunciation of the sensual world is a condition of this. The ascetic consequences of this point of view are, however, only found occasionally in the Hermetic writings. On the other hand it is all the more evident that one of their inspiring motives was the desire to defend the national, and above all the Egyptian, cults against Christianity, the victory of which they already regarded as almost inevitable. The *Chaldaean Oracles* belong to the same movement. It is a religious poem, composed about A.D. 200, containing a mystical doctrine of salvation based on a mixture of neo-Pythagorean, Platonic and Stoic dogmas.

II. NEO-PLATONISM

86. *Origin, etc., character and development of Neo-Platonism*

Alexandria, where the Greek and oriental worlds met and mingled, had been the birth-place of the Hellenistic-Jewish philosophy, neo-Pythagoreanism and the revival of Scepticism. It was on this soil, too, that neo-Platonism came to life. This last attempt of ancient thought to fashion our knowledge of the world into a philosophic system bore from the beginning the marks of senility upon its countenance. The shrewdness which it exhibited in its attempt to harmonise all that is thought into a comprehensive unity should not deceive us as to its lack of real originality. Neo-Platonism is the direct continuation of neo-Pythagoreanism and middle-Platonism, with which it is allied by its eclectic combination of Platonic, Aristotelian and Stoic ideas. The idea of a graduated scale of existence that pervades its system was borrowed from Posidonius (p. 270). It takes, however, precisely the opposite course. Posidonius started from empirical investigation and ascended thence to the upper world, while neo-Platonism concentrates its whole efforts on deriving the sensual from the supersensual world, so that what most interested Posidonius, nature as a sensible phenomenon, is so far separated from its opposite pole, the transcendental supersensual world, that all interest was lost in its investigation. The two systems, however, have one aim in common—the endeavour to build the whole of existing religious beliefs and superstitions into their system. This was utilised by neo-Platonism to introduce new intermediate stages in the form of the most miraculous hypostases between the primary divine being and the material world. The apparent success, too, of neo-Platonism in turning the Pythagorean and Platonic dualism into a dynamic or spiritualistic pantheism by means of Stoic monism is also deceptive in two respects; for in the first place, the neo-Platonists doubted in the last instance the possibility of theoretical knowledge of the ultimate basis of all being and sought a remedy in revelation received in a state of mystical ecstasy; and in the second place, the ascetic tendencies in the ethics of its most prominent representatives show clearly enough that the conception of the world in neo-Platonism is essentially dualistic and that it remained in spite of its apparent monism true to its slogan "Back to Plato!". Nevertheless in one respect neo-Platonism shows a far-reaching modification of real Platonism. The social and political ideas to which, in the *Republic* at least, Plato had sacrificed the individual are replaced in neo-Platonism by an individualistic tendency. The kernel of philosophic thought lies no longer in knowledge of the object but in the state of the soul of the subject which is exalted to its highest bliss, the ecstatic union with God, by means of asceticism and pursuit of knowledge. Thus neo-Platonism with its need of revelation instead of independent investigation carried to its end the development begun in neo-Pythagoreanism and the Greek-Jewish philosophy and thus completed the suicide of philosophy. Only the fact that the liberation from the bonds of the sensual is a self-liberation which the philosopher can accomplish with his own strength remains the last flickering of the splendour of the Socratic "autarkia".

Although neo-Platonism as a philosophic tendency presents a uniform whole, the characteristics sketched above do not appear with the same prominence in all its representatives. Some stressed more its speculative side and others the ethical; in some thought lost itself in scholastic elaboration of single ideas, while others followed a more learned tendency. Thus various schools were formed with centres in Rome, Syria, Pergamum, Athens and Alexandria, each of which has its own peculiar colouring, although all agree in the general tendency of their thought.

Ammonius Saccas is named as the founder of the neo-Platonic school. He was a member of a Christian family and was at first a day-labourer (hence his name Sack-bearer) and later won distinction as a teacher of Platonic philosophy in Alexandria. He seems to have died about A.D. 242 but left no writings behind him. It is therefore difficult to establish how far the doctrines of his great pupil Plotinus are derived from him, especially as our earliest information on this point belongs to the 5th cent. (Hierocles and probably from this source, Nemesius). Of his other pupils Origen (not to be confused with the Christian theologian of the same name, who also attended the lectures of Ammonius) did not distinguish God from *nous,* above which it was placed by Plotinus, and contested its distinction from the creator of the world (see p. 310). A second pupil, Cassius Longinus, the famous critic, philologist and philosopher[1] who was executed in 273 by Aurelian, was also not in sympathy with Plotinus' conception of the Platonic doctrines and defended against him the proposition that the ideas exist in themselves apart from the (divine) *nous.* This proves that the doctrines of Ammonius differed considerably from those of Plotinus, although they approached his more than those of the earlier Platonists. The real founder of the neo-Platonic school was Plotinus. This eminent philosopher was born at Lycopolis in Egypt in 204/5 and enjoyed the instruction of Ammonius for eleven years. He joined the expedition of the emperor Gordianus against the Persians in order to gain an acquaintance with the wisdom of the Persians and Indians and after the failure of this enterprise went to Rome (244/5). Here he founded a school over which he presided until his death. He was universally revered for his unselfishness, modesty, his noble character and moral purity and was held in high honour by the emperor Gallienus and his consort Salonina. The emperor indeed for a long time cherished the plan of entrusting him with the foundation of a "philosophers' city" on Campanian soil, which was to bear the name of Platonopolis. His personal life was regulated entirely according to his philosophical principles, that is in an ascetic manner. He limited his sleep and food to the minimum, abstained from flesh food, remained celibate and refused to sit to an artist who wished to fashion "the shadow of a shadow"; he praised his friend the Prætor Rogatianus for resigning his office, gave away his fortune, liberated his slaves and fasted every second day in his efforts to realise the Cynical ideal of freedom from needs. He attained four times the ecstatic union with God. He is supposed also to have possessed clairvoyant powers. He died in 269/70 in Campania. His works, the composition of which he began in his fiftieth year, were published by Porphyry (who also wrote a biography of him which is still extant) and arranged in six enneads, that is groups of nine treatises which are similar in content.

87. The system of Plotinus. The supersensual world

Although attempts have recently been made to establish some sort of development in Plotinus' philosophic thought which leads from an original "transcendentalism" to the immanence of God in the world and in which the theodicy is regarded as the chief problem in philosophy; and although it has been pointed out that Plotinus' life gives more the impression of a religious awakening than the pursuance of a systematic philosophy, it is expedient to present his philosophy, like that of Plato and Aristotle, as a systematic whole.

The system of Plotinus, like that of Philo, proceeds

from the idea of God and concludes with the demand for union with God. Between these two poles lies all that was taught on the emergence of derived being from God and on the other hand its return to God.

In his conception of the idea of God Plotinus carries to the extreme point the thought of the infinity and supermundaneity of God. Presupposing that the original must be outside the derived, that which is thought outside the thinker, the one outside the many, he found himself compelled to place the ultimate source of all being and knowledge outside all being and knowledge. The primary being is without limit, form or definition, it is the unlimited or the infinite. Not merely corporeal but not even mental qualities, neither thought nor will nor activity can be ascribed to it. For all thought has the distinction of thinker from thought and what is thought within itself; all will, the distinction of the being and activity, hence a plurality, within itself. All activity is directed towards something else; but the first must be a self-contained unity. Furthermore in order to think or to will or to be active, we need something as an object of this activity; but God requires nothing besides himself. He does not stand in need of himself either and cannot distinguish himself from himself. Hence we may ascribe to him no self-consciousness. Here the denial of the personality of God, for which the way had been prepared by Carneades (p. 263), receives affirmation as a fundamental principle. No definite quality can be ascribed to God. He is what lies beyond all being and all thought. The concepts of unity and good are the aptest positive terms for him. These however are also inadequate; for the former expresses the denial of plurality and the latter merely an effect on something else. God is indeed the source to which we must trace all being and the force to which we must trace all effects, but of its nature we can know nothing except that it is completely different from all that is finite and known to us. God is the absolute One.

In so far as God is the primary force it must produce all things. Since however it is in its nature exalted above everything and stands in need of nothing, it can neither communicate itself substantially to another nor make the creation of the other its aim. Production cannot be regarded (like the Stoics) as a division of the divine being, nor as an act of will. Plotinus, however, could not succeed in uniting these qualities in a clear and non-contradictory concept. He had recourse to imagery; the First in virtue of its perfection flows over as it were; it radiates another, etc. The emergence of the derivative from the primary being takes place by a natural necessity, which does not however signify any compulsion for the primary being or any change in it. Hence the derivative being adheres to that from which it has arisen and strives towards it. It has no being which has not been produced in it by its source, by which it is supported and filled. It owes its whole existence to the fact that it has been produced by the primary being. But the producer remains undivided in itself and outside what it produces. Hence Plotinus' System is more correctly named a dynamic pantheism than a system of emanation. Since the prior remains in its essence external to what is posterior, the latter is necessarily more imperfect than the former; it is a mere shadow or reflection of it. In that this relation is repeated at each new creation and everything owes its participation in the highest to its nearest cause, the totality of beings derived from the primary Being forms a descending scale of perfection, the diminution continuing until at the end of the scale of being it fades into not-being like light into darkness.

The first production of the Being is *nous*, thought, which is at the same time the highest Being, just as the predecessors of Plotinus had characterised the really existent, the ideas, as the thoughts of God, while Plato himself had ascribed reason and thought to the existent. Plotinus arrived at his "First" in passing beyond all being and thought. In the downward scale thought occupied the nearest position to the First. The thought of the First is not discursive, but timeless, contemplative thought that is complete in every instant. Its object is partly the First (of which, however, not even this most perfect thought can gain a completely uniform idea) and partly, as with the Aristotelian *nous*, itself, as what is thought, Being; on the other hand it does not apply itself to what is beneath it. In so far as the *nous* is the highest being, it possesses the five categories of the "intelligible" which Plotinus borrowed from Plato's *Sophist*—being, motion, immobility, identity, and difference. The later neo-Platonists, however, after Porphyry dropped these categories of the intelligible and contented themselves with the ten Aristotelian categories (p. 190), against which Plotinus (as against the four Stoic categories) had raised many objections and which he recognised only for the phenomenal world. The universal, which is more closely defined by the categories, Plotinus called the unlimited or the intelligible material. In this lies the basis of plurality which the *nous*, in distinction from the first, has in it and in virtue of which it is resolved into the supersensual numbers, one of which must correspond not only to each species but to each particular being as the original of its individual peculiarity. These ideas are conceived, in a form which was still more favoured by Plotinus than even Philo (p. 281), as active forces or spirits. Since they are not external to one another but are together, without however being intermingled, they combine to form the unity of the intelligible world, the Platonic self-created, which, as the realm of the ideas, is also that of beauty, the primary Beautiful in imitation of which all other beauty consists.

It follows of itself from the perfection of *nous* that it must create from itself another thing; and this creation is the soul. This too belongs to the divine supersensual world. It has the ideas in itself and is itself number and idea. As a manifestation of it is life and activity and like *nous* it leads an eternal timeless life. But it stands already on the border of that world; while it is in itself indivisible and incorporeal, it nevertheless inclines to the divisible and corporeal, for which by its very nature it cares and to which it communicates the effects which proceed from *nous*. It is therefore not so peculiar as *nous*. The first soul or the world-soul is not merely by its nature external to the world but does not work directly upon it. Plotinus endowed it with self-consciousness and deemed perception, recollection and reflection unworthy of it. This first soul radiates a second from it, which Plotinus called nature; only this is combined with the body of the world as the soul with our bodies. The world-soul however creates and comprehends a plurality of particular souls which are connected with it as their origin and extend from it to the various parts of the world. With these part-souls the lowest limit of the supersensual world is reached. When the divine force descends still further, matter is created as its most imperfect manifestation.

88. *Plotinus' doctrine of the phenomenal world*

In his view of the world of phenomena and its fundaments Plotinus adhered in the first place to Plato. The sensual world is, in contrast to the supersensual, the realm of the divided and changeable, the being which is subject to natural necessity and the relations of time and space and has no true reality. The basis of this world can lie only in matter, which we must postulate as the universal substrate of all becoming and change. It is as Aristotle and Plato had already described it—formless and without quality, the shadow and mere potentiality of being, not-being, deprivation, "penia". It is also—and here Plotinus expresses the logical consequence of the Orphic, Pythagorean and Platonic view—evil, the primary evil, and it is this because it is not-being; for Plotinus refers all evil to a deficiency, a not-being. From this all evil in the corporeal world arises and from the body the evil in the soul. Nevertheless matter is necessary. Light must finally become darkness at the greatest possible distance from its origin. Mind must become matter and the soul must bring forth the body as its abode. But in that the soul illuminates and forms what is beneath it, it enters into relation with it; in that it transmutes the supersensual into matter (which can only receive it in varying degrees), it creates time as the universal form of its own life and the life of the world. This activity of the soul (or nature, cf. p. 317) is however not an act of volition but an unconscious creation and necessary consequence of its nature. Thus it is the world without beginning or end, a doctrine which Plotinus shares with Aristotle (see p. 199), while at the same time he follows the Stoics in assuming a periodical recurrence of the same world conditions. But however necessary that this activity is, it consists always in the descent of the soul into matter and it is therefore called the fall of the soul.

In so far as this world is material it is regarded by Plotinus as a shadowy copy of the true, real, supersensual world. Since, however, it is the soul which creates it and impresses upon it the features of its original, everything is arranged in it according to numbers and ideas and is formed by the creative ideas which are the nature of things. Hence it is as beautiful and perfect as a material world can ever be. With a striking inconsistency, which occurs in a similar form in Plato and the cause of which is to be found in the sound sense which the Greeks had for nature, Plotinus (Enn., II, 9) repudiates the contempt which the Christian Gnostics had for nature. He does not recognise any concern on the part of the gods for the world that is deliberate or willed or directed to detail. The ideal of providence takes in him the form of the natural influence of the higher on the lower. Nevertheless he defended the belief in providence as such, in imitation of the Platonic and Stoic theodicy, with all the more success that his views on the freedom of the will and future retribution put him in a position to justify on other grounds precisely those evils which had offered so many difficulties to the Stoic theodicy. Plotinus also followed the Stoics (cf. p. 235) and especially Posidonius in his doctrine of the "sympathy of things"; but whereas the Stoics had only meant natural causal connection by this sympathy, it signified in Plotinus a working from afar which rests on the fact that through the universal vitality and animation of the world everything that affects one of its parts is felt by the whole and consequently by all other parts.

In the universe it is heaven into which the soul first pours itself. Hence in this the noblest and purest soul dwells. Next to it the stars were also glorified by Plotinus as visible gods. Exalted above change and time and hence capable neither of remembrance nor arbitrary action nor of an idea of what is beneath them, they determine this with the natural necessity that is founded on the connection and sympathy of the universe. Astrology, on the other hand, and its basic idea of an arbitrary interference of stars in the course of the world is contested by Plotinus, and astrological prediction is limited to knowledge of future events from their natural prognostics. The space between the stars and the earth is the dwelling place of all dæmons. Plotinus shared the ideas of the Platonic schools of these beings although he gave them a psychological interpretation in his theory of "Eros".

Of earthly beings only man had any independent interest for Plotinus. His anthropology is in all essentials a repetition of Plato. Nevertheless, besides the adoption of Aristotelian elements, he contributed much that was original and much that gives proof of fine power of observation especially in the world of emotion. He described in greater detail and in a more dogmatic tone than Plato the life which the soul leads in the supersensual world in which it, like the souls of the gods, is subject to no change or time and, without remembrance, self-consciousness or reflection, directly beholds the *nous,* Being and the primary Being in itself. He regarded its descent into a body (in heaven it has to clothe itself first in an ethereal body) as a natural necessity and yet as a sin on the part of the soul, inasmuch as it is drawn down by an irresistible internal force into the body which corresponds to its nature. He found the peculiar nature of man in his higher constituent, to which a second ego, a lower soul, is added by its combination with the body. This second soul depends on the higher but reaches down into the body. Like Aristotle he regarded the relation of the soul to its body as that of an operative force to its instrument. Thus he explained the fact that it encloses it unspacially and that it dwells within all its parts without being itself divided or mixed with it; that it perceives and shares everything that occurs in it without suffering any change thereby. He thought to apprehend the passive states of the soul and the activities of the soul, which are related to the sensual as processes which take place partly in the body and partly in it and the lower soul and are perceived only by the higher. On the other hand he represented the operation of *nous* and the higher soul as unconscious, its action becoming only conscious by reflection. He upheld the freedom of the will against the fatalism of the Stoics and others. His defence however was not very profound, and he repeated, too, the assertion that evil is involuntary. Virtue is free, but its works are bound up with the connection of the world. Plotinus repeats further the Platonic proofs for the immortality of the soul, which however is again made questionable by the fact that the souls in the supersensual world cannot remember their earthly existence. He extended the transmigration of the soul so as to include plant bodies, and the retribution to which it leads he developed into a repeated atonement that goes into the smallest detail.

89. *Plotinus' doctrine of exaltation into the supersensual world*

Since the soul belongs by nature to a higher world, its highest aim can only be to live exclusively in this world and to free itself from inclination towards the sensual. Happiness consists in the perfect life, which in its turn consists in thought. He regarded this however as so independent of external conditions that no Stoic could have expressed himself more definitely on this point. Its first condition is liberation from the body and all that is connected with it, purification. From this it follows of itself that the soul, being hampered by an alien element, gives itself up to its peculiar activity. Catharsis includes all virtues. Plotinus however, despite the abstinences which he practised himself and praised in others, did not require that this liberation should be effected by a life of asceticism. In discussing Eros he recognised, with Plato, that sensual beauty can lead us to supersensual. But the whole of his ethics is dominated by the idea that the basis of all evil for the soul is its combination with the body and that every activity has more value the less it brings us into contact with the world of the sensual. Practical and political activity is indispensable and the virtuous man will not avoid it; but it involves us too deeply in the external world; it makes us dependent on others. The ethical and political virtues are merely imperfect substitutes for the theoretical,

but these too are of very unequal value. Much higher stands
mediate thought and its artificial training, dialectic. It has to
do with the truly real, with ideas and the essence of things.
But this mediate thought presupposes an immediate, the actual contemplation of the thinking mind which is also contemplation of the divine *nous*. Even this did not content Plotinus. It leads us to *nous,* but not beyond it, and there still
remains the distinction of the contemplator and the contem-
plated. We attain the highest only when we are completely
buried in ourselves and when raised above thought in a state
of unconsciousness, of ecstasy and simplification, we are suddenly filled with divine light and become so directly one
with the primary being that all difference between us and
him disappears. Plotinus was from his own experience well
acquainted with this condition, which of course can only be
transitory. He attained it four times in the period during
which Porphyry was associated with him (*Vit. Plot.,* 23).
Among his predecessors there was at least a beginning of
this tendency to transcend thought. It appears clearly in Plutarch (p. 308) and it is most probable that Numenius was
moving in this direction and he in his turn will have been influenced by Philo.

In comparison with this spiritual exaltation to God, positive religion had a minor significance for Plotinus. He is however far from adopting any critical attitude towards it. His
system recognised beside God in absolute sense a multitude
of higher beings, which were to be regarded partly as visible
and partly as invisible gods. He expressed his condemnation
of those who (like the Christians) refused them the honour
that was due to them. He refers the gods of mythology and
their history to these gods with the traditional arbitrariness,
without however showing the eagerness with which many
of the Stoics had applied themselves to this study. Moreover
he utilised his doctrine of the sympathy of all things to provide a supposed rational interpretation of idolatry, prophecy,
prayer and magic, under which he included every inclination
or disinclination, every effect of the external on the internal.
He did not find it possible, however, to unite perception of

what occurs on earth or a personal influence on the course of the world with the nature of the gods.

Although he certainly laid the foundations on which his successors built in their justification and systematisation of popular religion, his own attitude to it was comparatively free. For his own personal needs the inner worship of the philosopher satisfied his ideal sense. "The gods", he says in Porphyry, *Vit. Plot.*, 10, when Amelius wishes to take him into a temple, "must come to me, not I to them".

90. *The school of Plotinus. Porphyry*

Among the pupils of Plotinus Amelius is shown in the little that we know of him as an unclear thinker of a similar type of mind to Numenius, whom he admired. Far more lucid is the learned Porphyry (properly Malchus) of Tyre or perhaps Batanea in Syria, who was born in 232/33, was taught by Longinus and later by Plotinus and died after 301, perhaps in Rome. Both scholar and philosopher, he attempted in a special work to show the agreement of Aristotelian and Platonic philosophy and wrote a number of commentaries on Plato, Aristotle, and Theophrastus. His introduction to the categories of Aristotle won great renown. The work is also called *The Five Voices* since it deals with the five concepts of species, kind, difference, characteristic and accidental. It was translated into Latin, Syrian, Arabic and Armenian and had great influence on the teachings of mediæval scholasticism. His biography of Pythagoras which has been partly preserved is a section of a history of Greek philosophy down to Plato. His work on the Homeric "Grotto of the Nymphs" is an example of absurd profundity in allegorical interpretation of a poet. He saw his mission more in exposition and explanation rather than examination or systematic development of the doctrines of Plotinus. He actually did everything to make them comprehensible and his works won much applause through the clearness of their exposition. In his sketch of the metaphysics he laid the greatest weight on the sharp distinction between mental and corporeal without differing in other respects from Plotinus' theories. In *nous* he distinguished being, thought and life, but he would doubtless have hesitated to speak on that account of three hypostases of *nous,* as Amelius had been led to do by a similar distinction. In his anthropology, to which he devoted several works, there appears the endeavour to unite the unity of the soul with the plurality of its activities and powers. The soul has the forms of all things in itself. According as it directs its thought to this or that object it assumes the corresponding form. Hence he allows the assumption of different parts of the soul only in a figurative sense. In the same way the universal soul determines the nature of the individual souls without dividing itself among them. The combination of the soul with the body is a perfect union without mixture, however, or change. Porphyry ascribes reason to animals but does not extend transmigration of the soul to the bodies of animals, while human souls for their part are not exalted into superhuman nature. He holds out to the purified soul the prospect of complete liberation from irrational powers in which, however, remembrance of earthly life is extinguished together with desire. The chief task of philosophy consists for him in its practical effect in "saving of soul". In this respect the most important factor is purification, the liberation of the soul from the body, which is even more emphatically stressed in his ethics than in that of Plotinus, although the purifying virtue, while placed above the practical, is nevertheless below the theoretical or paradeigmatic (what belongs to *nous* as such). For this purification he requires more definitely than Plotinus certain ascetic exercises—abstinence from flesh food, for which he polemises in a separate tract, celibacy, avoidance of theatrical performances and similar entertainments. In the struggle with sensuality he found a greater need for the support of positive religion than Plotinus. He too could not sympathise with much in the beliefs and cults of his time. He recognises that a pious life and holy thoughts are the best service of God and alone worthy of the supersensual gods. In the remarkable letter to the Egyptian priest Anebon, he raised such serious doubts against the prevailing ideas on gods, dæmons, prophecy, sacrifices, theurgy and astrology that we should suppose that he would have been bound to turn his back on all these things. This however was not his meaning. We must raise ourselves through the natural intermediate stages—dæmons, visible gods, and the soul and *nous*—to the First. From this point of view his dæmonology, which is filled with all the superstition of his time and school, provided him with the means of defending the religion of his people, which he supported in his fifteenth book against the Christians in spite of his own doubts. On one hand he believed that this religion had been falsified by wicked dæmons, so that its purification from that which offended him is only a restoration of its original state. On the other hand he was able to justify all essential constituents of popular religion in the light of reason. The myths are allegorical representations of philosophic truth; the images of the gods and the holy animals are symbols of the supersensual; prophecy is the interpretation of natural auguries which can be communicated by dæmons and the souls of animals; magic and theurgy are the influence on the lower powers of the soul and nature and on the dæmons. Even what he disapproved of in themselves, such as blood offerings, he permitted to public worship as a means of placating impure spirits. Only the private religion of the philosopher must remain free from them.

91. *The Syrian and Pergamenian schools*

What in Porphyry was merely a concession to the traditional form of belief was made by his pupil Iamblichus (of Chalcis in Cœlosyria *mor., c.* 330) into the central point of his scientific activity, if the ingenious misrepresentation with which this Syrian read his oriental Hellenistic religious syncretism into the works of Aristotle and Plato may be called science. His pupils at any rate gave him the name of "divine" because of this sophistry. In reality he made philosophy, the beginning of which an Epicharmus, a Plato and an Aristotle had recognised in critical doubt, into a caricature when he pronounced the maxim "Doubt no divine miracle nor any religious belief" and absorbed the whole pandemonium of the dying ancient world into his system. In his written works he is revealed far more as a speculative theologian than a philosopher; and uncritical as he was, he preferred to draw on the traditional theology from the latest and most garbled sources. Against the defects of earthly existence and the pressure of natural necessity he could find help only in the gods. In his fantastic thought every concept was condensed into its own hypostasis. His need of faith could find no satisfaction in the multiplication of the divine. According to the principle that between every unit and that to which it is communicated an intermediary must intervene, he divided the primary being of Plotinus into two, of which the first lies beyond all principles and is utterly inexpressible, while the second corresponds to the One and Good of Plotinus. In the same way he divided the *nous* of Plotinus into an intelligible and an intellectual world, of which the first is that of the ideas and the second that of living beings. He divided the intelligible world, despite its unity which should have excluded all plurality, into three parts which were extended further into three triads. The intellectual, too, was divided into three triads, of which the last was apparently made into an hebdomad. According to Iamblichus the first soul produces two others, from which, however, he distinguished the *nous* which belonged to them and gave this too a double form. Next to these supermundane gods stand the intramundane gods in three classes —twelve heavenly gods, which are multiplied to thirty-six and then to 360; seventy-two orders of subcelestial gods and forty-two of nature-gods (the numbers seem to be derived partly from astrological systems). These are followed by angels, dæmons and heroes. The gods of the people were identified with these metaphysical beings with the traditional syncretistic arbitrariness. In the same way idolatry, theurgy and divination were defended on grounds in which the most irrational belief in miracles was combined in the most extraordinary way with the desire to represent miracles as something irrational. Iamblichus combined this theological speculation with speculation in numbers, to which, like the neo-Pythagoreans, he attached a far higher value than to scientific mathematics, although he thought highly of these too. In his cosmology, apart from the theory of the eternity of the world which he shared with the whole of his school, what is most remarkable are his statements on nature or destiny, so far as he depicts this as a power that oppresses man from which he can only be released by the intervention of the gods. In his psychology the endeavour to preserve the intermediate position between superhuman and subhuman beings is even more strongly marked than in Porphyry. He followed the latter, too, in denying that human souls pass into the bodies of animals with greater emphasis because he did not, like Porphyry, ascribe reason to animals. To Porphyry's four classes of virtue (p. 324) he added as a fifth and highest "the single" or "priestly" virtues by which man can raise himself to the primary being as such. But he too regarded purification of the soul as the most necessary thing, by which it can alone be freed from its attachment to the sensual world and its dependence on nature and fate. This point of view is put forward in his work *On the Mysteries,* an interesting document of the occultism of that time that is a clever and skilful defense of sacrifice, mysticism, theurgy, etc. against Porphyry (see p. 324) on the basis of the proposition that man belongs to the higher only through the lower and that man, on account of his sensual nature, cannot dispense with these material intermediaries. At the same time he stresses the fact that only divine revelation can instruct us as to the means whereby we enter into union with God, so that the priests, as bearers of this revelation, must be ranked higher than philosophers.

Among the pupils of Iamblichus who are known to us Theodorus of Asina, who also attended Porphyry, seems to have been the most important. His views, which have been communicated to us by Proclus and were doubtless laid down in his commentaries on Plato, especially that on the *Timæus,* reveal him as the predecessor of Proclus in the attempt to carry out a triple arrangement in all parts of the supersensual world. The primary being, from which he does not, like Iamblichus, distinguish a second unity, is followed by three triads into which he divided *nous*—an intelligible, an intellectual (being, thought, life, cf. p. 324) and a demiurgic, which in its turn comprises three triads. Next come three souls of which the lowest is the world-soul or fate and the body of which is nature. What we know of his detailed account of this being bears a very formalistic character and degenerates into childish trifling. Of two other pupils of Iamblichus, Ædesius and Sopater, we only know that the former succeeded him in the headship of the school and that the latter won influence at the court of Constantine I, but was finally executed. Dexippus is known to us by his explanation of the categories, which however shows complete dependence on Porphyry and Iamblichus.

An offshoot of the Syrian school was the school of Pergamum founded by Ædesius of Cappadocia. To it belonged Eusebius, Maximus and Chrysanthius the tutors of the emperor Julian (332-363). An enthusiastic admirer of Iamblichus was the rhetorician Libonius, who was also one of the emperor's tutors. He was a devotee of the old religion as interpreted by the neo-Platonists. As we can see from his address to king Helios, he regarded the sun as the intermediary between the supersensual and the sensual world, a reflex of the Posidonian idea of "Syndesmos" (see p. 269). He entertained the greatest admiration for Cynicism, although he condemned its free thought, and held that it approximated closely to Platonism. He had a violent antipathy towards the Christians that was doubtless occasioned by his terrible experiences at the court of the Christian Emperor. He attacked them with literary (*Against the Christians*, three books, of which fragments are preserved in the work written by Cyrillus in reply) and official measures (exclusion from office and higher educational establishments). The work of his friend Sallustius *On the Gods and the World*, an extract of which has been preserved, was intended as propaganda for polytheism. Finally Eunapius of Sardes was a member of this circle. He wrote, apart from an historical work, biographies of philosophers and sophists intended to glorify this tendency of thought.

92. *The Athenian school*

A final modification of neo-Platonic science was caused by
the study of Aristotle, which had not died out in the school
during the 4th cent., although it had unmistakably lost in
influence and importance since Iamblichus through theo-
sophical speculation and theurgical activities. It was now resumed with all the more vigour and keenness the more the
school, since the failure of Julian's attempt at a restoration,
found itself in the position of an oppressed and persecuted
sect, and the more exclusively they saw their hopes confined
to scientific activity. In Constantinople Themistius devoted
himself during the second half of the 4th cent. to the explanation of the works of Aristotle and Plato. Although with
his rather superficial eclecticism he cannot be assigned to the
neo-Platonists, he was in conformance with them in his conviction of the entire agreement of Plato and Aristotle. The
Platonic school in Athens became however the chief centre
of Aristotelian studies. It was here that the combination of
Aristotelian with Iamblichan theosophy was carried out
which gave the neo-Platonism of the 5th and 6th cents. and
the Christian and Mohammedan systems derived from it
their peculiar stamp. Here we meet at the beginning of the
5th cent. the Athenian Plutarch, the son of Nestorius, who
died in 431/32 at an advanced age. He was the head of
the school and a popular teacher, who explained the works
of Plato and Aristotle with equal zeal with word and pen.
The little information we have on his philosophic views does
not go beyond the traditions of his school. It is mainly concerned with psychology, which he treated on an Aristote-
lian-Platonic basis. At the same time we hear that he learnt
from his father and continued to practise all sorts of magic
and theurgic arts. Syrianus was the colleague and successor
of Plutarch (*mor. c.* 430). This Platonist, who was highly
praised by Proclus and later writers, also possessed an exact
knowledge of Aristotle and was a zealous interpreter of his
works. But it was Plato whom he valued far more highly
than Aristotle (he recommended the study of Aristotelian

philosophy only as an introduction to Plato) the neo-Pythagoreans, the Orphics and the supposed Chaldean divine ut-
terances (p. 310) that he regarded as his leading authorities. Theology was the favourite subject of his speculation.
His treatment of this subject remained in systematic completeness far inferior to that of Proclus.

The successor of Syrianus was Proclus, who was the pupil
of his predecessor and Plutarch. He was born in 410 in Constantinople and brought up in Lycia, came to Athens in his
twentieth year and died in 485. Through his untiring diligence, his scholarship, his supreme mastery of logic, his systematic mind, and his work as a teacher and author he was
as pre-eminent among the Platonists as Chrysippus had been
among the Stoics. He was, however, at the same time an
ascetic and a believer in theurgy, and thought that he was a
reincarnation of the neo-Pythagorean Nicomachus (p. 302).
He believed that he was the recipient of revelations and was
unwearying in performance of religious exercises. He shared
the religious enthusiasms of his school, its beliefs and superstitions and its reverence for Orphic poems, Chaldean oracles and similar productions. He now undertook to work
the whole mass of theological and philosophical doctrines bequeathed by his predecessors into a uniform and methodical
system, which in after-times served as a model for the Mohammedan and Christian scholasticism. It exhibits great formal perfection but shares with these later systems the inner
want of freedom of thought from which it arose and the
lack of a really scientific basis and treatment. The most general law on which this system is built up is that of triadic
development. The thing produced is partly similar to that
which produces it, for this can only produce it by communi-
cating itself to it. On the other hand it is different from it as
the divided from the unitary, the derived from the original.
In the first respect it remains in its cause and the cause is, although only partially, in it. In the second respect it emerges
from the cause. Since however it depends on it and is related
to it, it turns in spite of its separation to it; it endeavours to
imitate it on a lower plane and to unite itself with it. The
being of what is produced in what produces it, its emer-

gence from it and its return to it are the three moments through the continued repetition of which the totality of things are developed from their origin. The ultimate source of their development can naturally be only the primary being, which Proclus followed Plotinus in describing as absolutely exalted above all being and knowledge, higher than the One, a cause without having a cause, neither being nor not-being, etc. But between this First and the Intelligible Iamblichus inserted a middle stage—the absolute units which form the unitary, super-essential number. They are also called the highest good and as such receive predicates which sound much too personal for their abstract nature. Next comes the sphere to which Plotinus had assigned *nous*. Proclus, in partial reliance on Porphyry, Iamblichus, Theodorus and Syrianus (cf. pp. 324, 325, 326, 328) divided it into three spheres—the intelligible, the intellectual-intelligible and the intellectual. He defined the basic quality of the first as being, of the second as life and the third as thought. The first two of these spheres are each further divided, partly according to the same principles of division, into three trades; the third is divided into seven hebdomads and these separate members of each series are regarded as gods and identified with one of the gods of popular religion. The soul, which is defined in the same way as in Plotinus, comprises three classes of part-souls—divine, dæmonic and human. The divine are divided into three orders. The four triads of hegemonic gods, the same number of "liberated" gods and the two classes of intramundane gods, the star-gods and the element-gods. In the identification of the popular gods with these metaphysical beings Proclus found it necessary to distinguish a threefold Zeus, a double Kore and a triple Athena. The gods are followed by the dæmons which are divided into angels, dæmons and heroes and are described in the traditional way with a large element of superstition. These are succeeded by such souls as temporarily enter into material bodies. Plotinus had created matter from the soul. Proclus derived it directly from the unlimited, which together with the limited and the mixed, forms the first of the intelligible triads. In its nature he did not regard it as evil, but as neither good nor evil. His cosmological ideas agree in all essentials with those of Plotinus, except that he regarded space as a body consisting of the finest light which permeates that of the world. With Plotinus he defended the doctrine of providence on account of the evil in the world. He followed him and Syrianus in his assumptions on the descent and future destiny of the soul. In his psychology he combined Platonic and Aristotelian theories, but increased the number of the potentialities of the soul in that he distinguished thought or reason from what is unitary or divine in men, which is higher than the former and with which alone the divine can be recognised. Furthermore, like Plotinus, Porphyry and Syrianus he ascribed to the soul an æthereal body consisting of light which like itself must be unoriginate and imperishable. His ethics required a gradual ascent through the five different virtues which we have met in Iamblichus (p. 327) to the supersensual, the final goal of this ascent being the mystical union with god; but the more firmly he was convinced that all higher knowledge depends on divine illumination and that only faith joins us with God, the less was he inclined to abandon those religious aids to which the neo-Platonic school since Iamblichus had attached so high a value and the effectiveness of which Proclus defended with the traditional reasons. His interpretations of myths are naturally inspired by the same spirit. He gave expression to his piety in a series of hymns to different gods.

In the hands of Proclus the neo-Platonic doctrines received the final form in which they were handed down to posterity. After him the school had a few eminent representatives, but none who could compare with him in scientific power or influence. His pupil, biographer and successor in the headship of the school, Marenus, an able mathematician, distinguished himself by a sober interpretation of Plato, but shared in the beliefs in theurgy. Damascius, the pupil of Marenus, who presided over the school from about 520 onwards, was an admirer and intellectual kinsman of Iamblichus. In his work on first principles he made a vain attempt to find a transition from the primary being, whose incomprehensibility he could not express strongly enough, to the intelligible by the insertion of a second and third unity. He was finally forced to the confession that it was not possible to speak of an emergence of the lower from the higher but only of one uniform indeterminate being. This conviction, which borders on agnosticism, did not prevent him from writing a work *On Paradoxa,* in which he entertains the maddest superstitions. Simplicius belongs to the last generation of heathen neo-Platonists; he was a pupil of Damascius and the Alexandrian Ammonius (p. 334). His commentaries to several Aristotelian works are of inestimable value and give evidence not only of the scholarship but also of the independent and clear thought of their author, although they do not go beyond the bounds of the neo-Platonic tradition. But in a Christianised Roman Empire philosophy could no longer maintain a position independent of the victorious Church. In the year 529 Justinian issued the decree forbidding the teaching of philosophy in Athens. The property of the Platonic school, which was of considerable value, was confiscated. Damascius emigrated with six comrades, among whom was Simplicius, to Persia but soon returned in disappointment from there. Shortly after the middle of the 6th cent. the last of the Platonists who had not entered the Christian Church seem to have died out.

93. *The Alexandrian school*

In Alexandria, where it had arisen, neo-Platonism seems to have survived until the end of the ancient world in a school which, despite active relations with that of Athens, nevertheless bears its own peculiar stamp. In distinction from the enthusiastic mysticism which prevailed in the Athenian school, it preferred sober research and replaced abstract metaphysical speculation by the study of mathematics and the exact sciences. Its exegesis of Plato and Aristotle is sensible and objective. In systematic philosophy it showed a preference for the latter, especially his logic. Finally, a peculiar feature is lent to it by its relations to the Christian school of the Catœchetes, which flourished in Alexandria after the time of Clemens. The combination of neo-Platonic philosophy with ancient polytheism was here not so close as in Athens, so that this school became gradually almost a religiously neutral educational establishment, in which adherents of the old and the new religion were found together in common endeavour. That finally made possible the adoption of Hellenic science by the Christian Byzantine Empire. Among the most distinguished representatives a woman is pre-eminent, Hypatia, the daughter of the mathematician Theon. She interpreted Plato and Aristotle and wrote on mathematical and astronomical questions. In the year 415 she fell a victim to the fanaticism of a Christian mob; whether the bishop Cyrillus was implicated is doubtful. A pupil of hers, Synesius of Cyrene, who was elected as bishop of Ptolomæis in the year 411, kept up a frequent correspondence with her on scientific questions which has been partly preserved. He himself was the author of a series of philosophic and religious works and represented in his person the union of neo-Platonism and Christianity, a sort of Christian humanism. Hierocles of Alexandria (who is not to be confused with the Stoic of the same name, p. 290) was a pupil of Plutarch, the head of the Athenian school. In his doctrines he combined Platonic, Peripatetic and Stoic elements in that he stressed the belief in divine providence and the purity of moral principles, but shows himself influenced by Jewish and Christian ideas in the assumption of a creation of the world out of nothing, a thought that had remained foreign to Greek philosophy. The physician and mathematician Asclepiodotus (second half of the 5th cent.) was distinguished by the moderation of his views, although he was not completely free of mystical belief in miracles. Ammonius, the son of Hermias, had been a pupil of Proclus and taught in Alexandria as an able interpreter of Platonic and Aristotelian writings. The following were pupils of his: the younger Olympiodorus, whose older namesake had taught at the same time as Hierocles in Alexandria, and the Christian Joannes Philoponus, who fought with Simplicius once again the old literary feud on the question of the eternity of the world. Nemesius, Bishop of Emesa in Phœnicia, whose book *On Human Nature* is seen to be a last representative of a development which goes through the whole history of Greek philosophy after Posidonius, stood under the influence of the Alexandrian school. Finally with Stephanus of Alexandria, who under Heraclius (610-641) was called to the university of Constantinople, Platonism entered into the Christian middle-ages.

94. *The Neo-Platonism of the West*

Once Plotinus had transferred neo-Platonism from Alexandria to Rome and handed it on to his pupil Porphyrius. In Italy no such uninterrupted school tradition or such a speculative development of the system took place as in the East. Here Iamblichan abstrusities were avoided. Chalcidius (*c.* 350) is to be mentioned as a commentator of the Platonic *Timæus* and Macrobius as the commentator of Cicero's *Somnium Scipionis* (*c.* 400); Marius Victorinus, a grammarian and rhetorician of the 4th cent., who wrote commentaries to Aristotelian and Ciceronian works, was the teacher of Augustine and initiated him into the neo-Platonic philosophy. By far the most important representative of Latin neo-Platonism was however Anicius Manlius Severinus Bœthius of Rome (*c.* 480-525). Although a Christian, his membership in the Roman nobility and his marriage with the daughter of the younger Symmachus brought him into relation with those circles who adhered longest and most firmly to the old religion. Appointed to the consulship in the year 510 by Theoderich, he was later suspected by him of participation in a conspiracy intended to bring about his downfall, and was imprisoned and executed. He was the author of translations and interpretations of the works of Aristotle and also a work on the Trinity. In prison he wrote his last work *On the Consolation of Philosophy,* the last of the series of ancient consolatory writings. We cannot expect new ideas from him, for he is no professional philosopher but only a layman interested in philosophy, like Cicero or Plutarch. Thus he entertained an eclecticism in the manner of the pre-Plotinian middle Platonism. While the work exhibits no single specifically Christian thought, it shows it-

self influenced by the *Protrepticus* of Aristotle, probably
through the mediation of Cicero's *Hortensius* (p. 178). The
form is that of the diegematic dialogue on the lines of the
Menippean Satire, with an alternation of prose and verse.
Contentually it shows a strictly monotheistic belief in God
and providence, which it defends against all objections with
warm enthusiasm. It is the last fine example that proves
what support ancient philosophy could offer to an enlightened man in life and in death.

95. *Conclusion*

Boldly almost impetuously Greek philosophy had in 6th
cent. B.C. trod the way which leads from myth to the
Logos. Trusting in the power of the human mind, the great
pre-Socratic Ionians, Plato and Aristotle built up their systems on a basis of science and superseded the mythical ideas.
Socrates, the minor schools which took their rise from him
and the Hellenistic philosophy of the Stoa and Epicureanism
were all united in maintaining that ethical conduct of man
depends on his knowledge. This intellectualism that proclaimed the autonomy of human reason formed the back-
bone in the organic development of Greek philosophy. But
at an early date this rationalistic tendency was crossed by a
religious influence, which originated in the last instance in
the East. This was Orphicism, which with its separation of
body and soul, matter and mind, god and the world grafted
dualism upon Greek thought and relied on divine revelations instead of rational proof. The Greek mind in men like
Pythagoras and his pupils, Empedocles and Plato endeavoured to comprehend this doctrine and elaborate it on rational grounds. But it remained something foreign in Greek
intellectual life. In the Hellenistic period and the Roman
Empire, when not only the orient was Hellenised but the
Greek world, too, was to a large extent orientalised, this
tendency received fresh support and strength from its old
home. Posidonius exhibits in a higher degree the tendency,
which had always been strong in the Stoa, to reconcile philosophy and religion. Now the power of philosophic specula-

tion which had been weakened by scepticism showed itself in neo-Pythagoreanism, the Hellenistic-Jewish philosophy and in neo-Platonism as no longer strong enough to dam the stream of religious mysticism which was now sweeping in full force into philosophy. However much we may admire the last revival of antique thought in the philosophic system of Plotinus, it nevertheless bears the stamp of a non-Greek nature and traces of decadence which become more numerous and more pronounced in his successors. In the hands of Iamblichus and Proclus philosophy was petrified into scholasticism, the characteristic of which is that it no longer sought to supersede mythical ideas by empirical research and independent rational thought, but saw its task in supporting the traditional religion with their reason and in presenting it as intellectually comprehensible. Here knowledge is replaced by revelation in ecstasy. After Greek philosophy had performed this self-castration it sank exhausted into the arms of religion; as Proclus expresses in one of his hymns to the gods:

"And so let me anchor, weary one, in the haven of piety."

This development was completed both in epistemology and metaphysics, ethics and politics. Here, too, Orphicism had familiarised the Greeks with an asceticism which was wholly contrary to their nature and in connection with this the idea of salvation, the saving of the soul. That is the exact opposite of the Socratic *autarkia* based on knowledge. The Greek was also familiar with the repression or limitation of natural bodily needs, but only from the point of view of inurance which was aimed at increasing the control and capacity of the body. On the other hand the Orphic asceticism, which was revived in neo-Pythagoreanism and neo-Platonism, served religious and cathartic ends, the liberation of the soul from the supposed impurity of the body. It finally absorbed the Cynical form of asceticism, which was aimed originally at ensuring the independence of the individual, and passed over with it into the Christian monasticism (Aug. *Civ. Dei*, XIX, 19). In the Aristotelian philosophy and especially in its last phase, neo-Platonism, asceticism was accompanied by the recedence of political ideas and the growth of individualism in philosophy which had been initiated by Cynicism and furthered by Epicureanism. This found further support in the fact that not only the Greek Polis but also all ancient states had been absorbed into the Roman Empire. The Stoic thought of a world-state comprising all men lived on in the form of the Christian world-church uniting all in one faith for the salvation of the soul.

NOTES

THE PRE-SOCRATIC PHILOSOPHY

[1] Now Lesina, an island in Dalmatia, Diels, *Vors.* 4, I, p. xxii.

[2] Perhaps in this point influenced by Anaximander, p. 29.

[3] This aphoristic manner of Heraclitus is not completely certain. Even if the three-fold division into the sections *On the All*, *The Statesman*, and *The Student of the Deity* does not, as is natural, proceed from Heraclitus, this nevertheless seems to indicate a definite arrangement and connected exposition from which only the most famous sayings have been preserved. The beginning (*Fr.* 1) and the silence of Aristotle (*Rhet.* III, 5p. 1407 b. 11ff.) would indicate this, for he would have been bound to mention such a singular form of philosophic writing.

[4] That Heraclitus did not mention air is proved by *Fr.* 31 and 36; *Fr.* 76 on the other hand where it is included presupposes the theory of the four elements and is probably to be ascribed to Stoic influence.

[5] Although we do not know the year of Parmenides' death it is hardly possible as Plato (*Parm.* 127A, *Theæt.* 183E, *Soph.* 217C) represents, that he met Socrates in Athens when he was an old man.

[6] Cf. above p. 54. This, of course, could be due to a misunderstanding in that Theophrastus' expression *strongyte* (round, bent) was understood as spheroidal, a mistake that was all the easier to make in that Parmenides compared not the earth but Being with a sphere (*Fr.* 8, 43), which the Pythagoreans regarded as the most perfect body.

[7] The third and fourth proofs were perhaps not directly concerned with the refutation of the theory of plurality, but the former was directed against the (Pythagorean or Atomistic?) assumption of an empty space, the latter against the reliability of our sense perceptions.

[8] According to another ancient interpretation, Hera was earth and Hades air.

[9] Of these two forces Hate is obviously borrowed from the Orphic cosmogony: Apoll. Rhod., *Arg.* I, 498 (*Fr.* 29 Kern), while Empedocles (*Fr.* 17, 25ff.) claims to have been the first to have conceived Love as a cosmic force. Cypris reigned in the Golden Age (*Fr.* 128). Cf. *Fr.* 130, 2.

¹⁰ The doctrine of the pores may have been borrowed by Empedocles from Alcmæon of Croton.

¹¹ See above, p. 38.

THE ATTIC PHILOSOPHY: SOCRATES AND THE SOCRATICS, PLATO, ARISTOTLE

¹ As is to be inferred on the one hand from the statements of our authorities as to the time of his death and condemnation (Diog., II, 44; Diodor., XIX, 37, 6; Xenoph., *Mem.*, IV, 8, 2; Plat., *Phæd.* 59D), on the other hand those in his age at the time of his death (Plat., *Apol.*, 17D; *Crit.*, 52E). Since the visit to Delos did not, as was formerly supposed, fall in Thargelion (May-June), but in Anthesterion (February-March), the speech for the defence must have been delivered about the middle of February, thus Socrates, who was then at least seventy years old, must have been born at latest at the beginning of the year 469, but probably as early as 470 or 471.

² Cf. the deliberate ambiguity at the end of the *Rep.*, X, 621D.

³ According to Plato (*Apol.* 36E) the verdict would have been reversed if only 30 of the heliasts (whose number presumably amounted to 500 or 501) had voted otherwise.

⁴ Two women, Lastheneia of Mantineia and Axiothea of Phleius, appear among the number of Plato's pupils (Diog. L., III, 46).

⁵ The priority of the *Parmenides* over the *Theætetus* and the *Sophistes* is fully established by the references in these two dialogues to the first. To this must be added further the change in dialogue form (*Theæt.*, 143C).

⁶ This is the next best way of 300BC.

⁷ This number is the product of 2x3x4x5x6x7. *Laws*, V, 738A.

⁸ The fearful, dangerous Man of *Phileb*, 29A is doubtless Democritus and *Laws*, XII, 967A—C is more applicable to him than to Anaxagoras.

⁹ On the Materia see especially *Tim.*, cap. 18-19, p. 48E—53C.

¹⁰ The expression which in *Theæt.*, 191C, is used in a psychological sense for the reception of impressions in the consciousness is borrowed from Democritus and perhaps goes back to Protagoras.

¹¹ Plato actually does not use this expression in his dialogues, but probably did so in his lectures.

¹² At the conclusion of the *Nic. Eth.* (X, 10, p. 1181b, 15ff.) there is a reference to this collection.

¹³ Aristotle does not discuss the affects either in the *Psychology* or in the *Ethics*. In the two books of the *Rhetoric* however we find for the first time in philosophic literature an exact definition of the different affects, which, according to Aristotle consist of

a mixture of pleasure and pain, the predominance of one or the other deciding the character of the emotion.

HELLENISTIC PHILOSOPHY. STOA. THE LATER CYNICISM. EPICUREANISM. SCEPTICISM. ECLECTICISM

[1] It is doubtful, whether the common concepts according to the Stoic conception were really derived from experience. Since in the sources they are repeatedly denoted by the term natural or innate, they are probably to be regarded as present in us before all experience. This of course does not mean the ideas with their full contents like the "ideae innatae" of Descartes and Leibniz, but merely that the predisposition to their development is born in us.

[2] The beginnings of the allegorical interpretation of myths date back to the 6th cent. B.C. with Theagenes of Rhegium. This method was also used by Parmenides, Anaxagoras, and his pupil Metrodorus of Lampsacus, partly in a physical and partly in an ethical sense. The Stoic Crates of Mallus, the pupil of Diogenes of Babylon, the head of the Pergamenian school of grammarians, introduced it into philology in the 2nd cent. B.C.

[3] These images and influences are the unmistakable offspring of Democritus and Empedocles.

[4] These are to be distinguished from the common concepts or spontaneous judgements of the Stoics; they have no independent reality separate from the particular things.

THE PHILOSOPHY OF THE ROMAN EMPIRE

[1] The work which has come down to us under the title of *Dionysius,* or Longinus' *On the Sublime* is probably not by the neo-Platonist L. but was probably written at the beginning of the 1st cent. A.D.

BIBLIOGRAPHY

SOURCES

The most complete collection of fragments, F. W. A. Mullach: *Fragmenta philosophorum Graecorum,* 3 vols., Paris, 1860, is now to a considerable extent replaced by other collections which satisfy more fully the demands of criticism. The pre-Socratic philosophers are contained in H. Diels: *Die Fragmente der Vorsokratiker,* 4th edn., 3 vols., 1922. A selection is offered by the *Historia philosophiæ Graecæ* by H. Ritter and L. Preller, ed. 9, Gotha, 1913.

GENERAL HISTORIES OF GREEK PHILOSOPHY

Burnet, J., *Early Greek Philosophy,* 3rd ed., 1920.

Burnet, J., *Greek Philosophy,* vol. I. Thales to Plato. London, 1914.

Döring, —., *Geschichte der griechischen Philosophie.* 1903.

Gomperz, Th., *Griechische Denker.* Eng. transl. *sub. tit.,* Greek Thinkers. 1901-5.

Joël, K., *Geschichte der antiken Philosophie,* vol. I. Tübingen, 1921.

Stace, W. T. A., *Critical History of Greek Philosophy.* London, 1920.

Zeller, E., *Die Philosophie der Griechen in ihrer geschichtlichen Entwicklung*, Eng. transl., 1877-97.

PRE-SOCRATIC PHILOSOPHY

THE MILESIANS

Diels, H., *Ueber Anaximanders Kosmos*—in Arch. Phil., X, pp. 228 sqq.

Diels, H., *Ueber die æltesten Philosophieschulen der Griechen*—in *Phil. Aufs. Zeller gew.*

Heidel, W. A., *On Anaximander*, C. P., VII (1912), pp. 212 sqq.

Wellmann, E., art. *Anaximandros* in RE.

Wellmann, E., art. *Anaximenes* in RE.

THE PYTHAGOREANS

Bywater, I. A., *On the Fragments Attributed to Philolaus the Pythagorean*. J.P., 1, 21 sqq.

Cornford, F. M., *Mysticism and Science in the Pythagorean Tradition*. C.Q., XVI (1922), pp. 137 sqq; XVII (1923), pp. 1 sqq.

Heidel, W. A., πέρας and ἄπειρον *in the Pythagorean Philosophy*. Arch. Phil., XIV, 1901, pp. 384, sqq.

Keith, A. B., *Pythagoras and the Doctrine of Transmigration*. Journ. Roy. Anth. Inst., 1909, pp. 569 sqq.

Robin, L., *La théorie platonicienne des idées et des nombres d'après Aristote*. 1908.

HERACLITUS

Bywater, I., *Heracliti Ephesii reliquiæ*. Oxon., 1877.

Diels, H., *Herakleitos von Ephesus*, ed. 2. Berlin, 1909.

THE ELEATICS

Reinhardt, K., *Parmenides und die Geschichte der griechischen Philosophie*, 1916.

Schneidewin, M., *Von griechischen Trugschlüssen. Socrates* 70 (1916), pp. 193 sqq.

Slonimsky, *Heraclit und Parmenides*. Giessen, 1912.

Tannery, P., *La physique de Parmenide*. Rev. phil., XIII, 1884, pp. 264 sqq.

EMPEDOCLES

Bignone, E., *Empedocle* (*Il pensiero Greco*), vol. X. Turin, 1916.

ANAXAGORAS

Cappelle, W., *Anaxagoras*. N. J. Kl. Alt., XXII, 1919, pp. 81 sqq.

THE ATOMISTS

Diels, H., *Leukippos und Diogenes von Apollonia*.
Liepmann, H. C., *Die Mechanik der leucipp-democritischen Atome*. Berlin, 1885.

THE SOPHISTS

Nestle, W., *Die Vorsokratiker*. 1908 (ed. 2, 1922), pp. 67 sqq., 183 sqq.

SOCRATES

Burnet, J., *The Socratic Doctrine of the Soul*. Proc. Brit. Acad., VII, 1916.
Bury, J. B., *The Trial of Socrates*. R.P.A. Annual, 1926, p. 17.
Jackson, H., art. *Socrates* in Encyclo. Brit.
Maier, *Socrates*. Tübingen, 1913.
Taylor, A. E., *Plato's Biography of Socrates* (Proc. Brit. Acad., vol. VIII, 1917).

PLATO

Jackson, H., *Plato's Later Theory of Ideas*. J.P., X, p. 253; XI, p. 287; XIII, p. 1, p. 242; XIV, p. 173; XV, p. 280.
Lutoslawski, W., *The Origin and Growth of Plato's Logic*, 1897.
Nettleship, H., *Lectures on the Republic of Plato*, 1898.
Shorey, P., *The Unity of Plato's Thought*. Chicago, 1903.
Stenzel, J., *Studien zur Entwicklung der platonischen Dialektik*. Breslau, 1917.

Stewart, J. A., *The Myths of Plato.* Oxford, 1905.
Stewart, J. A., *Plato's Doctrine of Ideas.* Oxford, 1909.
Taylor, A. E., *Plato.* 1908.
Wilamowitz-Moellendorf, U.v., *Platon.* Berlin, 1920.

ARISTOTLE

Gomperz, Th., *Greek Thinkers,* vol. IV, 1912.
Grote, G., *Aristotle.* 1880.
Jaeger, M., *Aristoteles.* Berlin, 1923.
Maier, H., *Die Syllogistik des Aristoteles.* Tübingen, 1896-
    1900.
Ross, W. D., *Aristotle.*

HELLENISTIC PHILOSOPHY

Atanassievitch, *L'atomism d'Epicure.* Paris, 1927.
Bevan, E. R., *Stoics and Sceptics.* Oxford, 1913.
Bevan, E. R., *Hellenistic Popular Philosophy.* Cambridge,
    1923.
Brehier, E., *Les idées philosophiques et religieuses de
    Philon d'Alexandrie.* 1908.
Davidson, W. L., *The Stoic Creed.* Edinb., 1907.
Hicks, H. D., *Stoic and Epicurean.* London, 1910.
Leisegang, H., *Hellenistische Philosophie.* Breslau, 1923.
Reinhardt, K., *Poseidonius.* 1921.
Taylor, A. E., *Epicurus.* London, 1911.

PHILOSOPHY OF THE EMPIRE

NEO-PYTHAGOREANS

Campbell, F. W. G., *Apollonius of Tyana.* 1908.

NEO-PLATONISTS

Inge, W. R., *The Philosophy of Plotinus,* 3rd ed., 1928.
Jones, Rufus M., *Studies in Mystical Religion,* 1909.
Whittaker, T., *The Neo-Platonists,* 1901.

INDEX

346

MERIDIAN BOOKS

12 East 22 Street, New York 10, New York